Best wishes for
health & happiness!

(Michael & Juliette)

(Micari, 5/2000)

THE URBAN WARRIOR'S
BOOK OF SOLUTIONS

A difficult business environment requires executives who are aware of the physical strengths and weaknesses that influence their performance. Dr McGannon has designed an effective approach to create that awareness.

ARNOUD DE MEYER, Associate Dean, Executive Education and Director General, Euro-Asia Centre, INSEAD

The McGannon approach is a business approach, he speaks in language we understand – assets, returns, investment, risk – and he understands our health objectives and constraints. He teaches that we should love life, he obviously does, and he is walking proof that to be healthy you don't have to be a health nut!

TONY TYLER, Director, Airport Services, Cathay Pacific

Michael McGannon is a remarkable doctor. This is a remarkable book.

RON CLARKE, MBE, AASA, ACTS

Dr McGannon's combination of sound analysis and practical advice has made a significant difference to my attitude towards my health. I am enormously impressed.

DAVID BELL, Chief Executive, *Financial Times*

Dr Michael McGannon's preventative medicine approach is unique and imaginative. It is a refreshing reminder to busy senior executives that physical and mental health must not be taken for granted.

KARMJIT SINGH, Assistant Director Corporate Affairs, Singapore Airlines

McGannon has lead to a complete change in my attitude to health, exercise and nutrition – and it is so easy despite my heavy travel schedule. I have now introduced the program to our Company and it is rated highly popular in our management development program. Managers want results. This program gives results in personal asset management, your health, in a practical, down to earth way that managers respond to. The program is easy to follow, even when you have a hectic executive lifestyle. I know – I have been there and done it!

D C ANDERSON, International Director of Human Resources, ICI, Singapore

Business people who are serious about their careers have to be serious about themselves, and you cannot be serious about yourself without taking care of yourself. Keep up the good work Dr McGannon.

JOHN WARRICK, District Manager, United Parcel Services

Dr McGannon introduced me to preventative health and I have benefitted tremendously from his health management program and *The Urban Warrior's Book of Solutions*. This book will have a positive impact on the health and lifestyles of many businessmen and executives.

PROF DR MOHD ZULKIFLI TAN SRI GHAZALI, Dean, Faculty of Civil Engineering, University Teknologi Malaysia

I have never come across a more dedicated medicine man in my life as Dr Michael McGannon. His interest in and enthusiastic drive to get the businessman's body super healthy make him one of a kind in the medicine world.

VERNON HERRIS, Nedcor, South Africa

All of us have but one vehicle to achieve what we want in life – our body. Dr McGannon has played a tremendously important role in making many of the Corporation's executives realize this simple but important fact, so often overlooked by busy executives. He has helped restore some balance for over-stressed and over-driven executives to ensure they maintain peak efficiency to continue being effective executives.

PETER A AEPLI, former CEO, Mister Minit.

I discovered a number of simple techniques and practical ideas that help my body and mind keep fit. The health management program, presented in a clear and practical way, contributes to a healthier and positive lifestyle. When I run my first marathon I will let you know the outcome!

LUC PEETERS, Director, Thilly Van Eessel, Belgium

Dr Michael McGannon helped me get back on the health and fitness track and take charge of my attitude.

DR TERRY THOMAS, Deputy Chief Executive, New Zealand Dairy Research Institute

A down to earth approach with lots of useful tips on how to cope with the pressures of business through exercise, diet and lower stress levels. Dr McGannon has a depth of research on which he amply draws.

TONY ROGERS, General Manager, ABSA Bank, Singapore

Dr McGannon is simple to understand, requiring minimal effort and almost guaranteed success.

A KAPUR, Chief Executive, ABN Ambro Bank

Dr McGannon enables you to realize benefits in managing your health and indirectly the interests of the company you work for.

K T LIM, General Manager, BP Malaysia

Dr McGannon alerted me to the fact that I was out of condition, and gave clear, pragmatic guidelines for returning to and retaining good health. By following some uncomplicated advice on nutrition and exercise, I am healthier, happier and more content than I can remember in a long time. The best thing of all is that my lifestyle remains much the same – no strict regimes, just a slow and steady return to good health and peace of mind.

ALEXANDER BLYTH, Invest in Training, Hong Kong

Dr McGannon gave me the motivation to stop thinking about my health and to start doing something about it. Eight months later sensible exercise and eating has become part of my life.

JOHN HASTINGS-BASS, Jardine Insurance Brokers

Dr Mike McGannon, a world authority on executive health, combines two rare virtues. The capacity to convey complex issues in simple, practical ways which we can relate to our daily life and, through his passion, commitment and humanity to inspire us to do a better job at managing our own key asset. . . our health. This book is essential reading for every manager.

JOHN HUMBLE, John Humble & Co. Ltd.

If we take time to care a bit more about our body, then we care at the same time about our intellect and our soul. We work with better results, less pressure! No doubt Dr McGannon's advice and recommendations are a key to our success. Work life balance is still one of our top breakthrough objectives. In following Dr McGannon's approach we can reach it.

MR KLEBER BEAUVILLAIN, President de Directoire, Hewlett-Packard

A logical process, which involves eating, drinking and exercising. It soon makes you realize 'you are what you eat'.

DENNIS B JAMES, General Manager, ICI

The work of Dr McGannon gives us the tools to enjoy a healthy and vigorous lifestyle.

DANIEL L RITCHIE, Chancellor, University of Denver

Dr McGannon's approach to business health is novel and stimulating. I don't think that anybody previously has managed to make the subjects of eating and drinking sensibly at all attractive. Dr McGannon has just the right combination of youthful American enthusiasm with a very serious underlying message.

RICHARD POWERS, Senior Managing Partner, Rowe & Maw, London

Dr McGannon's charismatic, yet low key approach, combined with a sense of humour and coupled with his evident professionalism makes him my favourite health guru. Convincing, credible, pragmatic and challenging.

ERIK VAN GALEN, Senior Vice President Boyden International and Governor of the American Hospital in Paris

Dr McGannon's whole approach – scope of concepts, testing, feedback and exercises – is extremely effective in creating the commitment and the proper action for a better quality of life.

PROFESSOR JEAN-CLAUDE LARRECHE, Professor of Marketing, INSEAD

Senior and successful executives in this region, as elsewhere, are deeply concerned about the pressures that their position puts on their life and the price that they may be paying. The sympathetic understanding with which Michael and Juliette approach the issues facing senior executives has clearly been developed through long experience of advising such people in their programs at the European business schools. Their focus on well-being and preventative measures to sustain health and effectiveness is very well received. Our delegates have been truly appreciative of the advice and guidance that has been offered by Michael and Juliette; they are all aware now of the need to take control of their own lives and they have an armoury of techniques with which to do that. Michael and Juliette have made an invaluable contribution to our event and possibly a lifesaving contribution to the well-being of many of our delegates. I cannot praise their program or their delivery too highly. Their book *The Urban Warrior's Book of Solutions* will bring to a much wider audience their philosophy and their approach to these crucial issues.

DEREK B SMITH, President Asia Pacific

Dr McGannon's approach is friendly, professional and not too finger-pointing, which allows each of us to feel at ease and very engaged.

PATRICE TRIAUREAU, Directeur Général, American Hospital of Paris

THE
URBAN
WARRIOR'S
BOOK OF
SOLUTIONS

Staying Healthy, Fit and Sane
in the Business Jungle

DR MICHAEL McGANNON MD

FT
PITMAN
PUBLISHING

London · Hong Kong · Johannesburg · Melbourne
Singapore · Washington DC

PITMAN PUBLISHING
128 Long Acre, London WC2E 9AN

A Division of Pearson Professional Limited

First published in Great Britain 1996

British Library Cataloguing in Publication Data
A CIP catalogue record for this book can be obtained from the British Library.

ISBN 0 273 61307 3

10 9 8 7 6 5 4 3 2 1

Typeset by Pantek Arts, Maidstone, Kent
Printed and bound in Great Britain by Biddles Ltd, Guildford and King's Lynn.

The Publishers' policy is to use paper manufactured from sustainable forests.

About the Author

Dr Michael McGannon, MD, earned his doctorate in Medicine in 1983 from Georgetown University (Washington DC) and his Postdoctoral Fellowship at Stanford University Medical Center (Stanford, California, USA). Since completing his research in preventative medicine and gastroenterology at Stanford in 1988, he has been the Medical Director of the Health Management Program at INSEAD, Europe's premier business school in Fontainebleau, France.

On the basis of his 8 years of teaching and research with many thousands of managers at leading business schools such as INSEAD, IMD (Lausanne, Switzerland) and SIM (Singapore Institute of Management) and within leading corporations, he established the first McGannon Institute of Preventative Health, a research Organization devoted to the awakening of the Inner Warrior by principles and practises described in this book. The mission statement of the Institute is as follows:

> **Our mission is to provide interactive health education and encouragement so that participants can autonomously upgrade their mental and physical abilities towards the balanced enjoyment and fulfillment of *all* aspects of personal and professional life.**

This educational process takes place at business institutes and within organizations' conference rooms throughout the world in the form of The Health Management Program. The HMP is an educational and motivational program designed to provide managers with the opportunity to reflect on and take stock of their most important asset: their health. The philosophy behind the program is that fit and healthy executives feel better about themselves, are more mentally astute and energetic, and thus better able to contribute to their company's performance.

Dr McGannon is also a medical journalist, writing extensively on issues such as stress, health and fitness in such international publications as the *International Herald Tribune* (Paris), the *Financial Times* (London), *The Business Times* (Singapore), *The European* (London) and *L'Impresa* (Milan).

Presently, Dr McGannon is setting up a multi-center research project dedicated to demonstrating the long-term impact of health and well-being on the corporate "bottom line." Moreover, in 1996, to make the programs and seminars available to locals and ex-patriots, further McGannon Institutes of Preventative Health Institute extensions are planned: 2 in SE Asia (Kuala Lumpur and Hong Kong) and in the United States.

All correspondences, queries for on-site workshops, UWIN (Urban Warrior Interactive Network) interactive software, CD-ROM, Passport Editions, McGannon Institute health newsletter and other tools designed to help optimize health, fitness and sanity should be addressed to:

The McGannon Institute of Preventative Health (Headquarters)
25, rue de Flagy
77940 Thoury-Ferrottes, FRANCE
Telephone: +331-64.31.04.21.
Facsimile: +331-64.31.04.22.
e mail address: McGannon @ INSEAD. FR

A PERSONAL NOTE
FROM THE AUTHOR

Dear Reader,

The story told within is a true one.

Today, more than ever, business life is going to demand more and more of your inner resources. When you fall off the fast track today, you risk doing more than just scraping your knee. There was a time, not so long ago, when being a sacrificial animal on the altar of success was part of the business mindset. Self-neglect resulting in dying of a heart attack or stroke or wallowing in depression was considered part of the 'territory'.

Fortunately, the mindset is changing. Much to their credit, business people are seeking, and finding, real balance in their lives. This book was written over the past several years to help you, the Urban Warrior, find the critical balance between personal and professional life and, in doing so, prevent you from falling off the fast track.

Practice moderation, not martyrdom, in all things. But never forget: these are not easy battles to be waged and we must approach this conflict, not in emotional fretting, but with calm analysis of the situation. In the way we decide to live lies the critical difference between living well and living foolishly.

To show the implications of this choice and to lay out some practical strategies for effectively implementing a lifestyle that the best suits your goals is the sole purpose of this book. May it serve you long and well.

Dr Michael B McGannon, MD
The Coach

"Life moves so much more rapidly now than it ever did before . . . the huge acceleration in the rate of growth of facts, of knowledge, of techniques, of inventions, of advances in technology . . . We need a different type of human being . . . who is comfortable with change, who enjoys change, who is able to improvise, who is able to face with confidence, strength and courage a situation of which he has absolutely no forewarning . . . the society which can turn out such people will survive; the societies that cannot turn out such people will die."

Frontiers of Human Nature, Abraham Maslow

CONTENTS

DEDICATION

This labour of love is humbly dedicated to:

Juliette and Jules – the best fellow warriors a man could be blessed with; and

Opa and Mamie – who taught me the meaning of the "inner battle."

FOREWORD

by Ron Clarke MBE AASA ACTS

I first became aware of the work Dr McGannon was doing at the INSEAD (the European Business Institute) with the Advanced Management people undertaking the various courses there in Fontainebleau, France, when one of our executive members remarked on how similar were the philosophies preached on the course and those we were advocating at Cannons Sports Clubs.

In fact, very early on in my athletic career I realized how distant most medical "experts" were from reality. In this, I happened to be encouraged by a doctor friend, Israel Zimmerman, who was disappointed with the general attitude prevalent among his fellow practitioners.

At that time, I was seeking the secrets of training for long distance running. I had this feeling that the current world records in my distances, the 5,000 and 10,000 metres, were far too slow, yet the experts were telling me how unbeatable they were.

When I trained harder and differently from other normal athletes, I was told there would be repercussions, that the human body could not take the strain I was exerting, that I would perform worse rather than better.

Well, I broke those records and by greater margins than they had ever been bettered before or since. My efforts yielded spectacular results, but they did so in the face of prevailing medical opinion and seemed to confound historical data and beliefs about human performance.

After thousands of years of spectacular advances in all the sciences, we still know very little about the most important of all – the human body and why it functions as it does. Michael McGannon is a latter-day pioneer in his field in that some years ago he realized the folly and frustration of treating disease. Until then he had been taught and encouraged to practice, like all of his fellows, the sanctity of healing.

"How about prevention?" he asked himself . . . "Surely we could be a thousand times more effective if we concentrated on ensuring people never get sick in the first place, rather than making sure they die as comfortably as possible?"

And so he moved to Europe and developed his preventative courses. He produced a "Book of Solutions" and he practiced what he preached in France at the INSEAD Advanced Management courses. In doing so, his role changed from the wait-for-symptoms approach to that of "coach," proactively preparing many thousands of managers for the biggest marathon of their life.

Over the years he has seen his message work. He knows that what he says is true, but old habits die hard and our Western society is besotted with self-indulgence and commercial exploitation.

Prevention is relatively simple . . . it is a matter of balancing life-styles (what we call *total living* at Cannons Sports Clubs). There is a sort of myth perpetuated out there that if you are to be healthy (and that is not merely to be free of disease but to be dynamically alive, as Michael demonstrates in these pages), you have to be a fanatical fitness crank, forever exercising and restricting meals to lettuce leaves and soy beans. This is just not so and is really the defense of those who do not want to know, for whatever reason.

> *Michael McGannon is a remarkable doctor. This is a remarkable book.*

Health, fitness, being alive and in control, is a matter of balance, of a sensible and rewarding approach to life.

Michael McGannon is a remarkable doctor. This is a remarkable book. Once you start to read it you realize that what he says is just common sense. And that it is possible to be healthy and yet "live well." In fact, living well is basic to enjoying health and fitness as you will quickly discover when you read these pages.

After all, in our way we are all warriors, planning our lives and defending our ground so as to optimize our talents and, in so doing, protecting to the best of our ability ourselves, our families, our friends and our interests for as long as we are able.

A little bit of help does not go amiss and this Michael has provided by publishing his philosophies for all to follow.

ACKNOWLEDGEMENTS

The story told within is a true one: a distillate of many years of experience in medicine spent listening to my colleagues, patients and students from around the world. In the same breath I would like to acknowledge my debt for the wisdom imparted and absolve all of them of any responsibility whatsoever for my failure to precisely analyze or understand their messages.

I, therefore, assume complete responsibility for the clarity and accuracy of the interpretation represented in the views contained herein, however flawed or seditious. For every individual, viewing the world with different lenses, there is a different interpretation. Whether a health professional or not, each of us perceives the miracle of the human body through our own prism.

For whatever benefit gleaned from these pages about one's role in maintaining the body and mind, the weight of debt is great and the contributors are numerous. Any insights resulting from the reading of this book must be traced back to the relationship between medical researchers/practitioners, nurses, orderlies and their patients, in their co-operative war against suffering. I refer to my medical colleagues, Western and Eastern alike, throughout the book as the "coaches."

For their valued feedback, anecdotal insights and evidence, I am also deeply indebted to the "warriors in the field," the many thousands of managers and professionals who have either participated directly in my university or corporate-based educational programmes. I refer to these patients-not-to-be throughout the book as the "players."

Why coaches and players? Because life in general, and business life in particular, is a game like any other, with rules, risks and rewards. If the coaches and players can agree the overall strategy on maintaining high levels of health and vitality, great things can be achieved and the game will have no losers.

Thanks go to Marco Wankewicz and Dr Kenneth Axen, PhD, of New York University for illustrations based on their original designs.

PROLOGUE: CHANGING ROLES

An Historical Perspective

Despite spectacular achievements of science over the past few centuries, life expectancy has not really increased dramatically over the past 50 years. Most of the serious threats to our lives stem from chronic diseases like heart disease, cancers, strokes, diabetes, not the acute infectious diseases that were commonplace at the beginning of this century. Experts in the field of preventative health generally agree that up to 80% of the premature deaths and illnesses associated with these conditions could be prevented or postponed by shifting responsibility to the patient-to-be through lifestyle control: proper nutrition, stress management, weight control, smoking cessation and adequate exercise. For this to happen, the roles of both the patient and doctor must evolve.

One of the few unfortunate downsides of the "miracles" of the technological revolution in medicine is that the primary focus for the responsibility for health has shifted to the doctor. The lay public has been convinced, with all the high-tech wizardry, that somehow medical practitioners are a type of modern day Mr Fix-It. In large part, we, as health professionals, have also drifted quite off track from the famous phrase in the oath attributed to Hypocrites*: *primum non nocere* (first do no harm). Since time immemorial, with all good intentions noted, doctors love to meddle with your health and you also love us to meddle. This maintains a dangerous illusion that something is being done for your health (much like buying a stationary bike and storing it in the cellar). Leeches used to suck blood, now they suck fat. Common sense has become dangerously *uncommon*.

One example of this mindset is the attention that has been focused on the efficacy of annual executive check-ups. Even when obligatory, they risk falling short of the mark of keeping the modern

---

* The famous Hippocratic Oath was, in all probability, not composed by Hypocrites, but by a temple cult, the Asclepiades, who worshipped Apollo. Apollo's son, Aesclepius, was the god of healing, frequently represented bearing a staff with a snake coiled around it.

warrior in the fighting shape necessary to perform his professional and personal duties. Most managers get very anxious about them and are interested in only one word after the whole process is finished: "normal" (see Appendix for ways to interpret the findings on check-ups). These high-tech, low-empowerment tools can play an important role, but they do not, by any means or measure, contain all the elements for keeping managers in the "fast track."

The high-tech aspect of such check-ups must be better focussed and the language used needs to be more "user-friendly." Unwittingly, by over-dependence on machines for diagnosis and treatment, the doctors have allowed technology to create an ever-widening distance, felt especially at the bedside, between themselves as Nature's assistants and the patient. The emphasis has been, up to now, on more lucrative technical screening, not time-intensive counseling and education, where it is needed. By not completely enlisting the individual as a co-conspirator in the war on diseases we all risk another lost opportunity.

Doctors, as coaches, must reassume their traditional roles as models of moderation, advisors and teachers. By using a more educative approach, people enjoy, on the personal level, greater autonomy, health and quality of life. Industry stands to benefit, of course, from a healthy workforce and is not besieged by escalating health claims and indirect costs of absenteeism, low morale and turnover. Only by upgrading the skills of the personnel can the direction of any organization optimize the combat readiness of the group.

In ancient days, medical health professionals in China practiced "health care:" the preservation of health, rather than "disease care," which is what we practice today. Often the manager is satisfied with the word "normal" before going back into the fray. And, in my experience, the managers know it. When asked whether their executive check-up was an important element in keeping their performance upgraded, only 15% could respond in the affirmatory. To maintain this balance, new tools and new mindsets need to be developed.

Changing role of the doctor: the option

No greater opportunity or obligation can fall the lot of a human being than to be a physician. In the care of suffering he needs technical skill, scientific knowledge, and human understanding. He who uses these with courage, humility, and wisdom will provide a unique service for his fellow man and will build an enduring edifice of character within himself. The physician should ask his destiny for no more than this, and he should be content with no less.

Dr Tinsley Harrison, MD

As of the 1990s, there will be essentially two ways to practice medicine: in a **reactive** way and in a **proactive** way. If we represented your life in a linear fashion, it would look like this:

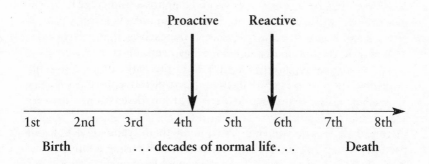

The major differences in the two approaches to practicing medicine are noted below:

Proactive		Reactive
Early: no symptoms yet	**Timing**	Late: symptoms manifest
Unlimited	**Options**	Severely limited
Limited	**Costs (human and economic)**	Unlimited
Fraternalistic: "coach"	**Doctor role**	Paternalistic
Active player	**Patient's role**	Passive players
"Could have"	**Language**	"Should have"
Low	**Risk of regret**	High
Shared	**Responsibility**	Lopsided
Win-win	**Overall situation (potential)**	Lose-lose
Open	**Information access**	Private
Home (familiar)	**Venue**	Hospital (depersonalised)
Mind/Body balance	**Overall focus**	Body as machine

By concentrating on the reactive approach, the health professional spends much of his effort waiting for the patient to present himself with a certain symptom (chest pain, breast lump, unwanted weight loss, blood loss). The doctor then "reacts" to the patient by developing the best possible "treatment ticket." It's not the doctor's fault: that's the way we are trained. Traditionally, during the education of the modern physician, the emphasis was very heavily weighted towards the curative "damage control" approach. It just seemed to all of us to be the most effective use of our limited time and energy.

Have we lost our primordial role of "healer?" Have we lost our time-honoured ability to re-align the ailing body with Nature's own laws that govern our body, mind and spirit. Benjamin Franklin once said, in cynicism of us: "God heals, the doctor takes the fee." Clearly, the role of the doctor must go beyond the prescription pad. The recent loss of faith and trust in the medical profession reflects this cynical attitude and suggests that the public is seeking a return to a more traditional role with expanded functions for doctors.

The proactive approach, on the other hand, offers such a feasible return to basics. It is best understood through its obvious similarities to ancient military strategy. Military planning and the healing arts are parallel in many ways: orientation of their respective strategies, there are adversaries (enemy and diseases), complete knowledge of this adversary is essential to victory and, the best resolution of disharmony is that which uses fewest precious resources and employs the least aggressive approach: victory without conflict.

Paraphrasing Sun Tzu, the mysterious philosopher-warrior who wrote on this subject 2,000 years ago: superior military strategists foil their enemies' plans first, then destroy the enemies' alliances and connections; then, his armies. The ultimate strategy (one could argue, a *failed* strategy) would be to use vast resources to lay siege to the cities and towns. Here, what could be seen as an exercise in pure ruthlessness, Sun Tzu would say was loss due to poor self-control and excessive emotionalism.

Likewise, in medicine, aggressive therapeutic modalities (chemotherapy, radical surgery, intense pharmocologic therapy) could scarcely be called an optimal strategy for dealing with chronic debilitating diseases like heart diseases, strokes and cancers.

From dike-tenders to coach

Over the past two decades, the landscape of medicine has changed dramatically. Now, medicine is entering an accelerated new phase, that of empowerment through education. During this new phase, the focus of responsibility shifts from being eccentric (outside oneself) to concentric (within oneself): DIY healthcare. It is no longer possible, nor desirable, for either the patient or the doctor, to restrict themselves to the practice of the "wait-for-symptoms" approach to heart disease, strokes and cancers. Doctors, appropriately, are learning the lessons slowly and are starting to complement their curative work in the hospitals and laboratories with educative work in the conference rooms of corporations and in classrooms.

> There is but one temple in the universe,
> and that is the Body of Man.
> Nothing is holier than that high form . . . .
> We touch heaven when we lay
> our hands on a human body.
> *Frederic von Hardenberg, 1772*

This book is written in homage to the happy and judicious marriage between the curative and preventative approaches, to the synthesis of each and every approach to optimal health and vitality, whether sponsored, sanctioned or re-reimbursed, with the objective to help the members of our societies enjoy as much of life as possible while being responsible for their own health.

Changing role of the patient: managing health as an asset

> Men travel abroad to wonder at the height of mountains, at the huge waves of the seas, at the long courses of the rivers, at the vast compass of the ocean, at the circular motion of the stars and yet they pass by themselves without even wondering at all . . . .
> *St Augustine*

The human experiment seems, at first glance, to be a miraculous defiance of the laws of probability. Take the human body: as with all things on the physical plane of existence, one easily witnesses a natural tendency for things to unwind, fall apart, age, degenerate and die. Each organism marches in this parade at a pace predestined and preordained by its genetic code, a continual unraveling at every second, until finally it requires a trip to the garage for some "rewinding." Anything that required energy to assemble will unwind to a more stable state. The way we manage this birthright is the whole issue in discussion here.

I must hasten to add that this book in no way subscribes to the current heresy of the "youth culture" to go against Natural Laws or to take short cuts. Rather, it is an appeal to go with the flow, the Tao, as the eastern half of the species calls it. That is, physical fitness and optimal health are best perceived as means to maintain our vitality, not as absolute ends in themselves. This means that much of the work of upgrading your health and fitness, for whatever life is going to throw your way, is up to you.

You will notice that even in its title, this book (your war manual), draws its inspiration from a tradition of warriors who always respect and prepare all their arms carefully before confrontations on the battlefield of life.

Ask any corporate executive, in all fields from marketing to human resources, from operations to information technology, what the critical link in the organization is, and most will readily reply "my people." That stands to reason: good people are the most expensive asset to recruit, to train, to keep *and* to replace. Clearly, there is no organization without people and a chain is only as strong as its weakest link; yet attitudes and policy towards "people" do not always reflect this.

If your company has recently bought a machine for US$250,000 to be used over the next ten years, you can expect that resources will be proactively mustered to maintain that machine. Therefore, logically, the same attitude must be applied to the human body and mind.

How then do we ensure that we will remain on the fast track effectively with the odds stacked against us? How can we increase our chances of winning, both personally and professionally? How do we balance the material and emotional needs of our family with our own professional ambition? Need we become sacrificial offerings on the altar of success or simply redefine success? The answer lies somewhere in the setting of priorities many years ago.

Shifting priorities

For most of us, the time during and just after university, was critical in setting priorities. When first confronted with the whole issue of "balance," some of us decided that for a while (say, during your 30s and 40s) we would go all out professionally, giving a full 85–90% of waking time to the company. This strategy would help achieve a certain "critical mass" of financial security, after which you could possibly tend to your personal life.

The unfortunate consequence of this thinking was that we found out, often too late, that the family, the principal unit of society, becomes an appendage of the career, like any other aspect of the CV: "married, two kids." Subconsciously, the *big three* priorities in your life may have been:

1. Work
2. Family
3. Self

In this scenario, too much time is spent *surviving* and too little spent actually *living*. Universal education (the arts, literature, poetry, the humanities) takes a back seat to more technical education. Our well-spring of philosophical wisdom starts to dry up and with it our ability to solve essential problems in our lives, such as our children and our marriage.

With the mindset of sacrificial animal, this is a lose–lose situation for all involved, including the health professionals. The people whose approval you sought have all moved out of your life or are dead.

Little did we know just how quickly these imbalances would come back to haunt us: time flew by and you had the sinking realization that you were living not with a soulmate and a tightly-knit family, but, in fact, with *strangers* (including yourself). Your health and confidence suffered to the long-term detriment of your family and company, and you lost your sense of humour and spontaneity. In a Faustian contract, you have convinced yourself that you must exchange irretrievably precious years of your life, marriage, parenting, health for one more rung on the corporate ladder.

Have you been mistaking your real career for your profession (medicine, law, business)? *Life* is the *real* career.

First things first

As professionals, a good place to start in bridging the gap between increasing demands and abilities is to take care of number one:

1. Self (health and sanity)
2. Family
3. Work

Corporations worldwide annually spend many millions of dollars on upgrading the managerial skills of their managers to help managers run their businesses well. By comparison, pitifully little is spent on upgrading the other skills necessary to run their businesses successfully for a long time. This mindset only perpetuates the lose–lose situation above.

Take a good hard look at a typical chap who slowly, but surely, lost control of his core asset, his health and sanity. In a race to get ahead, he has allowed his health to suffer and now the days are just flowing into each other without any real demarcation.

Let's assume for the moment that you are a business manager. One question: when it comes to your long-term business objectives (and, generally, how you manage your business) *is merely avoiding bankruptcy enough?* Obviously not. A smart executive never takes his eye off the profit margin. The same proactive approach is required when it comes to protecting your core asset, your mental and physical health; merely avoiding diseases, while an essential component, is not enough.

> **You cannot delegate your health and sanity!**

As a business leader, you want to develop a "health profit margin" while having fun at the helm. The challenge for the manager of the 1990s and beyond is to strike the balance between personal and professional life so that both sides profit!

The real obstacle lies not with the "players," but also with the ubiquitous folkloric understanding and antiquated, often demonic, business methods that abound. The stress, the rich meals (34% of interviewed managers eat in restaurants four or more times every week), the jet-lag, the isolation from their loved ones, the sedentary lifestyles, the macho nature of the business persona are now seen as significant inherent risks of the "terrain" to be dealt with, rather than just part of the job.

Changing role of the organization: payoff on the well-being investment

Changing trends for the better

Things have really changed in the past 25 years. Fortunately for managers, their families and their companies that depend upon them, the issue of staying healthy, fit, and sane is now once again on the business agenda – a far cry from the 1970s and 1980s, when mere profit margins were the manager's sole raison d'être and executive wellness was an optional fringe issue. The overall health of the managers is being perceived as part of the overall strategy for corporate survival.

Since my decision in the 1970s to carve out my professional homestead on the continent of medicine, I have been truly fortunate to be able to practice both reactive and proactive approaches. In the early days, as a student and house officer at Georgetown University (Washington, DC, USA), I saw that through long hours of hard work and study in the face of hopeless diseases, we were able to offer some relief and palliation. To a great extent and given the inherent limitations of the approach, we *were* effective. In 1988, when I completed my post-doctoral medical research in digestive diseases at Stanford University, California, one fact became exceedingly clear to me, one you should never forget:

> **The way things are arranged, you are worth more to the medical profession when you are *sick* than when you are *well*.**

My more recent proactive role over the past eight years has involved teaching more than 16,000 managers, from 500 or more international corporations from 40 countries worldwide and from all managerial strata, just how to appreciate the link between personal health management and professional performance. The results of my research are encouraging and indicate that corporate investment in this proactive approach is paying off already with positive signs of a reversal in the trend of the manager mindset.

In my experience, the response to this from forward-looking governments and companies (such as Hewlett Packard, Sime-Axa,

Singapore International Airways, Nokia, Standard Chartered, ICI, British Petroleum, IBM, Heineken, Thomson Electronics, PTT Netherlands, Malaysian Ministry of Home Affairs and scores of others) has been very positive. They have assumed a *proactive* role by creating programs which provide a structure to enable the harried manager to take a break from the grind and focus on upgrading their personal abilities: physical, mental and emotional.

I can see this approach reflected in the managers that I work with on a daily basis: they are getting more and more fit and taking on more and more responsibility for their own health. But congratulations may be premature as the job is far from done. In this era of down-sizing and cost-cutting, we will witness, I predict, a move to ask the manager to do more and more for less and less. Efforts to help the modern professional to balance work and home, heart and head, must persist as an integral part of corporate strategy.

HOW TO APPROACH AND USE THIS BOOK

To the Coaches

As a model for other health professionals to use, based on my long-standing experience with many thousands of professionals, whose business life has inherent hazards stacked against them, I propose a feasible model of coaching proactive medicine, based on my experience with both the reactive and the proactive approaches. One of my basic premises is that any health program, if it is to be effective, must provide these key ingredients for success:

1. **A pause for reflection to take stock of your core asset: personal health.** What are the facts as we know them? The players want to know. What are the adversaries (illnesses) and what are my arms to deal with them? Here is where a focussed and personal consultation, with the emphasis on education and implementation, could represent a successor to the check-up.

   Throughout the book, there are interactive exercises that are designed to emphasize the link between personal health and professional performance. That will help to provide a clear and concrete idea as to exactly where the players stand from a health and fitness point of view (the baseline). Everyone should be able to answer the question: "How am I *really* doing?"

2. **The most up-to-date information available** from the annals of medicine, East and West, that will enable the players both to make intelligent decisions about their health, as well as helping them to develop new skills to cope with the inherent demands of professional life.

   As everyone in the field readily recognizes, information is simply not enough: we must provide understanding. The players are much better informed and, with the information revolution, that trend will certainly continue with new fervour. This Promethean task has begun: we can no longer arrogantly profess to have a monopoly on this information, but, rather, need to work with our players to interpret and implement the messages coming from medical research.

3. A **specially-structured program,** conceived and designed with the realities of modern professional life in mind, to build players back into "fighting shape" and keep them there, at their speed and style, to their cultural liking. Interactive action plans in each chapter are designed to help players improve on their specific weak points, while observing the principle of minimal investment for maximal return.

4. **A self-designed and monitored follow-up program** designed to enable players to monitor their progress themselves, in *their* style, at *their* speed.

To the Players/Warriors

This book represents many years of careful listening concerning what aspects of your health and fitness you wish to upgrade and maintain to keep yourself competitive for the coming years. It is really about creating *options*.

When you are healthy: you have all the options regarding your cardiovascular fitness, nutrition, weight control, stress management and so on. Whether you exercise those options is up to you but our job is to give you **a choice.**

Once you become seriously ill: you have no real options because your control over your health has gone. Even the best doctor cannot save you after years of neglect and abuse. The control of your health is firmly in your hands. So come off the battlefield for a while, learn something about your body and mind with the idea of returning to Life's glorious battle, winning more victories and, above all, enjoying it more.

Optimal health management of oneself is largely the result of a balance between *lifestyle* (major influence) and intelligent *medical intervention* (minor influence). As such, it complements but cannot replace regular medical check-ups. When it comes to health management, do not try too hard to have perfect health: it's impossible.

As Sun Tzu put it:

> For this reason, to win a hundred victories in a hundred battles is not a hallmark of skill. The acme of skill is to subdue the enemy without even fighting.

What results can be realistically hoped for using this approach? One can expect both quantitative and qualitative improvement in all aspects of personal and professional life. In a word, to remain as active and vital for as long as possible and to die quickly and suddenly, without prolonged periods of hospital-bound or wheel-chair-bound illnesses.

> If life is a plane journey, the value of the whole trip is brought into question by a crash landing.
> *Senior Manager from Singapore*

A final word

In this very privileged position, one of the things that has astounded me most is the amount of personal and professional resources (time, energy, money) people are willing to invest to upgrade their personal and professional abilities. The problem is not one of "will power:" no one should ever doubt the motivation of professional people once the decision is made to tune up their bodies after years of neglect. This is a highly motivated group of people who are willing to show up for practice in preparation for the "big game."

People ask me again and again: "Can these diseases really be conquered?" and "Do I have a role in this struggle?" The answer to both queries is: "Yes." All scientific data indicate that if we are to have any impact on the major killers in the 1990s and beyond, we must teach "in the field:" in boardrooms and conference centers. The battle lines are drawn out there and that's where the battle against diseases will be won.

But do not engage yourself in a fretful way, but rather in a warrior-type way. Anticipate, in an intelligent way, the next move of the "enemy," that is infirmity and diseases, and develop alliances that help you make intelligent decisions about your health and fitness for battle. In a word, do not become *obsessive*. This mindset achieves nothing. Judgmental "mind-talk" not only detracts from the pleasure of life, but is also counterproductive to the accomplishment of your objectives. Practice moderation, not martyrdom, in all things. You do not have to look into the wide-open eyes of children in the leukaemia wards or in refugee camps, as I have had the honour of doing, to realize that life is an exceedingly precious and short proposition. You only go around once on this roller coaster, so learn to appreciate its "ups" and "downs."

You see, the pleasure of stoic self-improvement is not enough to sustain long-term progress. *To enjoy the fruits of self-improvement, you must uncompromisingly centre your lives around enjoyment of happy moments.* You are about to embark upon a journey of self-knowledge and self-awakening through exploration of the human body and mind, and it is through a more complete awareness of yourself and the enemy (diseases) that you will win all of Life's battles.

But never forget: these are not easy battles to be waged and we must approach this conflict, not in a state of emotional fretting, but with calm analysis of the situation.

> **In the way we decide to win this war lies the critical difference between living well and living foolishly.**

To show the implications of this choice and to lay out some practical strategies for implementing a lifestyle that best suits your goals is the *sole* purpose of this book. May it serve you long and well.

Dr Michael B McGannon, MD
"The Coach"
Fontainebleau, France
December 1995

1

STAYING HEALTHY: PROTECTING YOUR CORE ASSET

"When in doubt, I simply kept repeating the corporate mantra *'comes with the territory, comes with the territory.'* That seemed to do the trick."

THE JOURNEY OF AWAKENING

From ticker to time-bomb:
the anatomy of health bankruptcy

I would like to introduce myself. My name is Peter. I am now 47 years of age and this is my life.

My journey of awakening starts out with an anatomy of a health bankruptcy, a still photograph of me who, while very proactive and faithful to a healthy profit margin at work ("the bottom line"), was very reactive and negligent with regard to my core assets at work and home: my spouse, my family, my health, sanity, and happiness. A few years ago, I started my journey to awakening as a *real* time-bomb but I just couldn't hear the ticking.

My Profile

My university education was smooth, aside from the untimely death of my father at the early age of 51 years from "some heart problem." Mother subsequently became depressed, gained weight, and developed mild diabetes. Curiously, after the death of my father, I myself developed a bizarre ear problem, a ringing or ticking, that affected my balance from time to time. I actually used that as an excuse to stop my jogging program.

Three years after earning my degree in engineering, I realized that, even with that advanced degree, I would have to get my Masters of Business Administration if I had any hope of getting into the business "fast track." Professionally speaking, my investments in time and energy were paying off nicely and I seemed to be the master of my destiny.

I had even developed, several years after my MBA, my own version of "hero:" the fellow who would put in a full 16-hour day of negotiations in our Hong Kong office, jump on a plane for 14 hours to London, arrive 8 a.m., shower and hit the ground running to put in a 14-hour work day. Wow! High blood pressure seemed to me to be a small price to pay for such collective adulation.

Private Life

At that time, I was happily married to Jane, the mother of my two children, Christopher aged 12 and Julia, 9.

The intimate aspects of my relationship with Jane, in a word, had been better. She worked off and on and seemed content with her ladies' groups' meetings. The long hours and business trips of mine had stolen something away from our relationship. We had drifted apart and had discussed separation and even the "D" word, on numerous occasions.

Most of the time, when we went out to dinner, we would find ourselves at a loss for words. It was as though we were worlds apart, staring over each other's shoulders, not even touching hands, very alone. When in doubt, I simply kept repeating the corporate mantra *comes with the territory, comes with the territory.* That seemed to do the trick.

I thought for sure that the children had everything they might need or want. Sure, sometimes they whined and complained: Chris, about my missing his football games and judo tournaments; and Julia, about her piano recital. But they had everything they really needed to survive.

The worst part of the week was, of course, Saturday mornings. There was always a little tension as if we needed some time to re-acquaint ourselves, lots of pregnant, sometimes painful, silences. The whole family was making legitimate claims on my time and energy. Unfortunately, at a time when they needed my energy and attention the most, I was in need of being left alone to read my paper in the garden. Some day, I thought, they'll understand.

Back in the old days, as a student, I remember that I noticed when it was a beautiful day or not, I smelled the flowers, chatted with people at the bus stop and helped Jane prepare the evening family meal. Now it seemed that I did not really care about these things in life one way or another.

My home base was (and still is) in the UK, but I had lived in the USA and SE Asia for stints of five years apiece: truly a world citizen. By most standards, I was living the "good life." Things seemed to be going just fine on all fronts, except for that nagging ear ticking that sometimes kept me awake at night.

Over the previous five years, after many brief discussions with my family and with my spouse's tacit consent, I had decided to assume an even heavier workload, with lots of travel to the Far East (about 150 days per year), to achieve personal and company objectives. This decision, of course, involved more travel (my travel agent and hotel concierge are my extended family!), less time with my real family, and, of course, a more sedentary life.

Up until then, I never had much cause for concern or reflection. Sure, there was an occasional heart attack or cancer victim *at work*. But then one of those Saturday mornings, after returning from a prolonged business trip to Singapore, something happened that I did not expect. We were sitting around the breakfast table voting for the next vacation destination that summer. My young daughter, as of yet untrained in the fine art of diplomatic self-restraint, blurted out, "Dad, *you* can't vote! *You're* never here." I had heard it before, the only difference I remember was that I was genuinely distressed this time. I did not mention my feelings to Jane. It will pass, I thought.

But Jane, true to form, would not let these trivialities go by without mention. These conversations would, almost invariably, be followed by argument with her, usually in bed late at night, that made me feel uncomfortable.

"You're not being very careful with your time, Peter. At the moment, the children actually *want* you to come to their games and recitals. Do you know how rare that is these days? These years go quickly. Sooner than you think, this period of grace will be over and you will beg them to visit you. Only then they will make perfunctory visits to you out of a sense of duty, not desire. I don't know what's going on in your head, but try to be more careful with your time. All sorts of irreplaceable opportunities with the kids are slipping through your fingers."

Some time after that, though I cannot pinpoint the exact time, I found myself to be more withdrawn and drinking more alcohol, both alone and with colleagues. I was slowly and methodically isolating myself from those things I loved. I was rapidly changing for the worse and I did not want to hear about it. Although my family said that they understood my frequent absences, I still felt bad about being a "phantom father and spouse" and the half-hearted attempts to spend more time at home.

Several months later when driving back from services for a colleague at work who had suddenly died of a stroke, I decided to take stock at home.

Several months later when driving back from services for a colleague at work who had suddenly died of a stroke, I decided to take stock at home. One calm Saturday afternoon, I asked my children in the back seat how they might remember me. I expected nice words like "caring," "generous," "warm," or the like, and I was flabbergasted when Julia, with characteristic honesty, answered "never around, Daddy" and Christopher answered "angry, but just some of the time, Dad." The image of those two words, "absent" and "angry," etched into my tombstone started to haunt my dreams at night and recently even my daydreams. And the ticking just continued.

Physical and Intellectual Activity

Although a very active athlete (I adore football and badminton) as a university student, physical activity for me had become something of a luxury: restricted to an occasional game of tennis or golf on weekends, but only if and when time permitted. Even our once regular family hikes in the countryside had been phased out.

Once an avid reader of everything from spy novels to political analyses, I had been unable to get in any real reading since my last brief vacation 18 months before when I read half a novel. I probably read too many daily newspapers and management books and watched too much TV.

Nutrition

One word could best describe what and how I used to eat: rich. Lots of fatty meat like T-bone steaks, pork chops, bacon, lamb *at will*. I was not that keen on salads or vegetables (I could never tell exactly what fibre is), especially since my bout of "the runs" during my last trip to India the previous year. When I thought about it, I would take a one-a-day multivitamin.

Slowly, but surely, various imbalances that I thought improbable in my own life took hold. I had a weight gain of roughly one kilogram/year over the previous seven years. My form, that I subsequently stopped checking in the morning mirror, went from svelte to bloated amorphous. I used to say that I was "big boned," but my children would only laugh at that euphemism. At their insistence, I had tried the endless stream of "new diets" without any real success. I generally ate a late dinner, drank about 45 drinks a week (often more), smoked the occasional cigarette. I thought I was "in touch" with my body, mind and feelings.

Things began to change rather quickly in my life several years ago just as I turned 44 years old, head of an international division of a multinational company. I decided, with a little benign coercion from Jane and colleagues, to go for a medical exam, a check-up. After all, I reasoned, if I do it with my car, why not my body?

Going into this check-up, I was obviously well aware of the fact that I had many of the tell-tale signs and symptoms of someone who had been neglecting his body. It had become a ritual.

I dutifully presented myself to Doctor Blum, an old friend and confidante, with the usual list of complaints: I sleep poorly and always feel tired; chronic backaches and headaches plague me with increasing frequency; I bolt my food, heartburn and bloating ensue and lastly, mild depression strikes me from time to time (I think too much).

I was certain that, despite these nuisances, everything would be decreed more or less "normal" and that the same old lecture from Dr Blum would be as customary as my complaint list: lose some weight, stop smoking and drinking so much, watch your diet, get some more exercise and so on. Though an excellent doctor and good friend over the years, Doctor Blum was not a particularly good actor. As he performed my physical exam, his bushy eyebrows perked up and frowned as if in disbelief and dismay. He hummed and hawed as he jotted these findings into my medical dossier: he seemed in his own little world.

Just as he was finishing his entry, his nurse poked her head into the office and announced, somewhat out of breath.

"Excuse me, Doctor Blum, your 11 o'clock appointment is here and requires your immediate attention: blood pressure at rest is 220 over 115 and has severe headaches."

He was up and out the door before he could reply.

Wow, that must be serious, I thought, without really knowing what those numbers implied. Curious to find out something about myself, I leaned over his desk and read his last note in my chart:

History:

44 y.o. Male, senior manager, family history for heart disease and diabetes, here today for a routine check-up. Sedentary. Appears tired (? depressed?). Complains of poor sleep and backaches.

No meds.

Physical exam: obese male, mild sweating, poor dentition

(1) Blood pressure = 165/95 (last time it was ~ 135/80).

(2) Resting heart rate = 84 (last time it was ~ 72), normal sinus rhythm, with a few scattered ectopic beats.

(3) Body fat = 30% (last check was 24%).

(4) Waist-to-hip ratio = 1.05.

(5) Rectal exam: haemorrhoids, no occult blood, prostate: normal, no nodules.

Laboratory work from the previous week revealed normal ECG, elevated levels of cholesterol, triglycerides, fasting blood sugar.

Overall assessment: Syndrome X?

Health risk level: high for diabetes and heart attack.

Health age: 63.8 years of age.

Plan: (tough case)

#1. Elevated BP: stop smoking altogether, nicotine patch, relax, control stress, reduce alcohol/coffee intake.

#2. Excess weight (refractory), inactive. Watch fat in diet.

#3. Follow-up: borderline laboratory values. Return to clinic in one year. Decide on medication for BP, DM at that time.

Blum, MD beeper # 413

Just then, Doctor Blum came back to the room, slightly out of breath.

"Peter, I am going to have to run out just now. I must accompany a patient of mine to the hospital. Nothing serious, just for overnight observation. I see that you've read my note."

"Well, Doctor, we've spoken before: lose weight, stop smoking, less drinking, slow down. You know the old story of the man who, on the advice of his physician, had given up rich foods, smoking and drinking and was as fit and healthy as could be until the day of his suicide." I thought that office humour would make the doctor smile, but he clearly was not in the mood for my adolescent humour.

"Any questions or comments?" He was clearly in a hurry.

"Yes, I have known about the other aspects, the blood pressure being slightly high, the weight and cholesterol and so on. But, what is this bit in the Assessment: 'Health risk level: high for diabetes and heart attack. Health age: 63.8 years of age' mean?"

"Those figures, Peter, are handy statistical ways of letting you know that health-wise you are not really getting away with however you are living your life," he explained. "In a word, based on your lifestyle and family history, your body is ageing a lot faster than a normal person of the same 44 years. In fact, you a pretty good candidate for nasty problems, like diabetes or a heart attack."

I began to feel my face flushing warm and beads of sweat on my brow. My only real objective at that time was merely to resume work at a high level and carry out my professional responsibilities. As he seemed to drone on, I interrupted, exasperated.

"Doctor Blum, aren't there just some *pills* I could take to take care of these minor problems? You know, one of modern medicine's *magic bullets?*" I could feel an angry voice swelling up inside. *Must restrain that*, I thought. *Let's go back to work.*

I remembered having read in a magazine that the three most commonly prescribed types of medication in the world were blood pressure medication, tranquilizers and ulcer medication. I did not see the real meaning behind all of that for my case, but it all sounded good enough for me.

I knew that there had to be a quick way out of this one. While packing his doctor's bag, he responded.

"You will receive your whole report in several weeks, complete with my full recommendations regarding exercise, stress and diet. The usual, right? This time try to take them a little more seriously or you may find yourself looking down the barrel of a loaded gun. Listen, Peter, more and more, I am seeing the results of people who have given up on themselves and are dying of largely preventable diseases. I simply *cannot* do all the work here. Can't you at least meet me half way on these issues of your health? I won't be able to keep you off medications forever at this rate. You know what they say: 'Don't show up for practice, don't expect to play in the finals'."

I was starting to feel very adolescent and exposed without my denial to cover me.

"Yeah, Doc, I know and really do care, but I am pushing for that promotion I mentioned to you and time is short. It's not just that, exercise is boring, diet foods are boring, losing weight is boring." Although I was a little proud of my fast-track macho arrogance, I started feeling like a pampered celebrity: boring, boring, boring!

"Oh, is that it, Peter? You want to talk about something boring? Try spending five days in the local hospital like a caged animal, recuperating from a heart attack. Now, that's *real* boredom!" He carried on, "Incidentally, I may have to start you on blood pressure medications if your pressure does not come down by your next visit. That's it. Now, if you'll excuse me, I really must run."

I walked into the parking lot stunned, affected by more than my usual anxiety and irritation that accompanies these visits, not just because of my deteriorating health, but also because of the tone of Blum's voice: he was actually giving up on me. *I'm losing an ally and a friend at the same time. One by one in my life, I am sending them away only because they have had the courage and compassion to remind me that I'm slipping. Even my wife has long since learned that it's better not to discuss my health, my drinking, my smoking, my life in general. To discuss it would only ruin a nice afternoon. But how could I have gotten it so wrong for all this time? How could I have let myself go so far?*

Dr Blum, more a friend than a coach, had often warned me of the consequences, but it seems that every time he began his abstract litany of diseases, I phased him out, drifting off into other more pressing issues. As I drove back to the office, I decided that it was high time to finally get myself back into what I called "fighting shape." *This was it! No more fooling around! Today's the day! I am definitely not going the way of my father!*

I made a mental checklist of the possible outcomes of my type of "reactive" behaviour pattern and checked off the ones that I had seen colleagues in my company succumb to:

1. A heart attack: the BIG one, as I called it.
2. A stroke.
3. Various cancers.
4. Mental breakdown/depression.
5. Ulcers, alcoholism, diabetes . . . .
6. Overall poor life quality.

There was a check mark by each of the conditions!

But, alas, the impetus to change for the better created by the anxiety felt in Dr Blum's office quickly wore off as I plunged headlong back into my work and I slipped back into my reactive mindset. I didn't even open the finalized report from Dr Blum; I knew enough. I wanted to let the fuse burn down yet a little more.

In retrospect, I realize that I was going on the battlefield of life thoroughly unprepared, a liability to my team and to my family. With every birthday, the louder the ticking in my ears grew, and the more I squelched it.

All those things were complex abstractions that simply did not apply to me. I was going to beat the odds. How can such a smart guy like me not get the important signals that kept coming to me? Is a heart attack one of those macho happenings?

Months and years went by. I could have been more careful with my time, with my health. In the months and years that followed, I knew that I was responsible for the health of my body and mind (because that disease of the body really begins in the mind's attitude towards oneself), but like everyone else, I needed a little bit of a wake-

> *How can such a smart guy like me not get the important signals that kept coming to me? Is a heart attack one of those macho happenings?*

up call. And then a couple of years later, while closing some deals for my company in Hong Kong, it came. My wake-up call *finally* came.

Early Wake-Up Call

That fateful day started just like any other work day.

I had been involved in some critical negotiations for my company in Hong Kong, holed up at my favourite hotel for just two more days of gruelling meetings before returning home. My daily on-the-road routine, although somewhat stale, gave me a certain security and feeling of confidence: a rushed shower . . . quick breakfast gobbled, washed down by coffee and a cigarette . . . traffic jerking stop and go . . . finally getting to the office and looking over the faxes from head office and calls to make. On the way into the office, I was daydreaming about Dr Blum.

Two years had passed since the office visit with Dr Blum. Aside from the extra travel and the new "prosperity tissue" around my waist, the only things in my life that changed since my check-up is that my memory is slipping ever so slightly and that I am now taking blood pressure and ulcer medication every morning. Everything seemed more or less under control.

The day at work proceeded pretty much as usual: endless (sometimes pointless and trivial) meetings and calls punctuated the day with numbing frequency, leaving me with little time for myself at the end of the day. No matter, I've gotten used to this sacrifice: *comes with the territory.*

After a series of meetings that continued nearly non-stop until 10 p.m., I finally dragged my weary body back to the hotel *(they're always so friendly here)* for a night-cap and some sleep. Picking up the phone, I dialled 15 for the concierge, "Yes, please, a wake-up call at 6.30 tomorrow sharp. Thank you." Ready for another round tomorrow, then home on Wednesday. Exhausted, I fell asleep, comfortably anaesthetized by the alcohol, mulling over the day of work that awaited me.

Then, awakening suddenly in the early hours of the morning, I felt a presence in the room, as though there was someone sitting at the foot of the bed. As I often awake early in the mornings, my first reflex was to check the time: the red digital display on the TV console seemed to read much brighter than usual "2:47." I looked dreamily around the hotel room and noticed in my half-stupor that the city lights created strange images on the curtains as they were gently buffeted by the air-conditioning. Again, I could swear that I had heard or felt something in the shadows. As I had a long day tomorrow, I tried to ignore whatever it was and to get back to sleep.

Just then, as I was getting back to sleep, I noticed a vague pressure sensation (it was not really pain), which impaired my breathing. At first, it was a gnawing pain on my left side and jaw, then progressing to a severe crushing pain across my chest that made me feel like vomiting. This was most certainly not my usual type of indigestion that I was having.

It felt as though someone was sitting on my chest, pinning me to the bed. I could not move! Then a wave of panic seized my mind and thoughts of the family raced through my head. *This is the strongest case of heartburn that I have ever had. Am I suffocating? Is this the BIG one? It cannot be all that serious. What should I do? Should I call my wife? Where are my children right now? This cannot be happening!*

In my panic, my priorities seemed to shift so suddenly and so drastically, just as they had after the Dr Blum check-up several years ago. All I wanted to do was to speak with my wife and children. I now realize, in retrospect, that this was the beginning of my "awakening."

Groping for my eyeglasses on the night table, I clumsily knocked the ashtray to the floor, spreading a sickening stench throughout the room. Another wave of panic came over me. *What should I do? Sit tight? Call someone? Who should I call for help? What if this is nothing, a little asthma or bronchitis (my wife had become accustomed to my minor breathing problems and would know precisely what to do now). Humm . . . let's see . . . Reception: 12, Room Service: 13, Housekeeping: 14, Concierge: 15. That's it, the concierge would be the most discreet, least probing.*

While leaning back in bed waiting for the concierge to answer, I thought of how I really should have paid more attention to that Dr Blum about the cigarettes, the weight, the stress: so many "shoulds." Oh, well, too late for that now.

"Hello, concierge here. How may I help you, sir?" he asked cheerfully.

"Well, you see, I'm having this little problem with indigestion that's keeping me awake . . ."

I proceeded to explain my symptoms and what I thought was happening. As I told my story I detected an increasing tone of alarm breaking through his normally calm voice. Apparently, this type of thing was not at all new to him. He suggested calling an ambulance "just to be safe, sir." In the meantime, he was sending someone to my room to help gather my personal belongings. *I can't believe that this is happening to me.*

The waves of pressure in the chest came and went, increasing in severity and frequency sometimes moving across my chest and up to my jaw. I was still quite lucid and the only memory I had of the ambulance arriving was how sweaty and cold I felt, and how suddenly helpless I had become. As they loaded me into the ambulance, I could feel a tear trickle down my cheek as I thought of how many things in my life I would never get around to doing.

Obviously, this is more than heartburn. Whatever it may be, please, dear God, save me. I promise to get it right this time. What about my wife: should I call her? I really miss her now, I thought as they loaded me into the back of the ambulance. *Best not to scare her.*

It is just not supposed to happen this way. The kids haven't even graduated from secondary school yet. A condensed, surrealistic, version of my life flashed before me like a very clear, fast-forward, movie: my stellar university years, my corporate combats and victories, happy courtship scenes from my marriage with Jane, the birth of Christopher and Julia. *Where were the golden years, the payoff for all the sacrifice: my hobbies, golf, the farm, sailing, the grandchildren? What meaning does all this have?*

All of the rhetoric seemed to evaporate in front of me, as I was totally and utterly engaged in one of the biggest battles of my life.

Amidst the panic, I could not help but notice how remarkably well-equipped was the interior of this ambulance. I had an oxygen mask on now, intravenous lines, urinary catheter and monitor lines, beeping and hissing. Would all this be enough to save me? I felt very helpless and scared about what was happening: this was definitely not being treated as a routine case of indigestion!

"We could even do minor surgery and deliver babies, if those situations arose," chatted one of the two paramedics. I could see that he, though competent and professional, seemed a little nervous every time he glanced up at the portable heart monitor. In contrast to the hyper-alert demeanour of the paramedics was the calm demeanour of the doctor riding in the ambulance: his eyes almost closed, he seemed asleep. The morphine shot made me very comfortable but could not completely block the pain from breaking through. Somehow I was strangely free of panic, I was floating freely. *Was I having one of those celebrated "out-of-body" experiences? Had I died?*

I knew that I was still alive because I recognized the shopping malls and convention centre out the ambulance window as the ambulance whisked by the center of town. *Why couldn't this happen at home instead of 10,000 kilometres away from home? God, what I wouldn't give . . . .*

Static on the radio: "Unstable angina on the way in, arrival in four minutes." *Are they talking about me? OOWWWW!* The pain was back, deep, intense and so was the panic. I wondered if I could bargain my way out of this one. *"Anything, God, You name it, anything. Stop smoking? Lose weight? Slow down? You got them all! Just let me get through this one; to see the kids graduate from school, get married."* But I was not all that hopeful because I knew how weak my bargaining position had become over the years.

Day One: early Tuesday morning

The ambulance jolted to a halt in front of the emergency room entrance, and there was a flurry of activity that interrupted my divine negotiations. Then something very bizarre happened: the present moment seemed to freeze, as if I were watching myself in a movie in slow motion. People looking down at you as you are helplessly carried into the emergency department on the stretcher, bright lights, noise, the smell of the hospital, all reminded me of the sickening feeling I always had each time I went to the clinic for the check-ups. Thinking of that day in Dr Blum's office, a sinking feeling of remorse set in.

I hate these places, so alienating and all! Always the same at the clinic: the smells, the lights, lots of uncomfortable tests (were they all really necessary?), confusion, fear and then, relief at last that Doctor Blum had warned me, once again, that although there was nothing grossly abnormal, I really should stop smoking, cut back on coffee, lose some weight, work less, be more active and so on, and so on blah, blah, blah. There just wasn't time for those options. That incessant ticking in my ears urging me on: no time to waste! I'll be 50 soon. Anyway you have to die from something, right? "May I go now, Doc?" Already my mind had moved from there to the day's meeting and projects that required my attention.

That was all a distant memory now, matters out of my control and uncertain of my future, here in the emergency department of the local hospital 10,000 kilometres away from anything or anyone who really meant anything to me. Somehow I didn't mind the little pains of the intravenous lines and urinary catheter as long as it all worked. More morphine, more relief for now, floating free, watching the whole thing happen to my body.

Amidst the noise and chaos, I remember seeing the ambulance doctor now actually sitting quietly in a dark corner of my room in the Intensive Care Unit, apparently uninvolved with my care, just watching. It struck me that his serene demeanour and behavior seemed inappropriate for part of a medical team. Who could he be? Just as my attention was drawn to a vertical scar on his chest, peeking just above his surgical shirt, he started to speak. His voice

"The sad part of all this, Peter, is that it should NOT really have to happen like this."

though soft, was easily heard above the background din. "The sad part of all this, Peter, is that it should NOT really have to happen like this." Then he winked at me. "Talk to you later once you're all settled in the hospital . . . ."

I had heard and read of near-death experiences but always wrote them off as fantasies of a fevered, repressed or drugged mind. Strangely now, however, I felt at warm peace amidst this tense atmosphere, having given up control and surveillance for the moment. I was floating, unanchored above my body, unaffected by the flurry of activity below. Suddenly things in the next bed over seemed to change quickly for the worse.

"Code Blue! Code Blue! We're losing him!" shouted the resident doctor, as he approached the chest of the man with two metal electrical paddles with gooey gel spread over them. "OK, clear, everybody back!" and ZAP! The body of the man jerked up off the bed like a rag doll and the resident team stared intently at the heart monitor of that patient, as though waiting for a message from beyond. Apparently, they received that message and continued to shout orders and scurry around the bed like ants, inserting breathing tubes and administering ampoules of injectable fluids and drugs. With every wave of pain I felt snapped back inside my body, until the morphine of nitroglycerine, permitted the pain to disappear.

The last memory I had in the wee hours of that morning was that my condition had been stabilized long enough to schedule an emergency angiogram or cardiac catheterization. This is a procedure by which the medical and surgical teams can determine precisely to what extent certain heart arteries are blocked, by injecting radio-opaque dye into my heart arteries. Judging by the remarks made by the doctors at the "cath," I understood the stakes and realized that my life was, for that moment, in the hands of Dr Jason Lee, chief of cardiovascular surgery. I fell asleep, exhausted and scared, with the help of painkillers and sleeping pills, until noon.

Day One: Tuesday afternoon

As I ate my scant hospital lunch composed of Jell-O and ice chips, I was interrupted by Dr Lee, who was doing his teaching rounds in the Coronary Care Unit (CCU). He had in tow a bevy of young student doctors and surgical residents, and calmly explained to me that I almost had to be resuscitated twice prior to being stabilized.

"The major artery of your heart is about 95% blocked by plaque. Some of the heart muscle is at risk because it is downstream from the blockage. In fact, further heart muscle continues to be put at risk and that's why you have that occasional chest pain. This situation could deteriorate and cause a myocardial infarct or heart attack, an event that is all too common these days." He went on, "The other main artery is also significantly blocked. Both of these arteries serve the heart muscle and to do their job of delivering oxygen to the heart muscle downstream they must be bypassed with either an artery from your chest wall or a vein from your leg. Imagine those arteries in your heart to be a traffic jam that we must bypass to decompress the traffic jam. Only in this case, the traffic is the vital juice of life: your blood."

While Dr Lee spoke he took the clipboard of one of the students and drew a crude sketch of the heart with the arteries on the outside (they looked so small!) and then a close-up view of the arteries (see below).

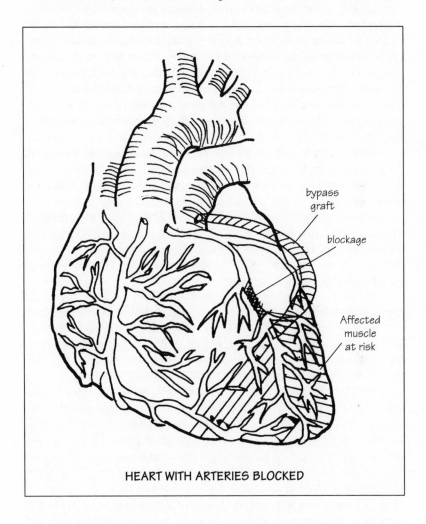

bypass
graft

blockage

Affected
muscle
at risk

HEART WITH ARTERIES BLOCKED

He mentioned that for now the numerous medications would keep the blood supply going to the heart and that he could fit me into his schedule in two days for a definitive procedure. *Fit me in? This fellow must be busy!*

"Excuse me, Doctor," I asked hesitantly, "why would my condition not be amenable to angoplaster?" I had a colleague at work who had done really well with that less invasive procedure.

"Do you mean angioplasty? Angioplasty will do the trick in some cases when there is a only small localized arterial blockage, that would be easy to get at. By inserting a balloon catheter into the arteries in the leg, we can thread the catheter up to the heart, guided by X-ray, and then, once near the blockage, we can inflate the balloon thereby crushing the waxy plaque. However, in your case, the catherization you had last night showed an entirely different picture: your arteries are severely affected, plaque up and down. For those reasons, angioplasty simply wouldn't work for you."

Doctor Lee was encouraging, "Do keep those questions coming. We encourage that here. The more you know about this whole scenario, the better your chances of avoiding being on my operating table again."

I had a thousand more questions, but Dr Lee had to finish his rounds. Maybe just one more.

"Excuse me, Dr Lee, how will I do long term, I mean, what are the chances of . . . uhh . . . ," I stammered, a bit more emotional than I had realized.

" . . . of a normal life?," he asked, "with proper attention, you have an *excellent* long-term prognosis. But I must add that your life will have to change and you will have to take better care of these new 'conduits' than you did the old ones. But, in general, the surgical literature says that if we use an artery that you don't really need, called the internal mammary artery, they will still be patent or open in about eight years in approximately 93% of cases, a little less if we use the leg veins: but, once again, that's with good maintenance. By 'certain changes,' I am referring to the way you live your life with regard to diet, exercise, stress and so on. Those are the things that caused this blockage. Anyway, you will probably not survive without the operation right now. Those blocked arteries are potentially posing a threat to viable muscle tissue."

"Doctor Lee, what do you recommend I do for the two days here. I'll go out of my mind watching the clouds go by my window and that cannot be good for my heart."

He answered, smiling, "That's for sure, but your condition should become stable enough to walk around the hospital hallways on this level by tomorrow afternoon. But don't worry about anything, you will be tethered to the portable heart monitors that send signals from your heart to a master control panel here in the ICU so we will be able to know not only your whereabouts, but also how your heart is healing and beating. If your heart starts any strange rhythms or whatever, we'll know about it before you will."

This was reassuring and I listened carefully to Dr Lee's continuing advice.

"If you take a walk about 25 metres down this hall here, you will find the hospital library. I would like you to meet our chief hospital librarian, Dr Charles, who is a retired internist and a very special man indeed. He is one person here at University hospital that commands everyone's respect. He runs our unique cardiac rehabilitation program which we, unlike many other places, start as early as possible, even before the bypass. That way, we know we have your undivided attention. People have a way of paying close attention just before heart-bypass surgery. You'll discover all that tomorrow morning. Just get some rest for now."

Day One: late Tuesday evening

Through the slit in my window curtains, as the sun went down and the city lights came up, I could see the cars and pedestrians passing by mutely, without any idea of the vital bustling transpiring within these walls.

The staff in the ICU, from the surgical residents and interns to the nurses to the cleaning lady, were a breed apart: modern day Florence Nightingales. They went about their daily chores, some of which were mostly unpleasant, with professionalism and compassion. I wasn't a particularly good patient: I did not like having to have myself cleaned and wiped, (especially after being given a laxative to prevent any strain on the heart due to difficult bowel movements), nor did I like them cleaning my bedpan, changing my intravenous lines, checking my cath sites for bleeding. They recognized my tears of helplessness as I lay there being attended to. They understood, I was sure, how I got there. I was definitely going to remember these folks.

Here were people with a real purpose, a mission of mercy, it seemed. Every action they took, whether dealing with frightened or cantankerous patients, or bathing dirty bodies, it was as though it was confirmation of their life mission to serve and love. All seemed to have plenty of time to explain things to me. All seemed to have that knowing look in their eyes that I had been brought back from the "great beyond."

The ICU itself reminded me of the battlefield hospitals that we see on TV: wheeling in the endless procession of the "wounded." Just as in war movies casualties often appear as naïve and young adolescent boys, the casualties here seemed also to have been cut down in their prime. In a very real sense, my survival was a victory for the ICU staff and I was determined right then not to let them down.

In this large University Hospital, strangely I felt more "at home" than in any of the hotels where I had stayed over the years. I also never felt more "awake."

At last, thankful for all the attention and feeling safe in their hands, I finally drifted off, sleepy and sore from my long trip to the brink, lulled by the rhythmic beeping of monitors and hushed voices, and very aware of the fact that my wife, for now, was the only person who I desperately wanted to see and touch. Never feeling quite so alone, I wanted desperately to hear her sweet voice. I longed to dream of us together, only to wake up in my bed tomorrow morning having had a very vivid nightmare of a faraway hospital.

My sleep was calm and only briefly interrupted by early morning admissions; waves of other people being pulled back from the brink.

Day Two: Wednesday morning

The next morning, to make room for more "wounded," I was moved out of the Intensive Care Unit into a step-down unit. There I had a quiet room with three room-mates and a telephone by my bed. The other three men seemed to be in their fifties and had all the tell-tale stigmata of fast-trackers: portable phones and briefcases on the beds (which they were not officially allowed to open). Every aspect of our lives was moni-tored and controlled. The hospital administration had even gone to the trouble of placing a large poster above the TV monitor:

> NO PORTABLE PHONES, PLEASE.

My first call was to the local office to let them know why I hadn't come in that morning. Already after 24 intense hours, it seemed to be weeks since I had been to the office; it was a million miles away. Our regional manager, James Reilly, was already in the meeting that I was to have attended. I spoke to Wendy, his secretary, who expressed shock and sadness at the news of my heart condition. She mentioned to me that James would get back to me as soon as the time permitted.

Replacing the receiver, I was suddenly gripped by fear about the prospect of making an infinitely more difficult call: to Jane and the kids. *What should I say? How detailed should I be? "What if nobody answers, should I leave a message? Will they say "We told you so, Dad?" Will I be a burden to them for the rest of my life?*

It seemed like an eternity in those three hours between that time and 2 p.m. when it was reasonable to call home. Several times between 2 and 2.30, I picked up the receiver and replaced it, hesitating and paralysed by these nagging questions.

"I know the feeling," a voice came from the adjacent bed, "Pleasure to meet you. I'm Raymond Young, call me Ray. Are you one of Dr Lee's patients?"

"Yes, I am. I came in yesterday morning," I replied.

"Well, I came in two days ago and it took me a whole day to get up the courage to call my wife. Probably felt that my credit rating was poor with her, having spent so much time away from home these past ten years. We'll leave what the whole thing means to the shrinks and the quacks though."

Ray was an interesting man: on the outside, a tough, seasoned, veteran of the game of business. He was very comfortable in his role helping several of the "new boys" get oriented and coaching them on what to do next.

I was struck by the honesty of feeling that Ray had with me, an absolute stranger. Ray had cut right through the formalities and lent a hand when needed. That seemed to be the rule around here. Throughout my hospital stay, patients and staff alike had a certain awareness that was genuine and immediate, with very little feigned formality or posturing. Clearly, these were people who had little time to waste.

"Yes, well, I suppose that it's really something that I will just have to get through," I said. "When are you scheduled for the operation?," I probed, returning his friendly ways.

"I go under the knife tomorrow at 7 a.m.," he said, "right after morning Mass. But I won't tell you that I'm not scared. You never know. Now I know how the prisoners on death row feel, waiting, waiting, waiting. The only difference is, Peter, that we get to walk out of here if all goes well, to live another day."

"I'm sure that you'll do fine, Ray. I'll keep you in my thoughts and prayers," I offered. "If you don't mind, I have to call Jane, my wife. Dear Lord, just let me get through this."

"Sure, let me step out to give you some privacy with your wife. See you in a little while," he said. "Hey," he said, winking as he slipped out the door, "you'll do just fine, too."

Well, here goes. I swallowed hard, sipping on the ice chips in front of me. "Uhhh, hello, Jane?," there was a terrible echo on the line. "This is Peter. Am . . . am I waking you up. No? . . . great. Uhhh . . . listen, Jane . . . uhhh . . . something has happened to me . . . No, honey, I'm fine but . . . uhhh . . . I'm in the local University Hospital, St Andrew's. I had a heart attack last night. No, no, honey, calm down now. Everything is just fine . . . they're really good and professional here. And I'm in good company. I had no idea how busy these places are. Me? Ohh, I'm OK, but I will need an operation in two days . . . a bypass . . . yes, that's right, a heart bypass." I wasn't doing very well to reassure her.

"Listen, Jane, tell the kids that everything is just great. Don't let them worry . . . when this whole thing is over . . . ." I attempted a brave front but I felt a lump in my throat that told me that I was close to tears. "Anyway, I really miss you and I'll call as things develop after I've spoken to the chief surgeon again," I needed to wrap it up, too hard to speak.

Dr Blum was right about this being really boring! I certainly had plenty of time to think about myself and my life and I was fed up with allowing my fear or denial, or whatever it was, to stop me from learning about my body. I decided right there to use my time until my operation reading about my condition, to educate myself.

Day Two: Wednesday afternoon

After speaking to Jane, I had to get out of that room and move around a bit. After a light lunch, I checked in with the head nurse in the step-down unit and attached my portable heart monitor, known on the ICU as the "executive's Walkman." As I made my way down the hospital corridor in bathrobe and slippers towards the library, I realized that annoying ticking in my ears had finally stopped. Strange and lovely silence!

Walking down the corridor is a special experience in a hospital as you continually risk being exposed by the famous back flap in the hospital gowns. Strangely, no one seems to really care about such things. Nobody seems to notice such things. These are not people who care much for protocol or decorum, their minds are on more important matters.

Once at the library, I knocked faintly on the door and poked my head in timidly. "Come in, please." That voice sounded vaguely familiar. As I turned towards the front desk I noticed a man in his late fifties.

"Dr Richard Charles, MD" the name tag read.

"Don't I know you?", I queried. I wasn't exactly sure, but it seemed that this was the same fellow that I had exchanged several words with in the ambulance last night.

"Dr Dick Charles, at your service," he smiled. "Yes, indeed. We met briefly the night before last. Glad to see you made it. You see, I'm a retired internist, and I split my time between riding ambulances and running this place. After my wife died about six years ago, I needed to occupy myself and I just couldn't say 'no' to some work when it was time to retire. So here I am. This is my 'classroom.' Welcome aboard! Now, how may I help you?"

Indeed, I noticed that there was a blackboard full of arrows and drawings, desks and chairs, pads of paper, all around medical graphs of the organs of the body on the walls.

"As I am going to be here for a couple of days, Dr Lee mentioned that you could help me if I wanted to learn something about my condition. You know, to kill some time. Frankly, I haven't a clue where to begin. I'm still wondering why this happened to me."

"Let me tell you a true story. For the 15 years prior to my bypass, we had a live-in housekeeper, a woman who was very much a part of our family whom my wife and I had grown to love very much. Though she never had the opportunity to get what we call a 'proper education,' she had a certain profound serenity that indicated a greater wisdom that years of education simply cannot impart. Over the years, she worked hard for us, provided well for her children and regularly attended church services.

"When I had my heart attack at the house one evening, she faithfully prepared my bag and escorted me on my stretcher to the ambulance. As they loaded me into the ambulance, she took my hand and, as her eyes moistened with tears, she said to me, 'Doctor Charles, why do these diseases happen only to rich people? Does too much money make you sad and break your heart?' When I returned home and she saw my bypass scar, she giggled,' calling my fellow bypass patients, the 'Zipper Club.' Now, she obviously could not understand the physiology of it all, but she seemed to be able to see that some people die long before their actual physical death.

"So welcome to the 'Zipper Club.' Good man, Jason Lee, one of the best. Did *my* bypass five years ago." As Dr Charles spoke, I noticed that same vertical keloid scar on his chest that I had seen the first night. "Ooh, right! you're still stuck in the 'why me?' phase. Don't fret, that'll pass. Everybody who actually makes it this far goes through that. Nobody really knows why you were one of the lucky ones to have made it this far. Most people with heart attacks just don't.

> *"So welcome to the 'Zipper Club.' "*

Just write it off to Fate for now. Jason Lee and his team will get you 'home' if anyone can. They are as good as they come, *anywhere*. But after that, you are going to be back in that big, bad, world, facing the same problems that brought you in here. As depressing as that probably sounds, we have to get down to work. Well, where would you like to start?" he asked.

"Just a quick question, Dr Charles," I asked, "it seems that there isn't much trivial talk around here. Everybody is so intense, so present. What's that all about?"

"Just no time to waste," he answered. "Now, where you begin will depend on what you are interested in and what you know. There will be some class work here in what I call the 'classroom.' There will be patients, coming and going, sent by their doctors to attend classes with me with similar conditions to yourself. And there will be others who are here just because they're curious.

"If you know next to nothing, like many of the outside world, may I suggest that you start with this pamphlet that I compiled for use by patients on this ward." He handed me the well-worn booklet.

"The Urban Warrior's Book of Solutions," I read the cover aloud. "That's a strange name for a medical book."

"It's not meant as a scholarly medical text or another self-help book, there are already enough of them. Nearly every bypass or Myocardial Infraction (MI) patient that comes into this hospital drifts in here and helps me by reading, reflecting and scribbling comments in the margins, which, by the way, I encourage: they are your active dialogue with the book. That's the way it should be. This is probably the only hospital-based interactive education program.

"Then, I go through and study the comments and doodles, look up the pertinent medical questions in what I consider the more important tomes, medical or from literature, and add to the book what I think might be of help to the patients. Medicine is full of controversy," he continued, "which is good if, at the end of the day, the discussions help shed light on pertinent issues. So much of the controversy is the sad result of self-serving interests. I'm not here to create consensus, but awareness, and to provoke reflection. You'll take it from there to wherever you can."

"But how do I use the book?" I asked.

"Consider it a practical manual to get you back into and keep you in shape. That's why you'll find something of interest to you. Just leaf through it with an opened mind and heart. Leave your impressions or thoughts in the margins, just as the patients before you did. Then, when I am here and not on rounds or whatever, ask me questions. It's full of exercises meant to provoke reflection, you know, 'stir up the mud' a bit. Take some paper and do the exercises at the end of each chapter. If you want something more in depth on any subject, just let me know. If you have any specific questions, that's why I'm here; every day except weekends from 8 a.m. to 8 p.m."

I started to open the book and saw that there was a handwritten dedication, just inside the front cover:

**To Juliette, my best friend and soulmate
from your most reluctant widower.**

I flipped directly to the first chapter entitled:

AVOIDING THE DISEASES OF AFFLUENCE

Give a man a fish, feed for a day.
Teach a man to fish, feed him for a lifetime.

In that chapter, there was a graph showing data from the World Health Organization (WHO), depicting the distribution of deaths around the world.

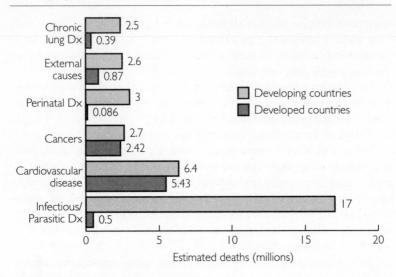

Total = ~ 50 million deaths (1990)
   Developing countries = 38.5 million
   Developed countries = 11.5 million

Annual deaths worldwide

I was immediately struck by the high numbers of "casualties" of the heart disease epidemic worldwide. I thought of all the ICUs crammed full around the world with people like me. But at 47, I thought I was a bit young for all of this. I read on.

Diseases of the body, and especially those of the heart have their origin in the mind and the spirit.

"Dr Charles, what do you mean by the statement, 'disease begins in the mind?' "

"Heart attacks, strokes and certain cancers," he explained, "are the result of insidious, smouldering, pathological, processes such as high blood pressure, high cholesterol, high stress, excessively rich foods, and excess body fat. More profoundly, they are due to processes that have their origin in the mind because it's the mind that controls the body. Fail to control the mind and it's the body that pays. Control the mind and the body will follow. Desires in your mind are like children, yield to them too much and they become impossible to manage."

Dr Charles's booklet went on to explain that these debilitating and often fatal diseases share similar pathological features: a progressive narrowing and blockage of critical arteries supplying the vital organs, i.e. the heart and the brain, respectively.

I also read how the process responsible for these diseases is called **arteriosclerosis** (literally, "arterial hardening") This process is far from being completely understood, but what is clear is that it begins in the late teens/early 20s, as evidenced by the astonishing report showing that arteriosclerosis was present in as many as 77% of 21-year-old soldiers killed in the Korean War. I never knew that these processes began so early in life!

As I read, engrossed by the lucidity and simplicity of the writing, I felt as though I, too, had a sense of urgency, no more time to waste. As never before, I was exhilarated by the possibility of going even further, having all aspects of health explained, how the heart works, how we nourish ourselves, how we can control better our emotions and thoughts. The next couple of pages of the book were entitled:

....

Yes, but first you are a human being

Though each organism in this parade marches at a pace largely predestined and preordained by its genetic code, all of us can profoundly influence our destiny and our health by the way we think and live.

....

I couldn't quite grasp the whole issue of genetics. Dr Charles seemed unoccupied, so I posed the question:

"Dr Charles, what role does genetics play in the whole health issue?"

"Well, that depends what you mean by genetics. Recent insights from the field of medical anthropology reveal that our rapidly changing lifestyles have outpaced our body's abilities to adapt. Our genetic code (DNA – deoxyribonucleic acid – and company) evolves at an infinitely slower rate than our high-tech lifestyle which is very much out of synch with the way our DNA is programing," he was careful in his choice of concepts and words to keep the whole discussion interesting on my level.

"You see, our genetic code cannot keep up and is still programing our bodies for high activity, optimal nutrition, physical, not mental, stresses and so on. Therefore, the body really still believes that we are cave-dwelling hunters and gatherers and programing our bodies accordingly. We must respect these 'design specifications,' otherwise, we invite problems."

"Could that be why fat and all things containing high percentages of fat: chips, fries, ice cream, bacon, taste so good? Are we programed to like fat?" I asked.

"Exactly, in cave-dwelling days, when famine was more the rule than feast, fat represented a perfect form of stored energy: calorically-dense (an energy yield of ~ 9 calories/gram fat) and light from a weight point of view (fat is less dense than muscle, bone or, even, water). As such, it was advantageous to eat as much fat as possible for fear of an imminent famine and we are still programed that way!"

"Could this be why we are having so many heart attacks, Doc?"

"In part. But not just heart attacks. The epidemics of heart disease, strokes, cancers, diabetes, diverticulosis and alcohol-related diseases are to a great extent the result of our disrespect for the design specifications and Natural Laws governing the human organism. We'll speak more of those laws and their balance over the next couple of days.

"Meanwhile, unaware of this mismatch, we jump on a plane, fly through several time zones at supersonic speeds, imbibe several glasses of strong alcohol, eat rich salty foods. We arrive for a few business meetings, maybe a game of tennis or golf and off again back home or another destination.

"All the while that we are caught unawares in the never-ending cycle (stress-coffee-alcohol-salty/fatty foods-inactivity), the genetic code is programing for an active hunter, whose only beverage was water, whose food was lean and who had to cope with just physical (external), not psychological (internal), stresses. We have gone from good old *Homo sapiens* to *Homo workaholicus obesus*. You must know the whole game pretty well by now, Peter."

"Yes, but are you suggesting that we have not benefitted from the great advances in society and medicine? Have we not become more comfortable and prosperous?" I asked. I, for one, was not prepared to go back to the days when disease and famine were rampant.

"Of course, in many respects, we have made great progress and I would never suggest that we go back to the cave-dwelling days. But we, perhaps, have lost the positive aspects of those days. In many ways, we have allowed technological wizardry to actually interfere with the healing relationship between the doctor and the patient. Before we know your emotional reasons for being here, we order tests to support our hypothesis.

"All that science may be getting in the way of the healing process. After all, you cannot measure the will to live or positive attitude, or faith. Yet they all play a role in healing. Though I cannot prove it scientifically, I'm absolutely certain. The feeling among modern day health professionals is if you cannot scientifically measure it or test it, it must not exist. They are missing an important essence in the art of healing."

Dr Charles explained further. "We're funny people, us doctors. Just love to tamper with your lives. And you, the patient, just love it when we do: you feel that we are getting something done. We tamper and Nature heals. However, when it comes down to it, to maintain your health options and stay well, one message should be clear: modern medicine can work high-tech miracles, but building up your health, fitness and vitality is *your* job. When it comes to cancer treatment or appendicitis, we can do the job, but when it comes to protecting your core asset best, no one takes better care of you than you! Don't ever forget it.

"For now, don't worry about the genetic component as you cannot change that anyway. Since heart disease is your particular problem, why don't you start with the chapter on heart disease and find out what aspects you actually can change and we can go from there," he suggested and went back to his scanning of medical journals.

THE HEART OF THE MATTER

Behold the heart: a fist-size organ, weighing between 280 and 450 grams (10 to 16 ounces), the most powerful muscle in the body, seemingly indefatigable, pumping silently, even whilst you sleep. While you are sitting there reading this page, your heart is faithfully pumping 5 liters *every minute* though countless meters of piping.

With every volley, the heart propels the blood that carries critically needed substances (oxygen, glucose, potassium, water, cholesterol and so on). These are sent along the arterial system, starting from the left

> *The heart, as the strongest muscle in the body, is a near-perfect pump that pumps almost 200 million liters of blood in a normal lifetime.*

ventricle and the major artery leaving the heart – the aorta.

In a flash, while you are running for a plane at Changi or Heathrow or when you are stressed at a board meeting, the heart responds instantly: it increases its rate and pumping capacity to meet your new needs to nearly 25 liters/minute, in conditioned individuals. In a normal lifetime, that amounts to nearly 200 million liters of blood.

To accomplish these fantastic engineering feats, your heart needs your help to protect it from the ravages of a modern business lifestyle: the stresses, the sedentary life, the rich foods, the jet-lag, the isolation from loved ones.

Unfortunately, these arteries can be up to 75% blocked by plaque before symptoms arise: in 50% of men, the first sign of coronary heart disease is usually a heart attack or sudden death, in most women, it's chest pain. That's one hell of a wake-up call! Wouldn't it be wonderful if at 10% coronary obstruction, you had low-grade 10% type of symptoms to warn you of a smouldering health problem. It just does not work that way.

As I continued my reading of the chapter on heart disease, I noticed some scribbled notes in the margins:

> We always say that when we have health, we have everything. But then when the demands of business life roll around on Monday morning, all that rhetoric gets quickly pushed to the back burner. Tomorrow I go for my surgery and can't push this one back.
>
> CB 1991

THE HEART – YOUR CORE ASSET UNDER ATTACK

Dr Charles looked up from his medical journals and started to talk about heart disease. "Next time you fly into Bombay, New York, or

London, Peter, on your way to the local office, drive past the local hospital. The chances are good that the operating rooms will be quite busy doing damage control for the 'diseases of affluence': Coronary Artery Bypass Graft Surgery (CABG), angioplasties, gall bladder operations. Why"

"Because the heart becomes tired," I guessed.

"Not really. The heart is probably as close to a perfect pump as they come. We doctors learned this lesson from Nature the hard way during the heyday of the artificial heart. To duplicate what your heart was doing in total silence, we had to develop an artificial heart for people who had to await heart transplants. Very complicated, beyond our wildest expectations."

"What is it then, if not the heart as a pump?," I pondered.

"It's those tiny conduits, the coronary arteries, that get blocked; the ones that our Dr Lee spends most of his time bypassing."

"Dr Charles, I feel as though I am really beginning to learn something with you here," I said.

"Well," he said, smiling, "your journey of discovery is just beginning. You've learned almost nothing compared to what you need to learn. While you may have information, you need *understanding*. And then, you need to implement that understanding. Let's face it," he said, pointing to his head, "if you don't change here, don't expect your body to change. Only then can you participate in your own evolution." He seemed very deliberate in his tone.

Dr Charles handed me a cup of warm tea. "Be patient with yourself and, for goodness sake, Peter, pay attention to those around you. That will get you there. Read the next couple of sections and then we'll speak." I read on.

I. MODIFIABLE RISK FACTORS FOR HEART DISEASE

Decades of research have identified several modifiable risk factors or "points of control" for both heart attacks and strokes. The main modifiable risk factors for heart attacks and strokes are (in order of importance):

1. Smoking (active *and* passive).
2. High blood pressure.
3. High blood cholesterol.

4. Physical inactivity.

5. Obesity (excess body fat).

6. Stress: personality and emotions.

7. Adult diabetes.

Moreover, the risk of heart problems can be amplified by the corporate work environment, which can be perceived as the antithesis of our cave-dwelling ancestors in two critical aspects: **high psychological stress** (which can lead to high blood pressure, smoking, illicit drug use, nervous eating, and depression) and **a sedentary lifestyle** (which can lead to high body fat stores, high blood pressure, certain cancers, and diabetes).

As the afternoon wore on, my earlier anxiety about being away from home, the call to Jane, the bypass operation, all seemed to matter little as I continued my journey of awakening.

The next section of the manual dealt with a subject that was near and dear to my heart, so to speak: smoking.

I looked up from my reading and my eyes met those of the doctor. "Dr Charles, I have smoked all my adult life, with little or no real consequences . . . " I said.

" . . . you mean, until now . . . ," he added.

I read on and had a healthy dose of reality testing.

Risk factor # 1:
Smoking – the mistress that will betray you

WHY DO WE BREATHE?

As a test of self-awareness, stop reading this page for a moment, close your eyes and what aspects of your body can you notice? Your heart beating? Perhaps, particularly if you are stressed or have had too much caffeine today. What else? Can you notice the blood coursing through the arteries? No. But you can always notice the ebb and flow of your breathing.

Of course, you cannot appreciate the physiology of gas exchange, but you are very aware of the lungs at work. The composition of the air around us (presuming, for the moment, a relatively clean atmosphere) is about 70% nitrogen (N_2), 20% oxygen (O_2) and infinitely smaller percentages of carbon dioxide CO_2 (not to be confused with its fatal cousin CO, carbon monoxide), hydrogen (H_2), methane (CH_3) and the rare gases.

Now take a breath of this ambient air. The oxygen herein contained travels through the nose, where it is warmed and humidified, down the trachea and bronchi (where no gas exchange takes place) to the spongy sacs (the alveoli) in the lungs where the stage is set for the next part of the journey: into the blood.

These alveoli can be visualized as a thin membrane surrounded by a woven basket of blood vessels (the capillaries) that drop off the normal "waste products" of metabolism, water (H_2O) and CO_2 and pick up, on the red blood cells, the critical molecule of life, O_2. The H_2O and CO_2 are exhaled, a fact that you have undoubtedly taken advantage of to clean your eyeglasses.

The way that Dr Charles explained the whole process of gas exchange made me realize the respect he had for this "temple" and just how badly I had been abusing it.

The oxygen is carried on special binding sites of the red blood cells through a vast highway of capillaries which converge into larger vessels that bring it to the major pumping station, the heart, where it is then sent off to all organs of the body, starting with the brain. This micro universe of respiration happens uneventfully 12 to 16 times every minute throughout your lifetime, filtering out all impurities that happen to have been mixed with the ambient air.

THE MAN-MADE CHEMICAL THAT NATURE DID NOT EXPECT

If you are a smoker, light up a cigarette or pipe, and place your hand on your chest to feel your heart rate. Why does the heart start to race? The answer is a simple affair of supply and demand. You see, among the > 2,700 identified substances in tobacco smoke, one of the most noxious is carbon monoxide, a product of incomplete combustion of ubiquitous carbon, found primarily in tobacco smoke and pollution.

Do you remember the oxygen-binding site on the red blood cell? Carbon monoxide takes the same trip as oxygen above, but instead of allowing oxygen to bind there, CO, *as it has an affinity for that oxygen-binding site 250 times that of oxygen*, bumps the oxygen off the site. This drops the effective oxygen concentration in the blood, the heart responds by pumping faster and faster, requiring, of course, more oxygen to do this. The heart gets caught in the dangerous and vicious cycle of too little supply coupled with excess demands.

TOBACCO SMOKE IN THE DISEASE HALL OF FAME

Cigarette smoking has long been established as the single most important cause of preventable disease and death in the world. It is estimated that every time you smoke a cigarette you lose at least 5.5 minutes of life, on the basis that the average reduction in life expectancy for smokers is up to eight years. Smoking kills three million people worldwide every year or one person every ten seconds. It is estimated that by the year 2025 [when Christopher and Julia are in their late 30s], *cigarettes will kill 10 million people per year!*

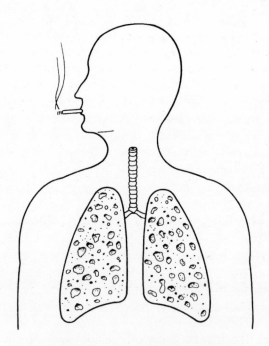

SMOKING: A BURNING ISSUE!

Roughly 50% of those who smoke today and who began in their teens will eventually die from it. Of that 50%, half will die in middle age, losing some 25 years of precious life.

Smoking is a real one-way dead end street, alluring young smokers early and keeping them hooked for a lifetime. Cigarette smoking is directly responsible for a full 21% of all mortality from heart disease.

Smoking a packet of cigarettes every day for ten years or more increases your risk for heart disease by 300% and increases your risk for lung cancer by 500%.

In fact, 90% of all lung cancers and chronic lung disease (emphysema and bronchitis) is due to either active or passive smoking. Evidence published in the journal of the American Heart Association, *Circulation*, revealed that in the USA alone, 53,000 non-smokers(who are passively smoking) die every year.

DOCTORS AND CIGARETTES

Unfortunately, we cannot look to doctors for the example. In developing countries, the percentage of doctors who smoke often exceeds 50% of the population! In Western Europe, the rate of smoking doctors ranges from 6% in Britain to 50% in Eastern European countries.

WOMEN AND CIGARETTES

Women, normally protected from heart disease and cancers until menopause, are now approaching and surpassing men in some cancers (lung) because of smoking. Moreover, there is a higher incidence of osteoporosis (thinning of the bones) in smoking women.

Pregnant women who smoke (passively from their surroundings or actively) expose their unborn infant to risk of accelerated atherosclerosis (as evidenced by the biopsy of the umbilical vessels) and nicotine addiction.

Moreover, a recent study, published in the Journal of the American Medical Association, strongly suggests that women who smoke have reduced fertility: 38% of non-smokers conceived in their first cycle, while only 28% of smokers did so. Smokers were more than three times more likely to take more than a year to conceive compared to non-smokers. The difficulty in conceiving may be due to a wide variety of factors.

HOW DO CIGARETTES KILL US?

Aside from the chronic lung diseases of emphysema, chronic bronchitis, asthma, infertility and ulcer disease, there is also the whole gamut of heart-related diseases. Moreover, cancers of virtually every system in the body are increased by smoking cigarettes: mouth, larynx, oesophagus, stomach, urinary tract, bladder and cervix. The causal relationship between cigarette smoke and these diseases is disputed by no one.

A sampling of some of the 2,700+ nasty substances found in cigarette smoke include (an asterisk* indicates known cancer-causing substances): *ammonia* (detergent), *cyanhydric acid* (used in gas chambers), *acetone/toluene* (solvents), *methane* (swamp gas), *naphthalene, carbon monoxide* (constituent of car exhaust fumes), *Phenol, DDT* (insecticide), *Toluidine*, Urethane*, Dimethyl-Nitrosamines*, Naphthylamines*, Pyrene*, Polonium-210** (radioactive), *Cadmium** (a heavy metal found in car batteries), *Vinyl chloride** (a plastic) and *Benzopyrene**. Interestingly, by scanning the brains of people using addictive substances, experts have found that substances like cocaine, barbiturates, nicotine and alcohol all tone down the metabolic activity of the brain: smoking makes you stupid! But that's what non-smokers have been saying for years.

PASSIVE SMOKING KILLS

You've been there. You find yourself cornered in a restaurant, bar or even, a corporate boardroom, in a meeting with someone who ignores your best interests by lighting that cigarette in closed quarters. Your eyes sting, your throat burns, your nose waters. You are a passive smoker.

Passive smoke inhalation is a major problem in our society. Even if you are a non-smoker you should be aware of the harmful effects of cigarette smoke. Be aware of smoky atmospheres, for example, restaurants, and ask to be seated in a non-smoking section or near the door where ventilation is increased. It is estimated that 35,000 non-smoking Americans die every year due to the passive inhalation of cigarette smoke.

Recent data published in the *British Medical Journal* suggest that 150,000 cases of chest infection and between 250,000 and one million cases of asthma are caused each year by passive smoking.

WHY, THEN, DO PEOPLE *STILL* SMOKE?

Simple: it's a legal addiction and addictive activities are part of our brain's organization. Just as we, as a species, are "addicted" to happiness, pleasure, sex, and food, we have all the wiring in place to practice pleasure seeking activity, however harmful. Many substances like cocaine, heroin, alcohol, and nicotine use this innate wiring that's involved in pleasurable activities like eating and sex. One cigarette will not kill you, smoked substances have been at the centre of all round tables until recently: it's the habit that will kill you *miserably*.

Reading this, I was becoming more and more at ease with this approach to addictive substances. Just then, I noticed an angry scribbled note in the margin.

Stop marketing this garbage to our children!

Tobacco is the only consumer product that, used habitually, will kill its user. Most smokers begin to light up in their turbulent adolescent years, and the manufacturers are aware of this. Get them hooked young and keep them for life.

Despite all this compelling evidence, the real danger is not yet fully appreciated. Worldwide consumption, according to the World Health Organization (WHO), tends to vary from region to region: the trends for smoking are down in developed countries, by 9% in the USA, 6% in Australia and New Zealand, and 25% in the UK. The trends for smoking are up in developing countries, by 42% in Africa, 24% in Latin America and 2% in Asia.

Three main reasons account for why people still smoke:

1. The social tolerance (which is changing).
2. Denial of the real problem.
3. A deceptively long delay of many years between the cause and the full effect.

As smoking is an addictive habit with deadly consequences, becoming a non-smoker can be a challenging, complex process. While giving up any addiction or dependency, resign yourself to an intense growth experience. Keep a diary of your withdrawal symptoms and your feelings towards them. Note the waves of intense longing for the drug as they come and go. Try not to react to them, just wait for them to pass.

Eventually, they will fade in intensity and frequency. Use the experience as an opportunity to offer it up to a favorite cause.

Non-smokers to be, take heart: carefully controlled studies found that acute withdrawal symptoms (irritability, shakiness, loss of lucidity, loss of concentrative abilities are over in four–six weeks. Then the real fun starts.

You are an addict forever.
Stay vigilant!

SMOKING ACTION PLAN

STAGE ONE: BEFORE QUITTING

1. *Admit to your addiction.* Don't fool yourself. Use your head. You are an addict. You must start with that stark reality. Even if this means that you, a respectable pillar of society, have the same "drug-seeking behaviour" as any other addict, that's all right. It'll be your secret. Now you are ready to stop smoking and become a lifelong non-smoker. Never negotiate with an addict!

    Imagine if cigarettes were illegal or in short supply: prohibition and its sequelae all over again. Education is the Key.

    I smoke _____ cigarettes a day and have smoked for _____ years.

    At ten minutes of lost life per cigarette, this represents a loss in years of _____ years.

2. *Demystify. Smoking is a joie de morire!* Smoking no longer has the romantic attachments of old that Hollywood spent so much energy perpetuating: Yul Brunner, Jacques Brel, Humphrey Bogart, all the tough guys died of lung or throat cancers. The world is a less rich place because of their premature exit.

    Smokers are predisposed to many life threatening diseases:

    1. _____
    2. _____
    3. _____
    4. _____
    5. _____

    > *The diagnoses that come with a smoking habit take no prisoners, leave no options. Cancer cures smoking.*

3. **Do not keep cigarettes around your house to tempt you.** Remember, pure air provides oxygen to power your brain and that of your children. Smoke-filled air is full of carbon monoxide and toxins that reduce oxygen flow to the brain – do not be deprived. Do not let anyone smoke in your home.

Do you practice	**Smoke avoidance:**
• Eating out?	Yes No
• Travelling?	Yes No
• In your house?	Yes No
• At business?	Yes No
• In meetings?	Yes No

4. **Prepare mentally to quit.** Warn your family and friends: this will keep *you* accountable. Do not quit when you expect to be under stress: choose a vacation. Plan it out! Plan, for example, to have absolutely ZERO cigarettes in the first two weeks, come hell or high water.

   Set a reasonable time frame for stopping smoking:

   I will stop smoking in ____ months on ___/___ 199__ .

5. **Develop a new reward system.** Stop viewing cigarettes as a reward for a long day or a job well done. Instead buy yourself some chocolate, go for a jog or a swim, or treat yourself to a massage. No substitute is going to be as dangerous as tobacco.

6. As many people smoke during lulls in the action because of boredom, **plan some engaging activity** for these times.

7. **Count the cigarettes and write them down.** Most smokers underestimate exactly how many cigarettes they smoke. Next to each cigarette put a * for those that you *honestly* enjoyed. Most smokers indicate that they derive pleasure from only 10% of their daily cigarettes. Smoke every cigarette with open eyes, at the exclusion of all other activity.

Cigarette smoke contains several hundred different toxic agents. Name a few:

1. _____

2. _____

3. _____

4. _____

5. _____

8. *Be prepared for difficult times and don't despair.* No one said it was going to be easy. Recidivism is highest in the first 90 days after quitting. Most relapses occur soon after quitting: 50% within the first two weeks and the vast majority within 90 days. It may take up to five or six times to get it right.

   When you know that you are going to be in a smoking environment (work, parties, bars, restaurants, friends' houses), prepare for the struggle. Decide ahead of time to avoid the smoke.

Passive smoke inhalation is clearly documented to contribute to: _____ thousand deaths in the USA, _____ thousand cases of chest infection and between _____ thousand and _____ million cases of asthma in British *non-smokers every year*.

9. *Never smoke blindly.* The typical caricature is the stressed manager lighting up a cigarette while there is one burning in the ashtray. Somebody is getting very rich off your lungs. If you are going to smoke, at least do so at the exclusion of all other activities. Make yourself aware of what you are doing to yourself.

10. *Smoke your first cigarette one hour later every day* and really start to enjoy your smoke-free environment. Also, reduce the number of cigarettes you smoke daily *by two each week*. Be firm with yourself. Try eating a piece of fruit when you would normally smoke a cigarette.

11. *Nicotine patch or gum?* Though some 90% of people manage to stop without any props at all (cold or warm turkey), you may benefit from the transdermal administration of nicotine if you have a real physiologic dependence on the drug. Ask yourself:

- Do I have my first cigarette within 60 minutes of waking up?
- Do I smoke more than 25 a day?
- Did I experience severe withdrawal symptoms during previous attempts?

If the answer to any of these queries is "yes", consider using a patch or gum to take the edge off.

STAGE TWO: ONCE YOU HAVE QUIT

1. *Take one day at a time. Every day is a victory and should be openly acknowledged between husband and wife.* Stand up for your new rights. Be tough. It's *now* or *never*. When people ask if you mind that they smoke, resist the opportunity to tempt fate. Saying: "I'm allergic to tobacco smoke," always works.

2. *View yourself as a long-term non-smoker.* Some managers confess to having resumed smoking after 15 years of abstention. You will have to stay vigilant forever. There will be times when you feel like smoking. If you fall off the wagon and have a cigarette, do not use it as an excuse to have a second and a third. It's not the end of the world. Climb back on the wagon and stay there. Don't confirm your worst fears that you will never be able to quit: self-confidence is at stake!

3. *Smoking and alcohol and caffeine are bedfellows.* Alcohol will lower your resistance to cigarettes. In the first critical weeks and months of a quitting program, knock off alcohol.

> **Ouch!! Two vices at once. Next is sex!**

> **Yeah, but at least you'll still be around to have sex!**

Watch your coffee intake as nicotine stimulates the enzymes in the liver that metabolize caffeine. Once you quit, each cup will make you more irascible and anxious, a set-up for the sedative effects of nicotine.

4. **Compensate previous damage from cigarettes with exercise.**
Cigarettes produce carbon monoxide (CO) which bumps
oxygen (O_2) off the red blood cell, effectively removing that cell
from the circulation so that your oxygen concentration drops,
your heart works harder and the vicious cycle begins. **Exercise**
can remove CO and replace the O_2 where it belongs.

The good news is that quitting smoking at any age improves
the time you'll have with your family and friends. For example, if
you quit before the age of 35, you reduce the risk of death to
the level of a lifelong non-smoker.

5. **Nicotine attacks?** Ride out the storm. It will pass. Do not act on
the impulse to smoke: get out, move around, go for a walk, do
anything to help you get through.

The chapter on smoking finished with a section that the previous readers had contributed under the heading, *Helpful Comments or Ideas.*

---

1. *Make your kids proud.*

---

2. *Help the kids to stop. We're showing them how to deal with life's stress. Our nicotine is their crack!*

---

3. *I want to see my kids graduate/see my grandchildren.*

---

4. Smokers, you've been duped! They are an insult to your intelligence.

When all else fails – you only need one reason for quitting: **you,** the father/mother, husband/wife, the partner, the colleague that no one wants to lose.

I noticed another scribbled margin note:

> After all, eventually everybody stops smoking. It just depends what position you want to be in: horizontal or vertical!

Risk factor # 2:
High blood pressure, controlling the silent killer

High blood pressure (also known as hypertension (HTN) is one of the four primary risk factors for heart attacks and strokes (along with smoking, cholesterol and inactivity). HTN is more than high blood pressure, it's a disease that involves coronary vessels, lipid (fat), glucose and insulin abnormalities and family predisposition. HTN is a silent killer in that many of you reading this may be at serious risk from those diseases without knowing or feeling bad: *a time-bomb.*

LIKE FATHER, LIKE SON

The late American cardiologist, Dr Samuel Levine, noted that in his study of families over many decades, when both the father and son had heart attacks, the average age of the first heart attack was 13 years younger for the sons than it was for their fathers. Therefore, every adult over 21 years of age should know his or her blood pressure as 90% of stroke victims have HTN and some with chronically high blood pressure have five times the chance of developing heart disease compared to those without high blood pressure.

Blood pressure (BP) at rest is part of a more complex relationship, involving flow (F, which is the output from the heart) and resistance to that flow, R. The heart, as a flow-dependent pump, itself depends on maintaining adequate flow (cardiac output) for its own blood supply. The relationship is best expressed by this formula:

$$BP = F \times R$$

Reasons for high blood pressure include increases in either or both of the flow or resistance variables.

WORST CASE SCENARIO: SUPPLY/DEMAND FIASCO

Many executives in middle life have chronic mental anxiety and uncompensated demands on top of some degree of coronary obstruction. So, the diminished flow (F) to the heart or brain, etc. can deliver less blood and oxygen downstream, while increased resistance (R) from tension makes the heart muscle work harder, increasing oxygen needs when less oxygen is being delivered.

Therefore, to control high blood pressure optimally and effectively, all variables must be controlled.

The *optimal range* goes from 90/60 to 135/85. But what do these numbers mean?

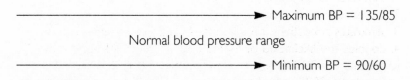

As it pumps, the heart goes through phases: contraction–rest–contraction–rest and so on. During the contraction phase (called systole), which is represented by the greater number, the pressure generated by the heart is transmitted directly to the arteries, which helps transmit a "pressure wave" throughout the arterial system to all organs (including the brain, kidneys and the heart itself) so that they can be perfused by oxygen and glucose.

A *systolic* reading in excess of 135 can be damaging to the arteries and the end organs as the arteries can lose their elasticity and harden (hence, "atherosclerosis"), unable to expand freely: rupture or blockage could result.

During the relaxation phase (known as diastole), the pumping chambers or ventricles fill with blood for the next volley. A *diastolic* reading in excess of 85 could mean that the heart is not relaxing adequately during this phase.

CLASSIFICATION OF BLOOD PRESSURE

Category	Systolic (mm Hg)	Diastolic (mm Hg)
Normal	< 135	< 85
High normal (Borderline)	135 – 139	85 – 89
Hypertension:		
Stage 1 (mild)	140 – 159	90 – 99
Stage 2 (moderate)	160 – 179	100 – 109
Stage 3 (severe)	180 – 209	110 – 119
Stage 4 (very severe)	> 210	< 120

THE INSULIN CONNECTION

HTN patients have insulin levels more than twice as high as normal people during glucose challenge tests. Elevated insulin in turn:

1. stimulates atherosclerosis;
2. causes sodium retention;
3. stimulates sympathetic nervous system (adrenaline); and
4. doubles the likelihood of high cholesterol in HTN patients (HTN patients >160/100), high cholesterol occurs in 70%, while in normal people (<135/85), it only occurs in 35%.

Although blood pressure can creep up with age alone, several life-style factors also contribute to this dangerous picture:

1. over weight: fat is a very vascular tissue through which the heart must pump much harder;
2. stress and emotions: due to chronically elevated adrenaline release;

3. excess alcohol consumption; and
4. lack of physical activity.

The key point here is to remember that high blood pressure can be well-controlled with little or no side effects and that once a stroke or heart attack plagues you, the quality of life can be compromised forever.

WHAT TO DO THEN?

The two-step approach appears to work best:

1. Proper diagnosis and evaluation.
2. Treatment.

Both steps involve lifestyle changes and/or medication. High blood pressure is a serious diagnosis and should *never* be given on the basis of a single reading.

Proper diagnosis and evaluation

There is an entity called "white-coat hypertension" which is high blood pressure actually caused by the doctor or nurse. The scenario goes something like this: you may be active, non-smoking, moderate in your alcohol use, not overweight and handle stress well. You show up for your annual company exam, a little anxious and your blood pressure is 165/100. Is it real? Should you be on medications, as your lifestyle is already close to optimal?

You know how to check the oil in your car, you should know how to check your own blood pressure!

Because blood pressure is a function of both *flow* and *resistance* variables (which are constantly changing), isolated blood pressure readings can often fail to discern the underlying heart status of the patient. The answer is that any elevated blood pressure reading should be confirmed during the course of at least two subsequent visits (with an average level of systolic greater than 140 or a diastolic greater than 90 required for that diagnosis) or, optimally, the patient could be monitored for 24 hours. Measurements should be taken after five minutes of rest and the patient should have abstained from cigarettes, alcohol and caffeine (coffee and tea) within two hours of the measurement.

If your pressure is still elevated, buy a well-calibrated blood pressure machine from your pharmacist, and take your pressure yourself at home under less stressful circumstances. After all, once the diagnosis is made, chances are good that you will be carrying that diagnosis all your life. Once the diagnosis is made, ask yourself the following questions:

1. Do you have a rather **sedentary** lifestyle (very little physical activity)?

2. Have you been particularly **stressed** lately?

3. Do you drink large amounts of **alcohol** (including wine, beer and champagne)?

4. Do you consume large amounts of hidden **salt** or **fat**?

5. Have you gained much **weight** over the past year?

6. Is **diabetes** part of your family or personal profile?

If the answer to any of these questions is "yes," you may have a secondary reason for having your blood pressure elevated which will be responsive to lifestyle changes.

Treatment

Many executives, who might initially be annoyed (classic coronary-prone behavior) at the finding that their blood pressure is elevated are later relieved to know that they were unwittingly placing themselves at risk by not getting enough exercise, letting their weight go up or consuming too much alcohol.

The goal of treatment is to avoid morbidity (illnesses) and mortality (death) associated with high blood pressure. Recent studies have shown that the following lifestyle changes lower blood pressure and improve efficacy and dosage of medication.

1. Weight reduction.

2. Moderation of alcohol intake.

3. Salt restriction.

4. Exercise/Walking program.

5. Stress management Program.

6. Relaxation techniques/Meditation.

7. Tobacco avoidance.

8. Dietary counsel/Calcium intake reduction.

BLOOD PRESSURE ACTION PLAN

Follow this action plan as closely as you can. It will help you learn how to improve and then maintain a good blood pressure. Results and ratings are indicated on your report.

My most recent blood pressure was measured at:

_____ systolic

_____ diastolic

This represents a rating of: *normal*, *borderline* or *high* blood pressure (circle).

If high, what category?   Stage _____

You need to have a good understanding of "blood pressure" to be able to control it. If you cannot complete this section without referring to "The Book of Solutions," then you need to invest more time learning about blood pressure. Reread the preceding pages on blood pressure before completing this section.

The "systolic" pressure represents: _____

_____

The "diastolic" pressure represents: _____

_____

There are five major lifestyle risk factors that will give high blood pressure:

1. _____

2. _____

3. _____

4. _____

5. _____

These key factors will influence your blood pressure. Record your scores and ratings here. Any that are not rated "acceptable" need attention. You should refer to the relevant action plan for each individual unacceptable risk factor.

Classifications and appropriate actions

Low and normal blood pressure participants (up to 135/85)

Lead an optimal lifestyle with regard to blood pressure control. Continue with regular checks to monitor your blood pressure.

Borderline or mild high blood pressure participants (136/86–159/99)

Although not at present severely hypertensive, you are "sitting on the fence" and could fall either way with regard to blood pressure and risk from disease. Most experts agree that for Stage 1 hypertension (systolic = 140–159, diastolic 90–99), a six-month approach using exercise, stress control, weight control, smoking cessation, lowered salt intake and so on is appropriate.

Then only if the hypertension worsens or if heart risk status worsens (like cholesterol going up, weight going up), medication should be considered, *in addition* to the aforementioned lifestyle changes.

Once you understand what your blood pressure represents and the key lifestyle habits that influence it, you can start to influence your blood pressure by concentrating on these factors. Record your blood pressure again after three months.

Moderate or severe blood pressure participants (> 160/100)

If your blood pressure is in this rating, you are suffering from hypertension. Once the diagnosis is made you need to start taking control of this key health issue as soon as possible.

Your goal is to avoid the morbidity and mortality associated with high blood pressure. As already mentioned, recent studies have shown that lifestyle changes – weight reduction, salt restriction, and moderation of alcohol intake – may lower blood pressure and improve the effectiveness of medication. Other measures to consider include: stress management, exercise, tobacco avoidance, increasing dietary calcium intake, biofeedback and nutritional *counseling*.

As you follow the advice given to manage these risk factors your blood pressure will start to decrease.

1. Watch **body fat** percentage (men, keep your body fat < 20%, women, < 23%). Start on a sensible weight reducing nutrition plan now. Refer to the Body Composition and Weight Control sections of Chapter 2.

2. Uncontrolled **stress** which causes chronic adrenaline release may be contributing to elevated blood pressure. You should develop an effective stress management strategy and follow the stress action plan at the end of Chapter 4.

3. Physical **activity** and **exercise** is crucial for the control of blood pressure. Follow the action plan at the end of Chapter 3.

Watch **alcohol** intake. If it is greater, on average, than 21 units per week, you must cut down on the amount of alcohol that you are drinking. Excessive alcohol consumption is the most common cause of reversible hypertension. Quit for two weeks and see the effect of alcohol on your blood pressure for yourself.

If you use **salt** in cooking or add it to food at the table, then you must cut down and then stop using salt.

Very severe blood pressure (> 210/120)

If you do fall within this category, you are at immediate risk from heart disease and stroke as a result of your blood pressure. At the earliest possible opportunity, seek medical help to control this key health parameter. You will need to consult with your GP for medication initially, but you can still control this issue by concentrating on nutrition and weight control, physical activity and stress management with the help of your medical consultant. With sensible medical intervention and lifestyle modification your blood pressure will come under control. When it does, a trial period off medication should be possible.

Monitor your progress by recording the relevant risk factors when you re-assess. If your blood pressure does not improve, you must seek medical advice.

What about the active hypertensive patient?

OK. So you are already slim and active and blood pressure is just not going away. You have accepted medication after having tried everything and you want to run a half or full marathon. A couple of provisos are in order:

1. *Watch dehydration.* If you run or engage in exercises (tennis, squash, badminton) that involve a lot of sweating, you run the risk of dehydration, especially in hot or humid conditions. Dehydration can be exacerbated by diuretics (like hydrochlorothiazide, which also causes problems of high uric acid, high blood sugar, and low sodium).

2. *Let your doctor know your exercise plans.* Your best drug of choice may well be *calcium channel blockers* (drugs like diltiazem, felopidine, isradipine, nifedipine or verapamil, which lower resistance by blocking calcium channels in vascular smooth muscle – see discussion above), *ACE-inhibitors* (drugs ending in -pril, like captopril, enalapril, ramipril) that also lower resistance, or *selective beta-blockers* (acebutalol, betaxalol, metoprolol).

Risk factor # 3:
High blood cholesterol

If you are serious about health and fitness, you must make a point of understanding and controlling cholesterol. Because of its asymptomatic nature (no symptoms), cholesterol represents an iceberg phenomenon to your health: another silent killer.

Moreover, despite a disciplined exercise program, designed to upgrade cardiovascular health, a preventative health strategy is sorely incomplete without some program to control this waxy substance. Since the cholesterol revolution was launched by the cardiovascular epidemic of the 70s and 80s, much research (including the Nobel Prize-winning research of Brown and Goldstein) has contributed to our understanding. But what is known for sure?

FACT ONE: CHOLESTEROL IS A FAMILY OF WAXY SUBSTANCES ABSOLUTELY ESSENTIAL TO LIFE.

It is involved in critical steroid hormone production, cell membrane production and fat digestion. The cholesterol family is classified in terms of density, starting with:

1. *Low density lipoprotein (LDL)*: the so-called "bad" cholesterol thought to be responsible for the deposition of waxy cholesterol plaques in the arteries, therefore, the lower the level of LDL the better.
2. *Intermediate forms*: including very slow density lipoprotein (VLDL), and intermediate density lipoprotein (IDL).
3. *High density lipoprotein (HDL)*: the so-called "good" cholesterol, it is the "clean up man," thought to be charged with the delivery of cholesterol to the liver for processing and elimination, therefore, the higher the HDL, the better for the heart.

FACT TWO: KNOWING YOUR TOTAL CHOLESTEROL IS *NOT* ENOUGH

For many years, doctors have been assessing the role cholesterol plays in health by referring to the total cholesterol level. Experts worldwide agree that to get a handle on the role blood fats are playing in your risk profile, you must also know the relationship between the total cholesterol and your HDL.

FACT THREE: THE REAL CULPRIT – SATURATED FAT

It is not the dietary cholesterol (found in seafood, eggs) that plays a major role in your cholesterol level, but saturated fats. Saturated fats (animal fats such as butter, cheeses, red meats and heavily saturated vegetable fats) stimulate cholesterol synthesis by the liver. It is estimated by the French Federation of Cardiology that up to 70% of your total cholesterol (TC) comes from liver production (such as when it responds to fat intake) and only 30% comes from dietary cholesterol (such as 250 mg/egg). That has major implications when it comes to diet.

FACT FOUR: REGULATION OF YOUR TC/HDL RATIO IS NEITHER DIFFICULT NOR TIME CONSUMING

The key is to lower your TC (total cholesterol) level and raise your HDL (high density lipoprotein) level. Never accept a diagnosis of "high blood cholesterol" on the basis of one isolated blood test because there exists *interlab variation* (6%) and *intralab variation* (3–4%).

KNOW YOUR LABORATORY UNITS

As international travellers, you should become acquainted with the various cholesterol laboratory units that may be used throughout the world. These are the necessary conversion factors to move easily between the three international systems:

1. grams/liter (g/l);
2. milligrams/deciliter (mg/dl); and
3. millimoles/liter (mmol/l).

Step 1 To go from the Continental European system of *gram/liter* (g/l) to the Commonwealth and American system of *milligram/deciliter* (mg/dl), multiply g/l by 100 to get mg/dl. For example, if your TC = 2.5 g/l (×100) = 250 mg/dl

> Write in your total cholesterol here (circle units): _____ g/l
> Convert it to the other system of mmol/l: _____ g/l divided by
> 0.39 = _____ mmol/l.

Step 2 To go from the Continental European system of *gram/liter* to the lab units of *millimole/liter* (mmol/l) divide g/l by 0.39 to get mmol/l. For example, if your TC = 2.5 g/l (0.39) = 6.4 mmol/l.
Note: regardless of the units, the TC:HDL ratio will be the same.

KNOW YOUR TC/HDL RATIO AND ITS MEANING

Heart disease risk	Male	Female
Lowest	< 3.5	< 3.5
Below average	3.5–4.4	3.5–4.4
Average risk*	4.5–6.4	4.5–5.5
2× Average	6.5–13.4	5.6–10.9
3× Average	> 13.5	> 11.0

*Average risk is approximately 25% chance of a heart attack by the age of 60.

Illustrative examples: which case are you?

Ideal situation

TC = 1,90 g/l or TC = 5.7 mmol/l ("normal")

HDL = 0,70 or 1.82 mmol/l (high) TC/HDL = 3.1(requires no attention)

Ideal ratio: less than 3.5 is associated with a **less than half the average risk** of developing heart disease. Recommendation: recheck it every year.

Marginal situation

TC = 2,00 g/l or TC = 5.2 mmol/l ("normal")

HDL = 0,40 or 1.04 mmol/l (high) TC/HDL = 5 (requires attention)

Marginal ratio: between 3.5 and 5.0 is associated with an average of developing heart disease – a 25% chance by the age of 60. If you are in this range, you are "sitting on the fence" and our job is to push you over to the right side. People who usually suffer heart attacks have ratios between 4.6 and 6.4.

Dangerous situation

TC = 2,80 g/l or TC = 7.3 mmol/l (high)

HDL = 0,30 or 0.78 mmol/l (low)

Important note: as HDL is the good cholesterol, the arterial "clean up man," you want a high HDL, certainly greater than 0.45 g/l. An HDL cholesterol level less than 1.0 mmol/l is also considered a risk factor for heart disease.

TC/HDL = 9.3 (requires definite attention)

Dangerous ratio: between 7.0 and 15.0 is associated with a tripled average risk for developing heart disease by age 60. We strongly recommend you to seek expert medical advice. As well as sensible medical intervention, you can improve your ratio by following the proposed action plan in that chapter.

CHOLESTEROL ACTION PLAN

This plan is both effective and feasible in the international business world. Results will be rapidly verifiable.

My total cholesterol is _____ g/l mg/dl mmol/l (*circle the units*)

Ideally, total cholesterol should be below _____ g/l mg/dl mmol/l (*circle the units*)

My HDL cholesterol is _____ g/l mg/dl mmol/l (*circle the units*)

Ideally, HDL cholesterol should be above _____ g/l mg/dl mmol/l (*circle the units*)

My total cholesterol/HDL cholesterol ratio is _____

This represents a rating of _____

The ideal cholesterol ratio is less than _____

Factors that help reduce total cholesterol include:

1. _____

2. _____

3. _____

TO LOWER YOUR TC

What you can do if your TC is > 2.0 g/l, 200 mg/dl, 5.2 mmol/l):

1. First rule, make sure your body fat is optimal (< 20% for men, < 23% for women).
2. Limit your consumption of animal fats in all forms (butter, cream, cheeses, red meats, organ meats).
3. Use low-fat milk products.
4. Avoid food fried cooked, or those containing coconut oils.

5. Increase intake of fruits, vegetables and grains.
6. Lower blood triglycerides by reducing alcohol and refined sugar.
7. Eat plenty of fish such as salmon, tuna, herring, mackerel.
8. Exercise, such as walking more regularly.

TO RAISE YOUR HDL

What you can do if your HDL is < 0.45 g/l; 45 mg/dl; 1.7 mmol/l:

1. Increase daily activity (see Chapter 3).
2. Quit smoking and avoid smokers (tobacco smoke lowers HDL levels).
3. Eat plenty of fish: salmon, tuna, herring, mackerel.
4. Moderate alcohol consumption to one–two drinks a day.

STEP-BY-STEP

1. Eat normally as you have been over the past several years. Count the total number of meals you have in a week which contain saturated fat (meat, cheeses, butter and so on). For example: meals with any fat = 16.

2. Count the total number of meals you typically eat in a week. For example: total meals = 20.

   Number of meals that will be eaten containing saturated fat will now be _____ per week.

3. Divide the first figure by the second and multiply by 100. This is the percentage of meals that contain some saturated fat – the chief stimulus of cholesterol in your body. For example: (16:20) × 100 = 80%.

   Saturated fat meals represent _____ % of all my weekly meals.

4. Cut back on meals containing saturated fat by 10–20% to start and then calculate how many meals containing saturated fat that represents.

OVERALL ARTERIOSCLEROSIS ACTION PLAN

Take a moment for reflection and complete this action plan to ensure that you fully understand the importance of arteriosclerosis to your health and the possible risk factors that may be present in your life.

> *Stop arteriosclerosis before it stops you!*

If you cannot complete all the questions, you should consider investing more time learning about heart attacks and strokes.

Health to me is (imagine speaking from the point of view of a heart attack or terminally ill patient):

1. _____

2. _____

3. _____

What are the major causes of illnesses and death in your country/ region?

1. _____

2. _____

3. _____

Atherosclerosis contributes to what percentage of premature deaths in our society? _____ %

Arteriosclerosis represents what process in the body?

_____

_____

Name several of the "target organs" for the long-term effects of arteriosclerosis:

1. _____

2. _____

3. _____

What are the seven major risk factors for the development of heart attacks and strokes?

Primary:

1. _____

2. _____

3. _____

4. _____

Secondary:

1. _____

2. _____

3. _____

Are there any of the seven major risk factors for the development of heart attacks and strokes currently present in your lifestyle? If yes, which ones?

1. _____

2. _____

3. _____

4. _____

5. _____

6. _____

7. _____

Here are some of the options once the development of heart attacks and strokes has occurred. Which ones, if any, can you envisage for yourself?

1. taking multiple medications ☐

2. bypass surgery ☐

3. angioplasty ☐

4. heart transplant ☐

II. STROKES

A stroke is the result of a disease of the blood vessels of the brain. Any interruption of the flow of blood that carries nutrients to the brain, even momentary, will cause damage to the part of the brain downstream from the obstruction. Generally speaking, there are two major types of strokes:

1. *Stokes by clot or embolism:* responsible for up to 70% of all strokes, these disable by *blocking* an artery of the brain with a blood clot. For example, an irregular rhythm of the heart, such as atrial fibrillation (estimated to cause up to 15% of all strokes), may allow blood to stagnate and clot. When the heart resumes a normal contraction, the clot is sent to the brain.

2. *Strokes by rupture of a vessel (Hemorrhagic stroke):* responsible for up to 10% of all strokes, these disable by *rupture* of an artery of the brain, thus spilling the blood onto the extremely sensitive brain cells (neurones). Up to 50% of these strokes kill the victims by increasing pressure within the skull.

Risk factors for strokes

The risk factors for strokes are as follows:

1. High blood pressure (weakens arteries).

2. Any heart disease or risk factor for heart disease increases the risk for strokes to *twice* that of normal heart status:
   (a) smoking;
   (b) cholesterol imbalance;
   (c) inactivity;
   (d) diabetes;
   (e) excessive body fat%.

3. Thickened blood states: cause clots to form.

4. Excessive alcohol.

Warning signs for strokes

The warning signs for strokes are as follows:

1. Sudden change in mental activity: speech, gait, thought.
2. Sudden falls.
3. Sudden headaches, especially with vision changes.
4. Weakness or numbness anywhere in the body.

The next chapter made me less nervous than the one on heart disease. It started with the age old question: What is cancer?

AVOIDING THE COMMON CANCERS

The society clever enough to perform sophisticated research on cancer is the society clever enough to invent sugar substitutes, children's sleepwear ingredients, food coloring agents, and swimming pool test kits that may cause it.

from *The Arrogance of Humanism* by David Ehrenfield

As a brief background, you must know that the body/mind is in a constant cycle of activities at the cellular level: a cell grows, it has some specific activity in the body (such as producing a specific protein), it dies and is replaced. All that countless times just in the time it takes to read this page! The organization of this cycle is vastly complicated and not yet completely understood. Cancer occurs when the meticulous control mechanisms go haywire and these "renegade cells" reproduce selfishly at the expense of surrounding cells.

A cancer is deemed *benign* or *malignant* as a result of several factors, among which are the aggressivity of uncontrolled growth, accessibility to treatment (chemical, surgical or whatever), and extent of spread.

Cancer and emotions

The immune system, our natural defense against infections and cancers, is under close control by the mind: you are well-balanced and you stay well, emotional instability, you get sick. This connection between mind and body has a long-standing history through many spiritual traditions worldwide. It is really only in Western countries that we, for the sake of analysis, separate the two.

One can never really understand the pathogenesis or treatment of any disease, certainly not cancer, without taking into account the emotional aspects of the disease. On certain cells of the immune system, there are receptors (antennae) that receive the messages and instructions from proteins in the part of the brain that controls emotions.

Research has shown that cancer patients who were cuddled, emotionally and spiritually cared for and who could communicate their situation, survived longer and died a more peaceful death.

What to do about cancer?

The treatment of cancer, as with the treatment of most internal imbalances begins with *you*. You vastly improve your chances of effective treatment and survival when you can detect and report symptoms as early as possible. Typical symptoms include: unusual lumps or nodules (anywhere), bleeding, unwanted weight loss, pain, appetite changes or wide mood swings.

The list below is meant to be an overview and in no way a list of all the possible cancers. There are numerous reference texts that can provide an exhaustive treatment of the subjects.

Cancer (comment)	*Lifestyle/Screenings*
1. Lungs (85% due to smoking)	Stop smoking NOW!
2. Prostate (very common in men)	(a) Watch early urinary symptoms: (change in stream, hesitancy, urgency, sexual changes in erection, blood in stool). (b) Proper rectal exam: (patient in knee-elbow position to adequately drain the prostate). (c) Watch saturated fat intake: (unclear connection).
3. Breast (very common in women)	(a) Watch early symptoms: (bumps, bleeding). (b) Proper breast exam/mammogram. (c) Watch saturated fat intake: (unclear connection)

4. Colorectal (intestine)
(common family history)

    (a) Watch early symptoms:
         (rectal bleeding, constipation).
    (b) Proper rectal/colonoscopic exam.
    (c) Watch saturated fat intake:
         (unclear connection).
    (d) Increase fibre.

5. Skin
(common family history)

    (a) Watch early symptoms:
         (change in moles, warts . . .).
    (b) Proper full body skin exam.
    (c) Watch prolonged UV exposure.

6. Liver
(common in Asia)

    (a) Watch early symptoms:
         (weight loss, nausea, anorexia).
    (b) Hepatitis B vaccine?
    (c) Know your carrier status.
    (d) Watch alcohol intake.

7. Stomach
(common in countries
with smoked foods)

    (a) Watch early symptoms:
         (weight loss, nausea, anorexia).
    (b) Watch smoked foods.

2

HUMAN NUTRITION
MADE SIMPLE

"It is not merely the *quantity* and *quality* of
foods we eat that causes disease, it's also *how* it is
eaten, *when* it is eaten, what we do *after* eating
it, and so on."

Day Two: Wednesday morning – back in class . . .

On my second day in hospital, I was awakened just as my room-mate Ray was being wheeled off for his bypass. My last memory of Ray that morning was him giving a wink and a thumbs up as he quipped, "See you on the back nine after lunch . . ." and he was off. After a light breakfast, I headed back to the library's special reading area. Settled back in the library with my cup of tea, awaiting the return of Dr Charles, I had decided to use my captive time well and get through as much of "The Book of Solutions" as possible.

The next chapter was on nutrition and food, a subject that I felt I had some expertise in. I had read all the new health books and had done some experimenting of my own. One of the aspects of the current flurry of health books that disturbed me was the simple idea of treating foods like medicine, without any real discussion of pleasure. Quel sacrilège!

My own feeling had always been that as we make our way through life, food and all the conviviality that goes with it was one of the great compensations for the trials and tribulations that we are asked to put up with. I was most curious to read what Dr Charles had to say about all that. Up to now, I had appreciated his less than orthodox, non-dogmatic approach to life. I had the feeling that a two or three day stay like this spent getting my life "back on track" would have done me a world of good ten years ago. Oh, well, better late than never . . . .

"Good morning to you!," came the friendly voice from behind. Dr Charles had a decidedly brisk pace to his gait. "Ready for another session of catch-up reading in the classroom?," he asked with a smile. His enthusiasm was contagious.

"I sure am. Should have done this years ago, Doc," I shot back.

"You pored through the first couple of chapters of 'The Book of Solutions'," he said while opening the door, "how far did you get this morning?"

"Well, I haven't gotten through all the solutions yet. I am really just beginning to understand *my* role in the problems of my own health. I suppose that is a good place to start, *at the beginning*. I got through the chapters on heart disease, arteriosclerosis and its relation to activity, smoking, cholesterol and so on. Good stuff."

"Any questions . . . comments?"

"Not just yet. But I am beginning to see what you mean about diseases having their origins in the mind," I said. "With the wrong attitude about food, exercise and so on, you can get really sick, just by not respecting the body. Disease, in a way, is a reflection of an imbalanced attitude towards a life more than anything else, isn't it?"

"Well, you're getting a little ahead of yourself. Let's save that discussion for some time later this afternoon when you get through the sanity chapter. By the way, there are other books here, as well. Real books, literature, poetry, drama, Dickens, Goethe, Shakespeare, Lao Tzu, Blake: medicine for the soul. Take a look around. Complement your technical education with a more universal education. You're welcome to take them back to your room."

"Thanks, Doc. This morning, I'm doing all of Human Nutrition before I quit today," I joked, as I settled into my seat by the window, pen and paper ready.

"A few years in a few hours. Sounds about right," he said, smiling. "Don't hesitate if questions come up. That's what I'm here for."

I flipped to my dog-ear in "The Book of Solutions" and dug in, tea at my side.

HUMAN NUTRITION

I. THE IMPORTANCE OF NUTRITION: THE BASICS REVISITED

The importance of the way that you nourish yourself cannot be overstated. *Every system* in the human body, with the exception of the central nervous system (the brain and spinal cord), regenerates itself using, in part, the foods we eat as building blocks. When you are injured, even by the minor wear and tear of everyday life, the body rallies all its resources and reparative powers to put you straight. If the food we eat or the way we eat it is less than optimal this process of regeneration suffers.

So, it is not merely the *quantity* and *quality* of foods we eat that causes disease; it's also *how* it is eaten, *when* it is eaten, what we do *after* eating it, and so on.

Loss of an important ritual

Rituals, the practice of doing something for the sake of being in the present moment alone or with others while offering something up, keeps some "magic" and structure to our lives. One by one, they are quietly disappearing from our lives and taking with them, our collective sanity. Some of the important rituals that make life bearable include: preparing meals together, taking afternoon tea, closing the shutters on the front of the house every evening, grace before meals, weekly or daily worship, going to the cinema together (popcorn and all), bedtime stories passed on from father to son and from mother to daughter. These rituals provided the thread of our family's moral fabric and kept us together in a frozen moment of communal transcendence.

There even used to be a time, not very long ago, when people would, as part of their normal lives, put down their plowshares and hammers to break bread, bow their heads and raise their glasses to the

sky in thanks. During that brief respite, those sharing in the ritual of "breaking bread" would exchange stories and smiles and forget the woes of survival. Because of that brief moment together people were happy and in harmony with the events and people who surrounded them. No one was allowed to drift off in an eddy of indulgent self-pity or depression: they were interrogated by concerned relatives until the emotional abscess was lanced and everyone would breathe a sigh of relief. Nutrition was a family event that stopped time, not a mere fill-up or pitstop in the rat race. It actually meant something!

In all likelihood, those folks were far less obsessive with their nutrition because they did not have to be. Because of the peace that the meal together brought to their lives, their minds were clear as to how and when to eat. Their bodies and minds were in synchrony with the Cycles and Laws of Nature. Rituals (the act of offering up something) gave a structured transcendence to their lives.

Then, very insidiously, something changed all that. Every lovely nuance of individual cultures (including language) started coalescing into one great modern culture. Traditional rituals are beginning to disappear due to decay from within and erosion from without. Quite regrettably, in homage to some golden calf called Time or Money, we are surrendering one of our most ancient and vital rituals: sitting at table. Instead of setting the pace of our own day, we allow time pressures to impose themselves. Then we tend to relegate nutrition to the status of a "fill-up," as if our body and mind were a simple machine, instead of a miracle of Nature.

One by one, our rituals that bind us together on this planet are being sacrificed to efficiency. Rituals that help to pay homage to the celebration of our victories over life's challenges (breaking bread with family, raising a glass of fine wine with friends, taking a little time to prepare a meal) may be accessible to us only on a CD-ROM and fingers previously singed by removing a lovely roast from the oven now have freezer burns.

Examples of the effects of loss of rituals on overall health abound. The Japanese, when they move to America, assimilate all too fully and become obese (and lose all that extra body fat when they return home to Japan), Yemeni Jews moving to Israel develop previously unheard of diabetes, throughout Asia rates of heart diseases are skyrocketing, as traditional diets low in fat are being replaced by diets of fast foods and prepared foods.

Take the whole issue of commercial fast foods. Even the name runs against a natural current. Fast foods are undeserving in **substance** because they are, on average, high in calories (the range is 900 to 1,800 calories or 33 to 90% of total daily calories for young people), high in sodium (many meals range from 1,000 to 2,515 milligrams), high in fat (some fast foods contribute up to 50% of daily fat intake in one meal).

More importantly, fast foods are undeserving in *format*. Rather than take time and love to prepare a meal that is destined to become part of our being, we voluntarily sit under bright lights, in uncomfortable chairs, listening to raucous music to eat a meal that is undeserving of the importance of the ritual. One is even expected to bus his or her own tray. That is, in part, why the family is disintegrating: because there are no structured rituals holding them together.

The loss of rituals can have a devastating effect on mental and physical health. In the moral sense, since we have largely abandoned the transmission of life's lessons from parent to child, the child has had to derive life's lessons from an infinitely more dangerous source: television (uninvited strangers in your home would be safer sources of influence). Instead of holding our elders in high esteem as vessels of wisdom, they are shipped off to old folks' homes. Unfortunately for the family, they tend to take their time-honored wisdom with them.

EXERCISE

Loss of an important ritual: modern foods

These modern fast foods may actually taste good during consumption but they may, in excess, cost dearly in health terms. Don't make your arteries pay for the caprices of your palate. Match the foods with their ingredients:

Food	Ingredients
1. Potato-chips (crisps)	_____
2. Diet soda drink (cherry)	_____
3. "Natural" candy bar	_____
4. Instant pancake mix	_____
5. Dog food	_____
6. Lite Italian salad dressing	_____

▶

Food	Ingredients
7. Breakfast cereal	_____
8. Instant soup	_____
9. Coloured candies for kids	_____
10. "Natural" cookies ("40% fat")	_____
11. Throat lozenges	_____
12. Instant tea drink	_____
13. Isotonic drink	_____

a. Bleached flour (wheat flour, niacin, reduced iron, thiamine mononitrite, riboflavin), sugar, soy flour, leavening, vegetable shortening (partially hydrogenated soybean and cottonseed oils), dextrose, eggs, buttermilk, salt, soy lecithin (an emulsifier) and non-fat milk.

b. Maltodextrin, malic acid, instant tea, aspartame (phenylalanine), natural lemon flavour.

c. Sugar, butter, whole milk powder, cocao mass, whey powder, lecithin (emulsifier), flavouring, may contain nut tracings.

d. Beef, mutton, poultry, bone, gels, food coloring, vitamins and minerals.

e. Potatoes, palm oil, spices, salt, glutamic acid, citric acid.

f. Carbonated water, sucrose, glucose, citric acid, sodium chloride, potassium phosphate, sodium benzoate, E211, vitamin C, calcium phosphate.

g. Sugar, corn syrup, dextrose, glycine, gelatin, artificial flavor, vegetable gums, colors include red 3, red 40 lake, blue 2 lake.

h. Water, distilled vinegar, salt, sugar, < 2% garlic, natural flavors, soybean oil, xanthan gum, sodium benzoate, potassium sorbate, calcium-disodium EDTA (preserves freshness), yellow 5, red 40.

i. Wheat flour, palm and sesame oils, freeze dried mushrooms, dehydrated sweetcorn, leeks, carrots, seaweed, sugar, monosodium glutamate (MSG).

▶

j. Corn, oat and wheat flours, vegetable oils (soy, cottonseed sunflower) salt, sugar, natural colours (annattol, carmine).

k. Enriched wheat flour, raisins, rolled oats, fructose, polydextrose, soybean oil, water, apple and pineapple juices, powered cellulose, corn syrup, dough conditioner (lecithin), < 2% apples, corn starch, leavening agents, ammonium bicarbonate, bicarbonate of soda, sodium aluminium phosphates, natural and artificial flavors, spices, pectin, citric acid.

l. Dextrose maltose, dextran corn syrup, malic acid < 2% artificial and natural flavors, calcium stearate, color additives, wax, blue 1, blue 1 lake, red 40 lake, yellow 5 lake, yellow 6 lake, yellow 6.

m. Carbonated water, sugar, citric acid, sodium benzoate E 211, caramel E 150, colour (E122).

Answers: (at end of chapter).

What happened to fresh meats and vegetables, prepared with love and attention? And fresh water to drink? We will have plenty of time in the 23rd century to eat "astronaut food."

Without investments of energy into these traditions they will die. Sit down to table and talk. Tell more stories before someone else does.

Listening to the body's messages

There are several good reasons why you need to pay attention to nutrition:

1. *Our energy and pleasure.* After all, one of the central reasons for eating food, from a physiological point of view, is to provide the energy sources necessary to carry out our daily functions effectively, both in the short and long term. Whenever pleasure is involved, time should be taken to enjoy these precious moments: eat slowly to savor the foods prepared for you. If little time is available, eat little.
2. *Our health.* The quality and quantity of the food that we eat will, of course, affect our overall health and performance (both physical and mental), now and for the rest of our lives. After all there really is no sense in making our arteries and intestines pay the price for over-stimulated taste buds and palates. A happy middle ground is, of course, desirable.

3. Our weight. When we perform a surgical procedure, the first fact that becomes evident to the surgical team is the *vascularity* of fat. That is, the amount of small, blood-filled capillaries that flow through the fat. The capillaries provide the conduits to and from the fat so that we can easily access this highly efficient storage form of energy.

The upshot of this is that the more "prosperity tissue" we have, the harder the heart has to work to get the blood through. Our daily diet is the major influence over our body weight and fat stores, as we'll see shortly.

But how do we know if we are nourishing ourselves well? In the rapid-fire fray of the harried business world, priorities are made and we are conditioned to ignore the signals our bodies and minds send us: we turn a deaf ear to ourselves until serious imbalances are incurred.

Tuning one's attention back into the body and mind after 30+ years of neglect is challenging and potentially confusing. It need not be so. The first step is to quiet the mind long enough to ask a few questions of yourself:

1. *Do you have bloating, gas or constipation?*

2. *Do you fall asleep at important meetings or after a large meal?*

3. *Are you excessively tired or even disoriented after a long business trip?*

4. *Are you irritable around meal time?*

5. *Do you have difficulty falling or staying asleep even though you may be exhausted?*

6. *Do you have frequent headaches, migraines? (Aspirin or other painkillers may only be muffling the real message.)*

7. *Look at your tongue: is it coated with a film? Is there a sour taste in your mouth? Is your breath foul smelling?*

8. *Look at your teeth and gums: are your teeth discolored? Are your gums receding from the base of your teeth? Do they bleed easily?*

9. *Look at your skin: is it dry and chapped? Is acne a problem?*

10. *Look at your hair: does it break or fall out easily?*

We are all different in the ways we respond to certain foods and that's why there are so many approaches because what works for you won't work for the next person. Is fat OK? Is chocolate OK? Is coffee OK? Can I mix proteins and fats and starches and so on? No one has all the answers for everybody but, if you learn to read the messages that your body is sending you, you can learn better than anyone else what aspects of your nutrition make you drag and what aspects make you fly: no mystery there.

II. THE ESSENTIAL NUTRIENTS AS BUILDING BLOCKS OF HEALTH

The human digestive system, though it prefers foods in their natural, uncooked state, is remarkable in its ability to transform seemingly un-nourishing substances like cookies, popcorn, doughnuts, and candies into the necessary elements of energy to carry on your daily chores.

Human beings, standing tall, with our heads towards the sun, our feet on the earth, are constantly seeking to integrate the elements that the sun and the earth have to offer to us. To accomplish this, we have developed a digestive tract, a canal more than 10 metres long, beginning at the mouth and terminating at the anus – this is best visualized as a mobile laboratory, with key stops or "stations" along the way. Let's take a brief look at the substrates that provide energy to this fascinating laboratory: proteins, starches, fats.

Proteins

These nitrogen-containing elements are the most plentiful organic compounds in the body. The primary element of proteins, *amino acids*, has many of the 20 of which are considered "essential" and, therefore, required in the diet: lysine, leucine, valine, isoleucine, threonine tryptophan, phenylalanine, methionine, arginine and histidine.

The principal constituent of most meats, protein, functions in the body to: form essential body proteins (hormones, enzymes, muscle), regulate water balance by maintaining osmotic pressure, buffer (keeping the body's pH near neutrality), make antibodies, promote growth and repair of living tissue, as well as provide a source of energy. Deficiencies of proteins, a major health problem in the world today, lead to marasmus (deficiency in calories and proteins, leading to muscle and fat wasting, anemia and loss of hair pigmentation), and kwashiorkor (deficiency in the quality and quantity of proteins, leading to bloated bellies and swelling of legs, muscle wasting, retarded mental and physical growth, and anemia and starvation).

From an energy point of view, our body is capable of converting every gram of protein into 4 calories of heat. Any protein consumed in excess of the body's requirements (estimated at 0.8–1.2 grams per kilogram of body weight every day) will be stripped of its nitrogen (deaminated) and the carbon backbone of the amino acids is recycled into the liver's citric acid cycle for energy, or fat storage if unused. The end-products of protein metabolism are water, carbon dioxide, energy, and nitrogen (in the form of ammonia and urea). Inability of the liver and kidney to excrete this nitrogen load can lead to the undesired build-up of these toxic substances in the blood. Therefore, a diet excessively high in proteins is unhealthy.

The protein family includes:

1. The muscle and flesh of fish, pork, beef, veal, lamb, chicken.
2. Milk, yoghurt and cheeses.
3. Soy products: tofu, soy milk.
4. Eggs and egg products, such as mayonnaise.
5. Some vegetables: beans, chick peas and lentils.

Carbohydrates (aka starches and sugars)

Thanks to the lay press, nearly everybody recognizes this term carbohydrates as meaning starches and sugars. In fact, they are subdivided into *simple* sugars (monosaccharides like glucose, fructose, galactose), *double* sugars (disaccharides like sucrose (glucose + fructose), maltose (glucose + glucose), lactose (glucose + galactose), and *larger sugar chains* (polysaccharides).

Examples of simple sugars in everyday life are the "natural sugars:" honey, molasses and brown sugar. Interestingly, all three products are composed of sucrose (molasses is the by-product of sucrose production). All simple sugars, except fructose, are utilized with the help of insulin, which shuttles the sugar into the cells for energy extraction. Examples of starches include potatoes, bananas, pasta, rice, and breads.

Starches constitute up to 60% of the modern diet. In simple terms, starches, energy yield is about 4 calories per gram. Interestingly, the ratio of carbon (C) to oxygen (O) in its structure $(C_6H_{12}O_6)_n$ is relatively high, 1:1. This becomes important particularly when it comes to energy utilization.

The carbohydrate family includes:

1. Bananas, sweet potatoes, potato family (yams).
2. Flour-based products: pasta and breads.
3. Refined sugar and honey.
4. Rice.
5. Cereals, including beers.

Fats

Here, the ratio of carbon (C) to oxygen (O) in its structure of fat $(C_{16}H_{32}O_2)_n$ is low, 1:8. That is why fats are more easily accessed during low-intensity (oxygen-sufficient) activities, such as brisk walking.

Among the many functions of fat in the diet (energy, insulation, prostaglandin production, cushioning), one critical function is to provide an essential fatty acid known as *linoleic acid*. Deficiencies of this compound lead to skin problems, impaired reproduction and poor fat transport.

Cholesterol

As discussed previously, one of the major fats of interest is cholesterol which provides three essential functions: cell membrane stability (without which we would evaporate), hormone production (cholesterol provides the precursor backbone of steroid hormones, such as vitamin D), and fat transport. Importantly, the liver makes most cholesterol. The dietary contribution of cholesterol to the total body cholesterol (check your cholesterol test in the laboratory report on your check-up) is less than 20%. Your body synthesizes about a gram per day of cholesterol; you consume, on average, about 0.4 grams, of which only 40% (0.16 grams) is absorbed. That means, for example, if your total cholesterol test is 220 mg/dl (or 2.20 grams/liter or 5.7 millimoles/liter), only 44 mg/dl (0.44 grams/liter or 1.14 millimoles/liter) comes from that egg or that prawn! If you ate a cholesterol-free diet, your total cholesterol would drop by only by 30 mg/dl. Most cholesterol comes from your liver's response to **dietary fat**.

As fats are largely insoluble in water (blood is mostly water), they require a transport mechanism called lipoproteins, which are classified according to their density:

1. *Very low density lipoprotein (VLDL):* forms by excess triglycerides (fat).

2. *Low density lipoprotein (LDL):* thought to be responsible for the transport of cholesterol from the liver to the arteries. It has, therefore,

been called the "bad cholesterol" and, to prevent plaque build-up that leads to heart attacks, it is recommended that your LDL blood level stays below 135 mg/dl (or 1.35 grams/liter or 3.5 mmol/ liter).

3. *High density lipoprotein (HDL):* thought to be responsible for the transport of cholesterol from the arteries to the liver to be metabolized and excreted in the bile. It has, therefore, been called the "good cholesterol" and, to help "clean up" the plaque on arteries, it is recommended that your HDL blood level stays above 45 mg/dl (or 0.45 grams/liter or 1.2 mmol/ liter).

Triglycerides

The other fats of interest are the triglycerides (composed of a glycerol ester backbone connected to three fatty acids of varying lengths). These fatty acids are classified as saturated, unsaturated or polyunsaturated, depending on the numbers of double bonds ($-C=C-$) present within the hydrocarbon chain.

Since fat's **energy yield** is about 9 calories per gram, it represents a major source of daily calories to the human body. The intake range for fat runs from < 10% calories a day in the poorest country to 60% daily calories in the most extreme case.

What is saturation vs unsaturation?

This is a question of **chemical structure**. Fat compounds are made up of carbon atoms linked to other atoms by chemical bonds: **single** bonds ($-C-C-C-C-$ . . .), or **double** bonds ($-C=C-C=C-$ . . .). Their chemical properties (boiling point, melting point, viscosity constants, solubility) change as the structure of the compound changes.

A fat compound with just single bonds ($-C-C-C-C-$) is called *saturated* and will generally be solid at room temperature, such as fatty meats, cheese, lard or butter. Conversely, a fat compound with single and double bonds ($-C=C-C=C-$) is called *unsaturated* and will generally be liquid at room temperature, such as oils. So, from a health point of view, one should switch from butter to margarine, right? Not yet and, perhaps, not ever. The reason for this is that in the process of making margarine, the double bonds of unsaturated vegetable oils ($-C=C-C=C-$) are hydrogenated to form saturated fats. Then various stabilizers and preservatives of color and texture are added to better simulate the original butter.

Recent studies suggest that these man-made transformed fats (i.e. margarine) may actually do the same thing as the natural saturated fats (butter) that they were made to replace: stimulate cholesterol in the blood and, possibly, cause clogging of the arteries. For now, the burden of proof is on the manufacturers to actually prove, not merely infer, a healthy connection between margarine and cholesterol. We are not there yet. The best advice is, therefore, to use **all** saturate fats (natural and man-made) *very* sparingly.

Mediterranean diet and health

In sum, independent of the *origin* of the fat, Nature or man, the *nature* of the fat, i.e. whether unsaturated (mono or poly) or saturated, will determine its association with heart disease: the more saturated, the greater this association.

This is best witnessed in the different eating habits of Mediterranean people and their northern European counterparts. The Finnish people and the Italians eat roughly the same proportion of fat in the diet, about 35–40% of total daily calories. The sole difference is the type of fats: Finns consume more saturated fats (meats, cheeses), while Italians consume more unsaturated sources (olive oil and fish).

This consumption of relatively "clean" fat, when combined with the beneficial effects of red wine and garlic, provides the extra edge on cardiovascular disease enjoyed by Italians. The shift from saturated to unsaturated fats may also impart an advantage over cancers of the breasts and colon (large intestine), but confirmation of this hypothesis is still in the research phases.

The table *on p. 80*, from the US Department of Agriculture, shows the composition of various common foods in the modern diet. Note carefully, not just the cholesterol content of various foods (remember dietary cholesterol only makes up 20% of your blood cholesterol), pay special attention to fat content and particularly saturated fat content.

The fat family includes:

1. Nuts and their oils.

2. Butter and creams.

3. All oils.

Composition of various common foods

Foods	Calories (approximate)	Total fat (grams)	Saturated fat (grams)	Cholesterol (milligrams)
Dairy products				
Milk, 2% fat	125	4.7	2.9	18
Yoghurt, low fat	145	3.5	2.3	14
Cheddar cheese, 28 grams	115	9.4	6.0	30
Mozzarella cheese, 28 grams	70	4.5	2.9	16
Cream, table or light, 1 tablespoon	30	2.9	1.8	10
Vanilla ice cream, half cup	135	7.2	4.4	30
Orange sherbet, half cup	135	1.9	1.2	7
Meat, poultry, fish, beans and eggs				
Beef liver, 56 grams	–	4.5	1.6	273
Pork loin	–	13.8	5.0	51
Chicken, light meat, with skin, 56 grams	–	6.2	1.7	48
Chicken, light meat, no skin, 56 grams	–	2.6	0.7	48
Chicken, dark meat, with skin, 56 grams		9.0	2.5	52
Chicken, dark meat, no skin, 56 grams	–	5.6	1.5	53
Shrimp, steamed and shelled, 56 grams	–	0.9	0.1	117
Tuna, canned, oil packed, 56 grams	–	4.6	1.2	37
Crab, cooked, 56 grams	–	0.9	0.1	57
Oysters, shucked, cooked, 56 grams	–	1.5	0.4	36
Navy beans, cooked, half cup	–	0.4	0.1	0
Egg, large	–	5.6	1.7	274
Fats and oils (in tablespoons)				
Beef fat	–	12.8	6.4	14
Chicken fat	–	12.8	3.8	11
Lard	–	12.8	5.0	12
Butter	–	11.5	7.2	31
Soy	–	13.6	2.0	0
Peanut	–	13.5	2.3	0
Olive	–	13.5	1.8	0
Coconut	–	13.6	11.8	0
Margarine (hard stick)	–	11.4	2.1	0
Avocado, half	–	18.5	3.7	0
Snacks				
Potato–chips (crisps), 10	–	8.0	2.0	0
French fries, (chips), 10 long	–	10.3	2.6	0
Peanuts, dry roasted, 1/4 cup	–	17.6	3.1	0
Peanut butter	–	15.3	2.8	0

Source: US Department of Agriculture

III. THE "LABORATORY ON LEGS": THE STAGES OF HUMAN NUTRITION

Technically speaking, the digestive system is not a part of the body's "internal milieu." Rather, it is a convoluted canal, with numerous access and exit points, which runs from outside the mouth to the anus, through the body. At each of the stations (the mouth, the stomach, the small intestine and the large intestine), the bolus of essential nutrients of proteins, carbohydrates and fats and vitamins is temporarily halted for inspection, exposed to digestive juices, transformed into more digestible morsels and then absorbed to be transported to the billions of hungry little furnaces, the cells of the body.

The various cells use these nutrients to generate heat to keep the "internal milieu" balanced and transform the nutrients in such a way to suit their highly specialized functions. The unused "waste products" are left behind in the intestines to move down the tract towards their fate.

The mouth: where digestion begins

As Pavlov once demonstrated with his dogs, even prior to placing the first morsel of food upon your tongue, the brain prepares the body for the feast in anticipation of the food: salivation starts from three pairs of glands, the stomach growls and starts secretion.

Salivation

Wholly undeserving of its bad reputation, perpetuated by tobacco chewers and camels, saliva not only helps dental hygiene by neutralizing (with bicarbonate) the acid produced by bacteria and acid foods, but also lubricates the mouth making speech a lot easier. The daily flow of saliva is on average between 1,000 to 1,500 milliliters.

From a digestion point of view, salivation starts when a combination of visual, auditory, olfactorial and psychological factors tell the body: "It's time to eat." Saliva contains ptyalin (α-1,4-amylase), a catalyst that starts to break down starches at an optimal acidity range of 6.5 (low pH indicates high acidity), and is de-activated at pH less than 4.5. Cooked starches, unlike simple sugars, are branched structures that require "clipping" of the branches into smaller chains of sugars by ptyalin prior to absorption in the intestine.

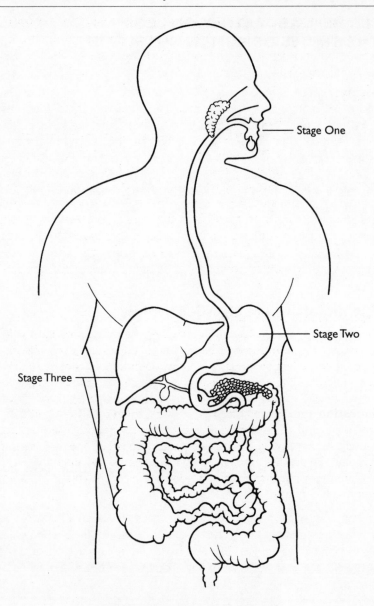

Stage One

Stage Two

Stage Three

The stages of human nutrition

Importantly, ptyalin is stable at mid-range pH of 4–11 and therefore, any "clipping" of starches that does not happen in the mouth, may impair optimal digestion, by leaving more work for an already overworked pancreas, as we'll see in a minute.

The tongue

For efficient grinding, the food must be kept between the tongue and the teeth. For this reason, the tongue has one of the riskiest jobs in Station 1, of rolling and flicking the food, with the aid of the cheek muscles, into the way of the crushing millstones. The tongue readily accepts this dangerous task as it is amply rewarded with the best task, as well, the tasting of the food. The tastebuds are actually specialized chemical receptors that transmit stimuli from the food in four basic categories: *bitter* (distributed at the back of the tongue, hence, the bitter aftertaste of some foods as they pass over this area on the way "down"), *sweet* (tip of tongue), *sour* (side of tongue), and *salty* (tip and side of tongue).

At this point, I recalled what Dr Charles had said about our genetic heritage and this shed a whole new light on my eating habits. We obviously eat according to what our body craves (it's even been postulated that when people do not get enough fat and cholesterol, they get violent!). The brain can detect whether it has enough sugar, fat or whatever, I thought, only if the food spends enough time stimulating the appropriate tastebuds on the tongue. All of a sudden, I wasn't afraid to eat fats and sugars, but decided to savour them slowly so that my body's cravings can be satisfied. It was starting to become simple: digestion and enjoyment begins in the mouth!

Then, on the next page, I found a very interesting way to approach cravings.

When you reach for . . .	. . . what your body wants is . . .	. . . instead, try . . .
Pork, bacon, ham, lamb, sausages, liver, pork brain, kidneys, tripe	**Animal protein**	Skinless chicken, turkey, veal, rabbit, game, tuna, salmon, bluefish, herring and mackerel: steamed or grilled, not fried
40%-fat cheeses, whole milk/creams, fat-based sauces	**Animal fat** (something creamy)	Low-fat milk/yoghurt (0–20%) cheeses
Candies, chocolate colas, sodas, cakes, candies, sugary cereals, syrupy fruit	**Something sweet**	Fresh or dried fruit, fruit juice, fresh fruits
Fast foods	**Something quick**	Whole wheat bread-sticks, unsalted nuts, pretzels or crackers, popcorn
Caffeine	**Something hot**	Herbal teas, hot apple cider, low calorie cocoa, tea

The teeth

Having been relieved, in large part, of their erstwhile role of defence and aggression, our teeth are, of course, the principal agents of mastication, or chewing. They are aided by powerful chewing muscles, all of which are voluntary muscles; that is, under your conscious control. Together, they can generate a pulverizing force of over 100 kilograms! All this thanks to a covering of enamel (hardest substance in the body) which is logically thick-est (1.5 millimeter) at the chewing surface.

If the eyes are the "gateway of the soul" and reflect the overall state of the soul's health, then the teeth are the "gateway of the body". Rising up like jagged white menhirs from shining pink gums, the teeth's apparent durability belies their general fragility. Properly cared for, the gums and teeth can stay intact in the jawbone for up to eight decades, protecting the body's health and the face's esthetic appeal. In fact, the most prevalent reason for lost teeth is gum neglect, not teeth caries.

Left undefended against the acidic activity of bacteria and food, the teeth are rapidly eroded away, like ancient monuments in acid rain, transforming the mouth into an odiferous worn facsimile of its former proud self.

In sum, Stage One, the mouth, from the digestion's point of view, has several functions:

1. First and foremost is **pleasure**, which begins the whole salivary process.
2. **Crushing** and **lubrication**, so that foods slide down the gullet easily.
3. Start of **digestion of starches** by saliva.

The stomach: the gatekeeper and protein cauldron

The stomach, from the digestion's point of view, has several functions:

1. **To act as a gatekeeper, holding foods until the rest of the digestive system is ready.** The stomach empties starches most rapidly of all foods (water is emptied from the stomach virtually instantaneously), then proteins, then fats, which are held until the downstream stations of the liver and pancreas are ready. This is why, all other factors being equal, you may expect to feel a sensation of hunger sooner after a meal of toast and fruit juice than after a ham and cheese omelette.

   In some cases of food poisoning, the stomach, sensing an unwelcome microbiological or chemical intruder contaminating the food, will not allow the food to proceed downstream. Instead of allowing the entire system to be contaminated, the stomach retches and forcibly expels the intruder.

   Other factors that **accelerate stomach emptying** are:

   (a) **hunger:** as the stomach has increased tonicity, it makes good sense that the foods be delivered to a hungry (hypoglycemic) person faster;
   (b) **physical activity:** low grade exercise, such as brisk walking, will aid emptying and digestion.

Factors that **slow stomach emptying** are:

   (a) **emotional state or pain:** stress of any kind (anger, aggression, depression, fear), as it triggers the "fight or flight" response;

(b) *food type:* fat contents in excess of 10% (cream = 20%) will slow emptying, giving the liver and pancreas time to prepare, and inhibit stomach secretion of acid, necessary for protein digestion. Fats and proteins, therefore, are best consumed separately.

2. *Cauldron for protein digestion.* In response to the presence of foods, particularly proteins, the outpouring of secretions from the stomach begins. Though there is considerable variation in acid response to proteins, in general, the more protein present, the greater the secretion of acid and the more fat or starches present, the less acid production there is in the stomach. Practically speaking, therefore, taken together with protein, starches may interfere with the optimal digestion and breakdown of proteins.

I paused briefly, pondering why, if the stomach is so involved with acid secretion, the stomach, composed of muscle protein itself, does not actually digest itself. Fortunately, Dr Charles was not busy, so I posed the question to him.

"Wow, you're really starting to think like a doctor now. Bravo. Well, you see, the stomach produces a protective layer of mucus that helps to prevent 'auto digestion,' as well as a very sophisticated series of physiologic pumps that keeps the acid where it belongs until the right moment. However, you must beware of several foods and drugs that will break-down this system of autoprotection and set you up for ulcers. They include: 1. Caffeine (a popular ingredient of headache medications). 2. Alcohol (watch this on an empty stomach). 3. Aspirin, some other painkillers and certain anti-asthmatic drugs. So, beware of these foods and drugs, because many a surgeon and stomach doctor have been called into the emergency room at 3 a.m. for bleeding ulcers, a diagnosis which carries a 10% mortality rate."

The small intestine: laboratory door

Once the stomach has finished liquefying and acidifying the meal's contents, it passes on the watery chyme to the small intestine where, in unison with the liver and the pancreas, and the lining of the small intestine itself, it goes about the business of supplying the body with nutrients and calories. Virtually all processing and absorption of nutrients occurs within the small intestine.

The liver

Throughout history, from Babylon to the Bible, from Pythagoras and Plato to Shakespeare and Galen, in Oriental medicine and African medicine, virtually every major culture has attached a special meaning to the liver, particularly with regard to emotions. Even a cursory glance at literature and history reveals a myriad of words for bile, the gall bladder and the liver connoting courage, melancholy, depression and anger.

As it turns out all that attention is for good reason. The liver, about 1–2 kilograms in weight, is first in number and complexity of functions, some of which are: the **detoxifying centre** of the body's unwitting imprudence, **energy storage facility for proteins, fats and glycogen** (that's why marathon runners stock up on starches a few days before the race so that the liver can store these as glycogen for use during the long run), **synthetic factory** (bile acids and about 70% of your total cholesterol). The liver is the body's Central Station.

The pancreas

The pancreas neutralizes acid from the stomach with bicarbonate (HCO_3^-), secretes lipase (chemicals that break down lipids or fats) and secretes insulin to regulate sugar. You cannot live without the pancreas.

The small intestine lining

This is where the true work of chemical transformation takes place. It neutralizes acid from the stomach with bicarbonate (HCO_3), as well as secreting lipase to break down fats.

The highly convoluted small intestine is divinely suited for its basic job of *absorption*. Any excess energy absorbed through the small intestine that was obtained by dietary fat, sugar or protein will be transported to the liver for conversion into triglycerides (fat) to form VLDL.

The large intestine: where digestion ends

The large intestine (colon), from 1–2 meters in length, is not involved in the digestion of nutritive chyme.

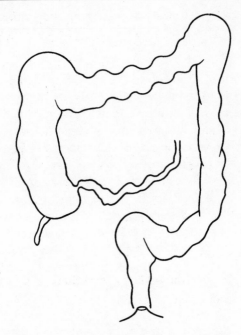

Normal configuration of large intestine

It is in charge, rather, of transforming the liquid chyme into solid faeces by absorbing the water and minerals. If water intake is too low, the colon will wring the chyme of water until the intestinal contents are hard and dry. This leads to constipation, a most undesirable condition in which waste products are retained until sufficient water is supplied.

Prolonged retention of faecal material and the attempts at forceful elimination thereof, could lead to a wide variety of intestinal ailments such as appendicitis (point A), spasm and painful distension and gas (point B), polyps (point C), diverticulosis (painful herniated outpockets through the muscular wall of the large intestine, point D), diverticulitis, colitis, haemorrhoids (point E) and, quite possibly, colon cancer. All this misery could be side-stepped by simply achieving an adequate water and fibre intake on a *regular* basis. Best time to drink fresh water is BETWEEN meals; with meals, water dilutes the efficiency of digestive juices and can impair nutrition.

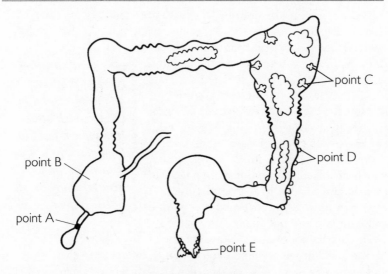

point C

point B

point D

point A

point E

Diseased large intestine

Dietary fibre

Why is dietary fibre so important to the health? In cultures where dietary fibre is high, the aforementioned intestinal complaints are virtually non-existent. But what is this miracle dietary fibre? It is a family of non-digestible carbohydrates that can absorb up to 15 times their weight in water, thereby, providing bulk to the stool and increasing motility and transit times through the intestines. In short, waste products are cleared. Best sources are fruits and vegetables.

Food compatibility

"Dr Charles, can we have a quick Question and Answer session?" I felt it was time to distil out some of his "pearls."

"No such thing with a doctor," he joked, "but, sure go ahead. I'll never turn down a curious student," he offered magnanimously.

"I really enjoyed reading about the digestive system. Why are we not as in tune with our systems as other animals," I asked, as I was starting to feel a little hungry myself.

"In the animal kingdom of which we are members, you see," Dr Charles explained patiently to me, "we are unique in that we have evolved a way of eating that puts all the three types of foodstuffs on our plate and in our stomach at once. It may be a feast for the palate, but often it turns out to be a disaster for the rest of the system. Susutra, the greatest surgeon of his day in India spoke of the elements "Vaju" (air), "Kapheh" (phlegm), and "Pittam" (bile), which, if mixed harmoniously, would lead to a balanced and healthy individual. If mixed in unwise proportions, they would cause disease and unbalanced character."

we put all the three types of foodstuffs on our plate and in our stomach at once. It may be a feast for the palate, but often it turns out to be a disaster for the rest of the system.

Dr Charles continued, "Nowhere else in Nature, which we seem so determined to escape, are the digestive and excretory systems so overburdened with the indulgences of the palate as in Humankind. And then we develop multibillion dollar industries to deal with the consequences of this folly: bloating, obesity, fatigue, weight control, indigestion, heartburn, constipation and so on. Bizarre how we chase our own tail."

"Even in countries where it is the tradition to mix it all up, like China and India, or the steak and potatoes in the States or fish and chips in the UK."

He explained, "Traditionally, all cultures used to eat in a more beneficial way, out of necessity. It was a question of economics. It also just so happens that eating that way was more in accordance with the design specifications of the body than how we eat now. Just because we have taken a few evolutionary 'wrong turns' on a global scale, doesn't mean that it's good for us. You don't have to be living in a so-called 'poor, under-developed, country' to be malnourished. Look at the rise of obesity and heart disease in developed and developing countries. I'm not saying that it's the only reason, but it is definitely a contributing factor."

"Can you please draw for me a simple way to remember what goes with what?," I asked.

"Certainly," he said graciously, "you've read already about the different foods: protein, starches and fats. Well, just remember this diagram.

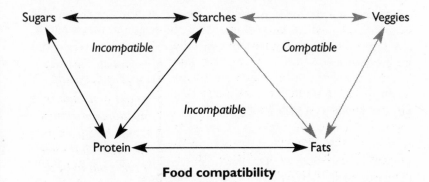

Food compatibility

"If you forget everything about these arrows and what goes with what, just remember, proteins and starches make for a tired digestive system and many uncomfortable symptoms."

Gas in the gut

"Is gas in the gut one of the symptoms of poor nutrition?," I asked.

"You have gas?," he joked, as he walked to the blackboard. "You're not alone, as this is a very common problem. Gas in the gut will definitely not kill you, unless you work in a submarine, but it will make your life miserable and, it's really very easy to take care of. Think of the causes. Remember that the air you breathe right now has a fairly standard composition: about 70% nitrogen, 20% oxygen and 10% carbon dioxide and hydrogen. Gas in the gut comes either from swallowed ambient air (60% of cases) or from production in the gut (40%). If you swallow air, because you bolt your food or chew gum, the oxygen is reabsorbed but the nitrogen is expelled as flatus. The key in that case is to slow down your eating.

"Interestingly, the combination of the acid from the stomach (HCl) and bicarbonate from the small intestine and pancreas is one of the sources of intestinal gas (CO_2). During a meal, 75 mEq of acid from the stomach may react with 75 mEq of bicarbonate from the pancreas generating 1,875 cc of CO_2 in the small intestine. While most of the gas diffuses back into the blood some remains to add to the intestine's gas load to be expelled later on.

"More commonly and more abundantly, gas comes from fermentation by bacteria in the large intestine (colon) of unabsorbed foods (like the hulls of beans or milk sugar lactose) to hydrogen and methane, both of which are combustible. In that case, watch injudicious mixtures of foods, particularly proteins and starches and watch the beans."

IV. OBESITY AND DISEASE

I had many questions for Dr Charles in relation to this section of the manual, and started with the most basic question of all.

"Aside from the obvious aesthetic aspect of being overweight and the psychological impact thereof, why is being overweight so serious for our health?"

"Obesity on such a grand scale as we are seeing it now is a relatively recent phenomenon of this century, so we are really just beginning to study the whole issue seriously. Unfortunately, obesity is not just poorly *understood* scientifically but also poorly *perceived* by the public at large. This is particularly true when it comes to upper body obesity. This type of obesity (described at length below under waist-to-hip ratio) is associated with increased levels of insulin in the blood

> *Obesity is more than being overweight. It is, more precisely, being overfat.*

(hyperinsulinelmia), which is thought to cause high blood pressure (a primary risk factor for heart disease) through three main mechanisms:

1. Increased water/sodium retention, which spells more fluid for the heart to pump.
2. Increased stress hormones in blood (noradrenaline), which increases the heart rate and contractility.
3. Increased vascular resistance to the heart's pumping.

Obesity is more than being overweight. It is, more precisely, being *overfat*, as measured and monitored by body fat percentage. The ideal body fat percentage is 15–20% for men and 19–23% for women. You see, increased body fat (greater than 20% for men, 23% for women) indicates a greatly increased risk of heart disease and a predisposition to elevated blood pressure, cancer, diabetes, accelerated 'wear and tear arthritis' of joints and breathing problems. Secondly, while the level of total cholesterol may in some obese individuals appear normal, lipid metabolism in these people is often awry. For example, the LDL portion of the total cholesterol is often increased, which correlates well with active plaque deposition."

> It is estimated that for every extra kilogram of body fat beyond the acceptable ranges (set generously at < 20% for men and < 23% for women) total cholesterol production rises by 0.20 g/liter.

Dr Charles continued, "There is new emerging evidence that these problems of obesity and cholesterol and blood pressure are all related somehow. They appear to be part of a larger constellation of findings known as **Syndrome X**. This syndrome, about which you all will be hearing a lot more in the future, is the relationship between what we call in medicine, the Fatal Quartet:

1. Upper body obesity.
2. Glucose intolerance (the inability to control blood sugar).
3. High blood pressure.
4. Elevated triglycerides.

But we are back to our genetic heritage, once again. Storing fat in our days of famine was a definite advantage because we never knew when the next hapless antelope would come along. We evolve much more quickly than our genetic code and now being overfat is distinctly *disadvantageous* and can have dire consequences," he said as he went to his handy blackboard and jotted down the following:

OBESITY AND DISEASE
1. Obesity predisposes one to adult diabetes.
2. Extra body fat spills into the bloodstream, thereby stimulating cholesterol synthesis.
3. Obesity makes the heart work harder → raises blood pressure.
4. Extra fat is dead weight, an extra kilo = more fatigue.
5. High triglyceride levels, uric acid levels.
6. Miscellaneous: Increased incidence of gout, gall stones, thromboembolism, hiatal hernia, arthritis

Moreover, studies have also indicated that the more overweight we are the higher our chances of developing certain cancers," he said, as he continued to write:

> OBESITY and CANCER
> Obesity may also influence the risk of certain cancers:
> 1. intestine (colon);
> 2. breast;
> 3. prostate;
> 4. gall bladder;
> 5. female reproductive tract.

Childhood obesity: a deadly legacy

Before delving into the section of the manual dealing with childhood obesity, I poured myself a cup of tea from the ever-present teapot behind Dr Charles's desk and asked him a question.

"Doc, I've always, since I can recall, been bothered by a weight problem, even as a kid," I confessed. "Is it possible to make our kids obese by forcing them to eat. You know 'eat up your plate now, the starving people in poor countries,' and all that?"

"Absolutely," he said. "Overbearing parents, charter members of the 'clean-plate club' can actually begin the whole pathological process of adult obesity by forcing, bribing, cajoling, rewarding, children to eat more than their little bodies are able to assimilate. That, combined with the media blitzing of fast foods and advertising, makes for a future generation of 'couch potatoes.' After all, up to 80% of obese children become obese adults.

"The accumulation of fat, due to excess intake or insufficient activity, can be stored either by *increasing the number* of fat cells (adipocytes) or by *increasing the size* of pre-existing cells, or both. When you lose body fat, say, through brisk walking, you shrink the size of fat cells, but not their total number. Most importantly for children, it seems that people who become obese as children have a higher **number** of fat cells, perhaps in response to excess fat intake and low activity levels, while most obese adults have bloated fat cells. That's precisely why liposuction is wrong because only the number of cells is changed, not the underlying lifestyle habits that made the remaining fat cells bloated in the first place.

"They are becoming obese because of three main factors:

1. decreased physical activity (addicted to TV at home and excessive work at school);
2. increased calorie intake (including sweets and fast foods); and
3. sedentary parents make for poor role models.

These kids will have the same confidence problems as their adult counterparts, but at an earlier, more formative, age. Imagine the psychological consequences of this deadly legacy."

"What can be done for kids, then?' I had noticed that both Christopher and Julia enjoyed fast foods and were becoming a little chunky around the midriff.

"Awfully tough to battle those fast food giants: pretty deep pockets. But they aren't the problem: they're just selling their wares. The real problem is that we don't educate our kids and help them compensate for the little excesses that come with being a kid. The trick, I think, is *don't deprive*, but *compensate*. I would try to get them to stay active and play sports to burn it all off. Make a deal with them: fast foods once a month in exchange for weekly hiking trips to the countryside or whatever," he explained, "anyway, if you yourself are overweight, any argument is a tough sell."

Obesity worldwide

Before reading this section of the *manual*, I asked Dr Charles for his opinions on worldwide obesity.

"Doc, why do you think that so many people from around the world are overweight? Is it all a question of ill-conceived nutrition and mixing?"

"Only in part. Otherwise, all the people in India and China, where rice and beef, pork and mutton are regularly served together, would be obese. Those countries, in my experience, have many overweight people, but first you have not defined what being overweight is," he said.

"Well, too heavy." I thought that was obvious. I had seen weight and height charts derived from insurance company statistics.

"What is more massive, more dense: fat, which floats on water, or muscle or bone, which sinks in water?," he asked me.

"Fat, of course," I said, confused as to where he was going with this.

"Right, so that when you are trying to control weight, is weighing yourself an accurate measure?," he asked.

"Aaaah! I see, finally. You mean all these years that I've been involved with the 'battle of the bulge', I should have stayed away from the bathroom scales?," I asked, relieved.

"Yes, in fact, one of the best ways to take a look at weight and its relation to the Fatal Quartet and Syndrome X is to look at body composition, best understood by two central concepts." He scribbled as he spoke:

Central concept:	As measured by:
Total fat % of total weight	Body fat %
Total fat distribution	Waist-to-hip ratio

For a full interpretation of your body composition and the role it plays in health, you should refer to both measurements, *not* absolute kilograms, because of what we just discussed regarding lean and fat compartments. Why don't you finish that chapter on weight and we'll grab some lunch."

The importance of knowing body fat percentage (BF%)

In the modern era of proactive preventative health, you should know your body fat percentage as this helps to accurately determine the overall level of health as well as your risk for diseases.

Consider that your total body weight is divided into two basic "compartments:"

1. the lean mass (muscles, bones and water); and
2. the fat compartment.

Whereas the lean compartment stays relatively stable until late in life when it diminishes rapidly during the shrinking phase, because of inactivity, the BF% compartment tends to expand and contract through life. The lean compartment is composed of water, muscle and other protein and bone mineral. When we overeat and become more sedentary, excess calories tend to be stored as fat, so increasing our fat mass, or body fat percentage.

The body fat that you are carrying around is an excellent source of stored energy: it is calorifically dense (~ 9 calories stored/gram) and it is

Your total body weight is divided into two basic "compartments"

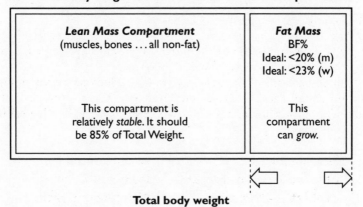

Lean Mass Compartment (muscles, bones ... all non-fat)	**Fat Mass** BF% Ideal: <20% (m) Ideal: <23% (w)
This compartment is relatively *stable*. It should be 85% of Total Weight.	This compartment can *grow*.

Total body weight

light (because of its specific density of ~ 0.90 gm/cc). It was very advantageous for our cave-dwelling ancestors to have a little extra body fat and is still considered in some countries to be a symbol of wealth and desirability.

However, if you have devised your lifestyle so that you make your living with your brain and your back is sore from golf, not from digging ditches, extra body fat can be quite disadvantageous.

There is a method that can be used by you at home to gauge your progress. Regardless of the actual method, you should know and monitor your BF% over time to gauge the effect of activity, diet and other lifestyle factors.

How to measure your body fat (women)

Materials needed: a tape measure.

Step 1: Use the tape measure to measure:
(1) the abdomen (half inch above the belly button);
(2) the right thigh (just below the buttocks);
(3) the right calf (halfway between the knee and the ankle).

Step 2: Then find the constant that corresponds to the measurement at each site and insert into the following formula:

Body fat = (abdomen constant + thigh constant – calf constant) – 21

Abdomen inches (cms)	Constant	Right thigh inches (cms)	Constant	Right calf inches (cms)	Constant
25 (64)	30	14 (36)	17	10 (25)	14
26 (66)	31	15 (38)	19	11 (28)	16
27 (69)	32	16 (41)	20	12 (30)	17
28 (71)	33	17 (43)	21	13 (33)	19
29 (74)	34	18 (46)	22	14 (36)	20
30 (76)	36	19 (48)	23	15 (38)	22
31 (79)	37	20 (50)	24	16 (41)	23
32 (81)	38	21 (53)	26	17 (43)	25
33 (84)	39	22 (56)	27	18 (46)	26
34 (86)	40	23 (58)	28	19 (48)	27
35 (89)	42	24 (61)	29	20 (50)	29
36 (91)	43	25 (64)	31	21 (53)	30
37 (94)	44	26 (66)	32	22 (56)	32

For example: 34" abdomen (constant = 40)
25" thigh (constant = 31)
16" calf (constant = 23)

Approximate body fat = (40 + 31 − 23) − 21 = 27%

How to measure your body fat (men)

Materials needed: a tape measure.

Step 1: Use the tape measure to measure:
(1) the buttocks (widest part with heels together);
(2) the abdomen (half inch above the belly button);
(3) the right forearm (widest part between elbow and wrist).

Step 2: Then find the constant that corresponds to the measurement at each site and insert into the following formula:

Body fat = (buttocks constant + abdomen constant − right forearm constant) −19

Buttocks inches (cms)	Constant	Abdomen inches (cms)	Constant	Right forearm inches (cms)	Constant
28 (71)	29	26 (66)	23	7 (18)	21
29 (74)	30	27 (69)	24	8 (20)	24
30 (76)	31	28 (71)	25	9 (23)	27
31 (79)	32	29 (74)	26	10 (25)	30
32 (81)	34	30 (76)	27	11 (28)	33
33 (84)	35	31 (79)	28	12 (30)	36
34 (86)	36	32 (81)	29	13 (33)	39
35 (89)	37	33 (84)	30	14 (36)	42
36 (91)	38	34 (86)	30	15 (38)	45
37 (94)	39	35 (89)	31	16 (41)	48
38 (97)	40	36 (91)	32	17 (43)	51
39 (99)	41	37 (94)	33	18 (46)	54
40 (102)	42	38 (97)	34	19 (48)	59

For example: 37" buttocks (constant = 39)
35" abdomen (constant = 31)
7" right forearm (constant = 21)

Approximate body fat = (39 + 31 – 21) – 19 = 30%

How to calculate your total calories stock

(How many calories are stocked as fat and how to mobilize your fat depots.)

Weight = 90 KGs body fat percentage = 30%

Write your *body* fat percentage here: _____ % and your weight in KGs: _____

Step #1 : calculate lean mass (LM): (KGs of muscle, bones and water)

Lean mass = total body mass – body fat mass
Body fat mass = 90 KGs × 30% = 27 kg fat
Therefore, LM = 90 KGs – 27 KGs fat = 63 KGs

My LM = present weight _____ KGs – _____ KGs fat = _____ KGs

Step #2: calculate optimal weight (OW): (use the upper limit of normal body fat of 20%)

At body fat 20%, the lean mass must be 80% of optimal weight. Therefore, in *this* example, 63 is 80 % of 79 KGs. (Divide 63 by 0.8) Optimal weight (at BF% of 20) = _____ KGs.

Step # 3: calculate energy stored as fat (difference between present weight and optimal weight = KGs extra fat)

Therefore, in *this* example, 90 KGs – 79 KGs = 11 KGs extra stored fat. Every kg of fat is roughly equivalent to 9,000 calories (1,000 gr @ 9 ml/gr).
So, 11 KGs × 90 ~ ml/kg = 99,000 calories stored as fat.

Step # 4: decide on a gradual time frame to mobilize fat stores

This person decided on a time frame of one year, which is a good idea as this means that 99,000 calories stored as fat are to be utilized gradually over a long period of time, little by little, thereby increasing chances of success.

Therefore, 99,000 calories stored as fat ÷ 365 days = 270 calories/day.

Time frame = _____ days = _____ cal/day.

The real trick here is to **take your time**. For example, if you chose 18 months to liberate this stored energy, you would now divide 99,000 calories stored as fat by 548 (days in 18 months), and you would need to create a calorific deficit of only 180 calories per day to mobilize 11 KGs of FAT!

Walking away from most diseases: the first "W"

As I was about to read this section of the manual, Dr Charles preempted the text.

"What do you think is the best single activity that you can do for your extra body fat stores if you've had 20 free minutes?," Dr Charles asked.

"I don't know," I admitted. All I could think of were highly intense and distasteful activities, "running, marathons, squash."

"Not quite," he said. "Look at this graph." (see opposite).

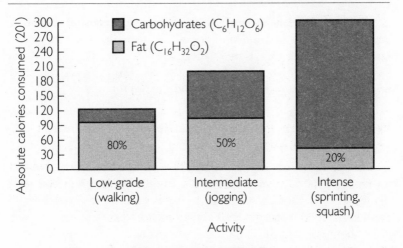

How energy is utilized

"I know this is a bit of biochemistry, but just bear with me for a moment and it will all be clear. Look at what happens to energy use during three examples of exercise: low intensity (brisk walking), intermediate intensity and high intensity, such as sprinting or squash. Interestingly, the ratio of carbon (C) to oxygen (O) in the structure of carbohydrates $(C_6H_{12}O_6)_n$ is high, 1:1. That is precisely why they are the preferred fuel during high-intensity (oxygen-deficient) activities, because there is plenty of oxygen available.

"Now look at the structure of fats $(C_{16}H_{32}O_2)_n$. Here, the ratio of carbon (C) to oxygen (O) is low, only 1:8. That is why these are easily accessed during low-intensity (oxygen-sufficient) activities, such as brisk walking. Of course, more absolute numbers of calories are consumed during intense exercise, but most of them, about 80%, are coming from glycogen stores in the muscle and liver."

"Doc, do you mean that jogging is a bad sport?," I asked.

"Well, that all depends on *why* you are doing that sport, something we will talk about tomorrow during the fitness talk. Say, for example, that your objective is to lose body fat: if you have just 15 minutes and cannot change into your jogging attire, warm up and cool down, etc., then walking in your work attire, particularly after meals, is a more efficient use of your time, given your objectives. If your objective is to condition the heart, something a little more intense, such as jogging, is more effective."

This was really beginning to make me think and I returned eagerly to the next section of "The Book of Solution."

Waist-to-hip ratio (WHR): the distribution of fat

The other central concept to weight control is *where* exactly you are distributing your body fat, as measured by the WHR. The ideal WHR for men is ~ 0.95, for women ~ 0.85. The WHR correlates well with decreased HDL cholesterol, high blood pressure, high blood trigly-cerides (fats), glucose intolerance and insulin resistance (potentially pre-diabetic conditions).

I looked up and posed some initial questions for Dr Charles.

"Clearly there is more to obesity than initially meets the eye. Are there different *types* of obesity with different risks attached? Don't women generally tend to have more body fat and still have less heart disease?"

"The answer to both queries is 'yes.' Though Hippocrates first classified the body forms into 'habitus apopleticus' and 'habitus phthiscus,' the real appreciation for the importance of exactly where body fat accumulated came with a French doctor, Jean Vague. In 1947, he differentiated two patterns of fat distribution." Dr Charles pointed to the following table in "The Book of Solutions:"

"Android" (man-like)	Pattern of distribution	"Gynoid" (woman-like)
Apple-shaped	Body habitus	Pear-shaped
Upper-body (belly)	Where fat is distributed	Lower-body (hips, buttocks)
< 0.95	Optimal waist-to-hip ratio	< 0.85
Diabetes Increased triglycerides Increased blood pressure Increased coronary heart disease	Diseases at risk	None

He continued, "There has been, over the past three decades, mounting evidence that, indeed, as your WHR climbs above the upper limit of normal (for men < 0.95, for women < 0.85), the risk of dying from cardiovascular disease rises **significantly**. The reasons for this are clear: there is a highly significant correlation between the rising WHR and glucose intolerance (a predisposition for diabetes), higher total cholesterol and triglycerides, lower HDL, higher systolic and diastolic blood pressures. It is estimated that people with increased abdominal obesity, have up to 15 times the risk of developing diabetes than people with normal ratios.

"Consistently, studies show that women can carry up to 25 kilograms more fat than men without higher risk because of the more gynoid (pear-shaped) distribution. The association of upper body fat with high blood pressure can even be identified among young children."

I returned to the pages of the manual.

....

How to measure your waist-to-hip ratio:

Materials needed: a tape measure.

Step 1: Stand erect and relaxed, without pulling in your stomach.

Step 2: Using the tape measure, take the circumference of your waist at the level of the navel (belly button).
Waist circumference = _____

Step 3: Using the tape measure, take the circumference of your hips over the buttocks at the widest point.
Hip circumference = _____

Step 4: Divide the waist circumference by the hip circumference:
W/H = _____

V. WEIGHT CONTROL: STOKING THE FIRE WITHIN

The only truly effective way to lose body fat is to change the behavior that caused the problem in the first place: no change between the ears, no changes around the waist or in the coronary arteries. For most people, taking off weight can be far easier than maintaining that weight loss. As discussed, the bathroom scales will serve no purpose as muscle, by volume, is heavier than fat, so, as you begin to mobilize the fat compartment (that is, decrease the body fat percentage to the ideal 15% or less) and increase your muscle mass, you may eventually actually *gain* weight.

The only difference this time is that your weight gain is the right kind: muscle mass. Using only the weight on the bathroom scales will only succeed in derailing your weight control program. Therefore, use the WHR or body fat percentage to gauge your success, not the absolute kilograms! That's the best single way to derail an otherwise motivated person involved in weight control.

Recent scientific research has demonstrated that you need not put on tennis shoes and jog against your will at noon to stay fit. But you must understand the central concept of metabolic rate (calories/day) and to do this you need to appreciate two central issues:

1. How to safely speed the metabolic rate up (avoid unwittingly slowing it).
2. The Glycemic Index.

Metabolic rate: cornerstone to weight control

The diagram shows a balanced relationship between calories eaten and calories expended.

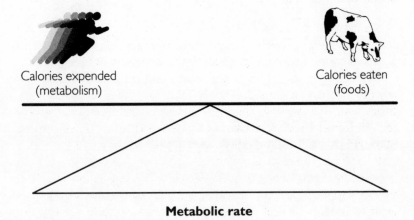

Calories expended
(metabolism)

Calories eaten
(foods)

Metabolic rate

Such a balance is impossible unless proper attention is paid to calories in (quality and quantity) and calories out (metabolic rate).

Are you storing or burning calories?

Check the items that are a regular part of your life and find out what message you send to your body.

The metabolic rate is then *increased* by:

1. **Spontaneous activity:** how generally active you are during the day.
2. **Exercise** (every 15 minutes of *brisk* walking within 30 to 60 minutes of eating increases the metabolic rate for at least 45 minutes).
3. **Eating/snacking intelligently** (dried, fresh fruits).
4. **Caffeine use** (watch dehydration).

These activities will speed calorie consumption by the body: that is, doing these things will burn stored energy (fat).

NB: as the metabolic rate increases, the red blood cells release oxygen more easily and the oxygen is, therefore, delivered more efficiently to needy tissues.

The metabolic rate is then *decreased* by:

1. **Inactivity:** (stores calories as fat).
2. **Dieting: calorie deprivation.** (*Note:* both inactivity and dieting *conserve* the body's calories as the body perceives no calories coming in, and seeks to conserve energy stores.)
3. **Starvation:** the body is dying of hunger and therefore *conserves* calories.

These items slow calorie consumption: that is, doing these things will *slow* the metabolic rate. A slower metabolic rate will, in an effort to conserve calories, burn progressively less fat and more muscle protein.

So, in direct response to energy needs brought about by fasting or any other form of calorie deprivation, the body does several "logical" things: first, your own muscle protein (including the heart muscle protein) becomes a source of calories. For every kilogram of weight lost, 300+ grams are from the body's own protein sources and the rest is water and salt. The result is weakness.

Secondly, during calorie deprivation, the body instructs the fat cells in the body to increase *lipase* activity, thereby breaking down fat into fatty acids for energy. Therefore, during fasting, up to 2,500 calories are expended, of which 90% comes from fat; loss of weight is slow because only 300 grams of fat per day can provide the energy needs slowed down by calorie deprivation. In addition, fasting can cause, in prolonged states, an increase in uric acid levels, leading to gout.

In practical terms, unlike the widespread and dangerous short cut approach of *diet pills*, there are several safe and effective ways to increase the metabolic rate. They include:

> *In the Western world, the obsession with dieting has been paradoxically linked to the increases in obesity and poor health.*

1. *Eat! The body uses energy to process the food you eat.* Conversely, skipping meals or other forms of calorie deprivation slow the metabolic rate. Snacking on fruit (fructose, water and fibre) between meals will maintain the metabolic rate.

2. *Walk after meals.* Metabolic studies show a synergistic relationship between low-grade activity (like brisk walking) and food. For every minute of walking briskly within 30 minutes of finishing the meal, your metabolic rate will be elevated for three minutes!

....

"That's quite interesting, Doc," I said. "You mean if I go for a brisk walk for 15 minutes after my meals, I will continue burning the calories just eaten for 45 minutes after my return!"

"Yes, it's really that simple. By *brisk* walk, I mean about one cycle per second. That is, roughly speaking, walk to a pace of 'one and two and three and . . . .' It doesn't make any sense to walk faster than that because the body only has a certain amount of blood. If you exercise too vigorously after meals, say, jogging or running up stairs, your body will send blood to the leg muscles instead of the digestive tract. You'll get an upset stomach."

....

The Glycemic Index of foods

The approximate Glycemic Index of various foods represents the extent to which those foods raise the blood glucose level and consequently, the insulin levels. As insulin is a 'storage hormone' (one that promotes fat storage – see physiology of insulin, below) any food causing a surge in blood insulin levels, will promote fat storage. During weight control, limit your consumption of foods with a high Glycemic

Index (Glycemic Index > 50)*. Below are the Glycemic Index values of various common foods.

High glycemic foods	> 50	Low glycemic foods	< 50
Glucose /Refined sugar	100	Orange juice	46
Baked potato	98	Rye bread	42
Honey	87	Apples	39
Cornflakes	83	Ice cream	36
White rice/Bread	72	Whole milk/Kidney beans	34
Candy bar	69	Lentils	29
Raisins	64	Raw carrots	16
Banana/ Corn	61	Peanuts	11
White pasta/Peas	51		

To thoroughly understand this important concept, a brief digression into insulin physiology is necessary. You sit down to a meal. The first morsel is, say, bread, moistened by the saliva in the mouth and digestion has begun. The salivary enzymes begin the process of starch breakdown into smaller sugar units even while the tongue mashes the food against the hard palate on the roof of your mouth. The food descends to the stomach, one of the body's gatekeepers, not by gravity but by muscular contraction.

The stomach further mashes this starchy mixture and propels it all into the proximal small intestine where these sugary building blocks are absorbed into the bloodstream. Within 30 seconds of a rise in your blood sugar level after a meal, your pancreas gland is stimulated to secrete insulin. The primary effect of insulin is to facilitate transport and storage of various substances (like sugar and fat) into various organs (like the muscles and fatty tissues).

*Foods that have a **high** Glycemic Index (> 50), as they deliver a rapid rise in blood sugar and insulin levels, are best consumed *after* exercise to speed recovery. Those with a **low** Glycemic Index are best consumed roughly 60 minutes *before* exercise to ensure adequate energy during exercise.

Dr Charles interrupted at this point to expand on the text: "I think it's important that you have at least a general idea what actions you are asking the body to perform. Take a quick look at the actions of insulin in response to a meal of sugar and starches." He jotted this table on the board:

PRINCIPAL ACTIONS OF INSULIN

Muscle:
1. Increases glucose entrance into muscle cell.
2. Increases uptake of amino acids, building blocks of proteins.
3. Maintains muscle protein by decreasing muscle degradation and increasing protein synthesis.

Fat:
1. Increases glucose entrance into fat cell (adipoctes).
2. Sharply depresses the liberation and synthesis of fatty acids.
3. Increases triglyceride deposition.

*Importantly, fructose, the sugar of fruits, does not require as much insulin for transport into cells, probably because of the ketone group at position 2.

"This action on fat tissue is very critical as fatty acid released into the blood interferes with other aspects of glucose metabolism. Moreover, in obese individuals, the muscles' ability to metabolize glucose is impaired. A diet high in carbohydrates (starches), despite the absolute calorie load of 4 calories/gram, may, therefore, be partly responsible for high insulin surges. Insulin is, therefore, best perceived as the "storage hormone" of the body and anything that stimulates it, will promote fat storage. In simple terms, starches (breads, rice, pasta, potatoes) and refined sugar stimulate insulin. That's the connection between sugar and starch intake and weight (i.e. body fat) control.

"The effects of optimizing body weight are dramatic in all regards, particularly so with regard to high blood pressure, independent of changes in salt intake. In fact, one of the positive results of weight reduction comes from the restriction of simple and complex sugars and the resultant effect on insulin levels."

This section of the manual concluded with a table showing the levels of sugar consumption worldwide (see Table opposite).

Sugar consumption worldwide

Rank 1970	Rank 1991	Country	Metric tons (thousands) 1970	Metric tons (thousands) 1991	% change
2	1	Former USSR	10,247	13,000	+ 27
3	2	India	3,767	12,056	+ 220
1	3	USA	10,547	7,994	− 24
4	4	Brazil	3,495	7,276	+ 108
5	5	China	3,150	7,100	+ 125
7	6	Mexico	1,992	4,200	+ 111
6	7	Japan	3,029	2,846	− 6
16	8	Pakistan	625	2,662	+ 326
11	9	Indonesia	888	2,629	+ 196
14	11	Turkey	662	1,631	+ 146
18	12	Philippines	613	1,512	+ 147
29	16	Thailand	372	1,189	+ 220
10	17	Argentina	952	1,140	+ 20
99	18	Canada	1,074	1,100	+ 2
12	21	Australia	721	835	+ 16
41	24	South Korea	212	780	+ 268
27	27	Malaysia	402	700	+ 74
39	31	Taiwan	236	540	+ 129
31	32	Chile	337	518	+ 54
61	39	Saudi Arabia	90	400	+ 334
30	40	Sweden	370	380	+ 3
33	44	Switzerland	318	307	− 3
63	47	Zimbabwe	90	294	+ 227
43	49	Israel	176	255	+ 45
40	53	Finland	224	213	− 5
55	54	Singapore	106	190	+ 79
44	58	Norway	175	177	+ 1
46	60	New Zealand	158	165	+ 4
67	64	Hong Kong	80	155	+ 94
92	96	Kuwait	26	40	+ 54
58	100	Myanmar	95	35	− 63

Source: United Nations

VI. AVOIDING DINING OUT TRAPS

Everyone enjoys eating out occasionally. Business people are obliged by the nature of doing business, to dine out more frequently than others. Many business people interviewed indicate that it is precisely because the lack of control inherent in dining out that they get into health problems. This need not be so. You should select the restaurant and time. Ask how your meal is prepared. Try to finish dining by 9:30 p.m. and leave time for a walk.

These menus are designed to help you accomplish two goals:

1. to learn to apply the rules of food compatibility; and
2. to learn to easily identify the saturated fat content of your meals.

ACTIVITY

In the menus below, use your new knowledge to decide whether:

1. the meal's components are physiologically compatible (C) or incompatible (I);
2. the meal represents a saturated fat (S) load or an unsaturated fat (U) load.

Circle your answers. Incorrect answers should be checked with the text.
The *optimal meal* from a health point of view would be one which is compatible (C) and unsaturated (U): C/U.

Answers: (at end of chapter).

Western Menus

1. Marinated salmon with mixed salad	C or I	S or U
2. Avocado stuffed with shrimp and scallop salad	C or I	S or U
3. Roasted lamb with beans	C or I	S or U
4. Beef stew with carrots	C or I	S or U
5. Grilled lamb kidneys with green beans	C or I	S or U
6. Steak and French fries	C or I	S or U
7. Pork chop with lentils	C or I	S or U
8. Roasted rabbit with pasta	C or I	S or U
9. Chicken (without skin) sautéed with green peas	C or I	S or U

10. Steak tartar with vegetables	C or I	S or U
11. Broiled salmon with wild rice	C or I	S or U
12. Fried fish with fried vegetables	C or I	S or U
13. Tuna with tomatoes, onions and mushrooms	C or I	S or U
14. Trout with almonds and steamed potatoes	C or I	S or U
15. Mussels with wine and onions and seafood salad	C or I	S or U

Answers: (at end of chapter).

Chinese Menus

1. Chinese soup with chicken and vegetables	C or I	S or U
2. Chinese soup with pork and noodles	C or I	S or U
3. Vegetarian spring roll	C or I	S or U
4. Tom yam kung (Spicy prawn soup with lemon grass)	C or I	S or U
5. Roasted suckling pig with vegetables	C or I	S or U
6. Pork and fried rice	C or I	S or U
7. Lacquered duck with vegetables	C or I	S or U
8. Spicy fried rice with vegetables	C or I	S or U
9. Chicken with peanuts and fried vegetables	C or I	S or U
10. Shrimp with hot sauce and vegetables	C or I	S or U

Answers: (at end of chapter).

Indian Menus

1. Jhinga Kesari (Saffron flavoured tandoori prawns)	C or I	S or U
2. Tandoori Murgh (Half a chicken marinated in spices)	C or I	S or U
3. Seekh Kabab Gilafi (Lamb with tomatoes and onions)	C or I	S or U
4. Tandoori Bateyr (Farm raised quails)	C or I	S or U
5. Jhinga Curry (Prawns cooked in an Indian curry)	C or I	S or U
6. Rogan Josh (Lamb cooked in a traditional gravy)	C or I	S or U
7. Dum-Biryani (Steamed lamb and rice with spices)	C or I	S or U
8. Kandahari Pulao (Rice with almonds and raisins)	C or I	S or U
9. Aloo Lajawab (Potatoes with mint and spices)	C or I	S or U
10. Kabab-E Chaman (Spinach and lentils griddled fried)	C or I	S or U

Answers: (at end of chapter).

Malaysian Menus

1.	Kari Ayam with rice (Chicken curry)	C or I	S or U
2.	Ayam Masak Merah with vegetables (Chicken in red sauce)	C or I	S or U
3.	Ikan Masak Tempoyak (Fish in durian sauce)	C or I	S or U
4.	Sotong Masak Lemak with rice (Squid in coconut curry)	C or I	S or U
5.	Sambal Sotong with vegetables (Squid in spicy sauce)	C or I	S or U
6.	Daging Masak Merah with vegetables (Beef in red sauce)	C or I	S or U
7.	Udang Serimpi with vegetables (Prawns in nut sauce)	C or I	S or U
8.	Sayor Lodeh with steamed rice (Vegetable in coconut sauce)	C or I	S or U
9.	Dalcha Kambing with beans (Lamb dalcha)	C or I	S or U
10.	Udang Sambal Petai with beans (Prawns in bean sauce)	C or I	S or U

Answers: (at end of chapter).

VII. NUTRITIONAL SELF-ASSESSMENT: KEY CONCEPTS RECAPPED

1. Body fat percentage should not exceed:
   (a) 10–13%
   (b) 15–20%
   (c) 21–23%
   Key concept: _____

2. Dieting (calorie deprivation) is clearly the best and most efficient way to control weight:
   (a) True
   (b) False
   Key concept: _____

3. Dietary cholesterol plays a major role in blood cholesterol levels:
   (a) True
   (b) False
   Key concept: _____

4. What is the best way to burn excess body fat?:
   (a) Low intensity exercise such as walking
   (b) High intensity exercise such as running
   Key concept: _____

5. It is better to eat fruits:
   (a) At beginning of meal
   (b) At end of meal
   (c) Between meals
   Key concept: _____

6. Drinking water during your meal aids the digestion of food:
   (a) True
   (b) False
   Key concept: _____

7. Performance (physical and psychological) declines when as little as ___ % of our total body water is lost (the body is 60% water):
   (a) 5%
   (b) 10%
   (c) 30%
   Key concept: _____

8. Losing excess body fat lowers blood cholesterol:
   (a) True
   (b) False
   Key concept: _____.___

9. Protein, fats, carbohydrates and alcohol have the caloric
   value of _____ cal/gram, _____ cal/gram,
   _____ cal/gram, _____ cal/gram, respectively:
   (a) 4, 9, 4, 7
   (b) 4, 9, 9, 4
   (c) 4, 9, 4, 9
   (d) 4, 7, 4, 7

10. Snacking promotes weight gain:
    (a) True
    (b) False
    Key concept: _____

11. It is easier to digest food when it is well cooked:
    (a) True
    (b) False
    Key concept: _____

12. It is normal to feel tired after eating:
    (a) True
    (b) False
    Key concept: _____

13. Butter and cheese belong to the same food group:
    (a) True
    (b) False
    Key concept: _____

14. Muscle turns to fat when we stop using that muscle:
    (a) True
    (b) False
    Key concept: _____

15. Match the food to its food group: P = protein, S = starch, F = fat.

Eggs	_____	Pasta	_____	Butter	_____
Cheese	_____	Soy	_____	Banana	_____
Oil	_____	Nuts	_____	Bread	_____
Potato	_____	Meat	_____	Rice	_____

Answers: (at end of chapter).

VIII. NUTRITION CLINIC

Just as I was about to begin this section of the manual, Dr Charles interrupted: "By the way, there are a couple of sections after this one, as well as some interactive exercises. I'm going upstairs to attend teaching rounds with the students. Why don't you go over them. They're short, about 20 minutes. Then, I'll give you a tour of the staff cafeteria, where you can try out the principles. How's that sound?"

I was flattered, but a little worried that my condition was rather fragile to be walking all over the hospital. "Do you really think that that's a good idea, given my condition?"

"I couldn't really imagine a better place to develop a health problem than somewhere with 50 doctors and nurses. Besides, you've got your heart monitor on and we'll call up to the step-down unit to let them know. OK?"

"Sounds great to me," I said. I read on.

The "Whats" of eating for success

By watching how your body and mind *react to certain foods*, you will learn which foods really serve *you*.

Rule # 1: cut back on saturated fat (the main dietary determinant of blood cholesterol)

As discussed earlier, a high fat diet is responsible for the stimulation of cholesterol synthesis by the liver (which leads to heart attacks). In fact the type and quantity of dietary fat is more important than the amount of dietary cholesterol itself when determining the blood cholesterol levels. The trimmable fat in meat contains much of the total saturated fat in meat; fish on the other hand contributes a higher percentage of unsaturated fat. Moreover, fat is associated with cancers (notably, of the colon and breast).

- Choose lentils, beans and fish as protein sources instead of fatty red meats.
- Choose egg whites for cooking instead of whole eggs.
- Choose poultry, without the skin: the skin contains lots of fat.
- Try low-fat dairy products: 20 % fat instead of 40% and skimmed milk.

- Try meals which are baked, poached or steamed instead of fried.
- Try vegetable omelettes instead of ham and cheese.
- Use butter sparingly (avoid margarine as it contains preservatives).
- In general, avoid high-fat foods: ham, salami, bacon, kidneys).

In countries, such as Australia and the USA, where these measures are now regularly encouraged and practiced, there has been a *dramatic* fall in heart attack deaths. In countries such as Great Britain, where diet has just begun to move away from heavy fats, heart attack death rates are, as of yet, unchanged.

Rule # 2: Load up on fresh fruits and vegetables

Load up especially on those that are deep yellow, orange and leafy green. Those are high in beta-carotene, a cancer-preventing vitamin A derivative.

In brief: at least once a day, eat carrots, spinach, broccoli, red pepper (highest naturally occurring source of vitamin C), mango, cantaloupe, a banana or orange. The fiber contained within acts as a therapeutic "bottle-brush" for the intestines, pushing and cleaning as the food passes through.

Rule # 3: Build your diet around plenty of dietary fiber

Fiber (or *roughage*) is that part of your food that is not digested or absorbed. As a result, it speeds the other foods through the digestive system such that fewer calories, less fat and cholesterol are absorbed. As such, fiber should be an integral part of any weight-control program. Furthermore, fiber can protect against colon cancer, constipation and painful hemorrhoids. Sensible choices include apples, carrots, oranges, strawberries, potatoes, brussels sprouts and bananas and all vegetables with edible skins.

Rule # 4: Develop a habit of eating fish four times a week

Not only is fish a superb source of low-calorie protein, but it contains large helpings of heart protective omega-3 fatty acids, niacin, copper magnesium and zinc. Other sources: tuna salmon, trout herring, lobster (never eat the green liver because it can concentrate PCBs and metals) and bluefish, clams, mussels, shark, swordfish, oysters, bass, bluefish.

Warning: watch fish taken from waters that are contaminated with PCBs (bluefish, bass), mercury (halibut, shark, swordfish), and bacterial contaminants (clams, mussels and oysters).

Rule # 5: Develop a healthy fear of sugar

Refined sugar (candy bars, pastries, table sugar, soft drinks, ketchup, mustard) is our society's "stimulant of choice," which simply whips up the organism, accounting for many of our complaints: chronic fatigue, irritability, sleeplessness, overweight and headaches. Check discussion of Glycemic Index.

In brief: never eat sweets before or during long trips or business meetings as they will rob you of the stamina necessary to stay alert.

The "Whens" of eating for success

Rule # 1: Never eat within one hour (preferably more) of going to bed

In brief: these calories are stored as fat if not burned immediately. Moreover, we ask for a case of heartburn (esophageal reflux), if we lie down before the stomach has completely emptied.

Rule # 2: Within 30–60 minutes of eating walk for 15 minutes

In brief: a brisk walk just after eating will immediately start to burn the calories that you've just eaten for up to one hour after you have finished your walk. As such, it is a very efficient way to combat weight gain and the sleepiness that often follows a meal. It also encourages peace of mind.

Rule # 3: Shift most of your daily calories to earlier in the day

"20–10–40–10–20" is ideal.

    20% of daily calories for breakfast;
    10% snack (fruit);
    40% of daily calories for lunch (preferably before 2 p.m., while your
        metabolism is still high);
    10% snack (fruit);
    20% of daily calories for dinner.

Research has shown that we can easily burn 70% of our daily calories if eaten before 2p.m. It doesn't really mean that you consume fewer calories. Now you'll be smarter as to **when** those calories are consumed.

The "Hows" of eating for success

Rule # I: Eat at least five times a day and never skip a meal

By snacking strategically between meals, you can accomplish three important health objectives:

I. You keep your metabolism (calorie consumption) high. Dieting, a form of starvation, slows our metabolism and is, therefore, a very inefficient method of weight control.
2. You maintain your blood sugar level (therefore, also energy levels) constant.
3. You will be less ravenous for your main meals and therefore, eat less.

Rule # 2: Stay properly hydrated

Dehydration causes fatigue, constipation, headaches, and a poor overall metabolism. This means that you should drink eight to ten glasses (two liters) of fresh water or clear juice a day.

In brief: coffee, tea, soft drinks, and alcohol do not count (as they are diuretics they cause water and mineral losses). Enjoy them, but do not count them in your daily total.

Rule # 3: Try to eat your food slowly so as to savour it

"Eat all your drinks and drink all your foods." Chew all foods slowly.

In brief: digestion begins in your mouth. You will notice that if you drink your two glasses of water at the beginning of the meal, you will not feel like attacking your food. Some useful guidelines are as follows:

I. When you eat food, there is a tremendous outpouring of digestive "juices" that are, in turn, absorbed by the foods, thereby increasing the volume of the food. If you eat too quickly, to satisfy the empty feeling in the stomach, you risk feeling overfed. Try this: just before you are completely satiated, stop eating. For the next few minutes, as the foods absorb gastric liquids, you will feel quite satisfied without having taken more calories.
2. Drink two to three liters of water (or equivalent) per day, *between* meals only. If you must drink liquids during meals, only sip very small volumes of fluids that are at room temperature.
3. Snack healthfully between meals (speeds metabolism).

4. Never, ever, skip meals (slows metabolism).
5. Never drink alcohol on an empty stomach (25% is directly absorbed through the stomach lining).

If you have digestive problems, feel tired or heavy after eating, follow the rules of food compatibility listed below for ONE MONTH and observe the results.

I. *Do not eat protein and starches at the same meal.* Proteins require an acid milieu (pepsin) and starches require an alkaline milieu (ptyalin) to be digested. This chemistry cancels out in the stomach. Result: proteins putrefy, starches ferment.

2. *Never drink with meals, except fermented drinks.* Beer, wine or champagne are OK with meals. Water dilutes digestive juices.
    Sip plenty of cool, fresh, water every day, between meals.

3. *Eat all food as low on the food chain as possible and as close to their original raw state as possible.* According to the Worldwatch Institute, to produce a pound of feedlot steak costs the world two kilograms of grains, about 10,000 liters of water, four liters of gasoline and 15 kilograms of eroded topsoil. To make more grazing land for cattle, the tropical rain forest, a vital source of oxygen and a treasure-trove of natural medicines for man, is destroyed at the rate of 4% per year. High temperature and long cooking hours will "kill" the vitamins and enzymes in the food.

IX. EXAMPLES OF BREAKFAST, LUNCH, AND DINNER THAT "WORK"

Normally, the metabolic rate is high in the morning, as you are getting your day going, so it makes great sense to adhere to the age old maxim:

> *Eat a breakfast of Kings,*
> *Eat a lunch of Princes,*
> *Eat a dinner of paupers.*

Breakfast options

I. Whole wheat or rye bread with butter, coffee or tea without sugar.
2. Yoghurt with non-acid fresh fruits, coffee or tea without sugar.

3. Freshly squeezed orange juice and fresh fruit salad.
4. Whole wheat cereal with yoghurt, banana and raisin.

Lunch and dinner options

A green salad at every meal will facilitate digestion and the transit of food.

PROTEIN-dominant meals (no bread, no potato)
1. Roasted chicken with green peas.
2. Leg of lamb with beans.
3. Onion and mushroom omelette.
4. Fish or seafood or steak (rare) with vegetables.

STARCH-dominant meals (bread is OK, no protein)
1. Pasta cooked with olive oil, garlic and fresh tomatoes.
2. Wild rice with onions and mushrooms.
3. Potato stew with green beans, onions and tomatoes.
4. Vegetable soup with garlic bread.

At the table

Ask questions for optimal choices:

- What is my time frame? In a hurry? Solution: eat *light*!
- What is the oil and fat content? Watch palm and coconut oil!
- What is the saturated fat content? Pork > Lamb > Beef » Shellfish » Fish
- How is the meal prepared? Fresh = steamed < Grilled < Broiled < < < Fried

Before and between meals

Fruit and water (including teas).

It had been a busy morning and I was rapidly approaching information saturation. Mercifully, I came to the last part of this interesting chapter on Nourishment and I needed some exercise to weave the whole thing together. I found it in the part on objective oriented approach.

X. THE NUTRITIONAL ACTION PLAN: PUTTING IT ALL TOGETHER

Nutrition for energy (battling fatigue)

1. Go for 15 minutes brisk walk after lunch.

2. Don't mix proteins and starches.

3. For high stamina, avoid alcohol at lunchtime.

4. Snack intelligently between meals (to avoid low blood sugar): fruit.

5. Diminish coffee intake.

6. Drink two–three liters fresh water/day (between meals!) or the equivalent: fruits, soups or veggies.

Nutrition for effective and lasting weight control

1. Eat foods with a low Glycemic Index.

2. Go for 15 minutes brisk walk after lunch.

3. Eat a light dinner and walk briskly afterwards.

4. Snack between meals (to control hunger): fruit.

5. Drink two glasses of water just before lunch and dinner.

Nutrition for optimal health

1. Stay "regular" with fiber and vitamin C: fruits and veggies.

2. Don't mix proteins and starches, ever.

3. Prefer fish and skinless chicken to red meats.

4. Eat foods as close as possible to their natural raw state: avoid deep fried foods!

5. Every month, do a fruit fast (at home): just juices and fresh fruits *all* day to clean out all digestive residue in the gut.

6. Drink two–three liters fresh water/day (between meals!) or the equivalent: fruits, soups or veggies.

Dr Charles had come back at around 12:45, full of pep and vigour.

"Ready to get some food?" he asked, "you must be starved. Your brain must be complaining for fuel, the way you've been working here."

"Most definitely," I responded, "my stomach is growling and after this morning, I know why. Good old Pavlov." We walked toward the cafeteria laughing. Looking around the cafeteria of the hospital staff, I realized that this group was not immune to poor choices.

"Doctors' days are just as much rat races as yours are," explained Dr Charles, "crack of dawn patient rounds, operative procedures until noon, rushed lunch, speaking with your mouth full of food, washing the whole mess down as quickly as possible with a diet soda. Afternoons are crammed with consultations and hospital admissions. Evenings are occupied with teaching rounds with the residents. Result: overweight doctors treating overweight patients."

I was impressed by Dr Charles' self-effacing candour. I could remember my own company cafeteria: trays full to overflowing with all sorts of fatty foods, desserts and in the lonely corner, a diet soda standing watch like the tribute to the guilty conscience. We were getting it all wrong.

After a refreshing lunch, Dr Charles and I walked quietly around the hospital gardens, chatting calmly. We then parted ways, he to his afternoon consultations and I back to the library to read up on exercise and stress. My time was running short before my operation and I had "miles to go before I sleep." The chapter on Human Nutrition ended with a refreshing quote:

Neither abstinence from fish or flesh, nor going naked, nor shaving the head, nor wearing matted hair, nor dressing in rough garment, nor covering oneself with dirt, nor sacrificing to Agni,* will cleanse a man who is not free from delusions. Anger, drunkenness, obstinacy, bigotry, deception, envy, self-praise, disparagement, superciliousness and evil intentions constitute uncleanness; not verily the eating of flesh.

The self-indulgent man is a slave to his passions . . . . But to satisfy the necessities of life is not evil. To keep the body in good health is a duty, for otherwise we shall not be able to trim the lamp of wisdom, and keep our minds strong and clear.

The Sayings of Buddha

*Agni: the Hindu god of fire.

XI. ANSWERS TO INTERACTIVE EXERCISES

Loss of an important ritual

1. e; 2. m; 3. c; 4. a; 5. d; 6. h; 7. j; 8. i; 9. l; 10. k; 11. g; 12. b; 13. f.

Avoiding dining out traps

Western Menus

1. C/U; 2. C/U; 3. C/S; 4. C/S; 5. C/S; 6. I/S; 7. C/S; 8. I/U; 9. C/U; 10. C/S; 11. I/U; 12. C/U; 13. C/U; 14. C/U; 15. C/U.

Chinese Menus

1. C/U; 2. I/S; 3. C/U; 4. C/U; 5. C/S; 6. I/S; 7. C/S; 8. C/U; 9. C/U; 10. C/U.

Indian Menus

1. C/U; 2. C/U; 3. C/S; 4. C/U; 5. C/S; 6. C/S; 7. I/S; 8. C/U; 9. C/U; 10. C/U.

Malaysian Menus

1. I/S; 2. C/U; 3. C/I; 4. I/S; 5. C/U; 6. C/S; 7. C/U; 8. C/S; 9. C/S; 10. C/U.

Nutritional self-assessment

1. **b** (for men), or **c** (for women). Key concept: follow BF%, not absolute KGs, for effective weight control.

2. *False.* Key concept: calorie deprivation, of ANY sort, *slows* metabolism and conserves calories.

3. *False.* It is estimated that dietary cholesterol (ex. eggs, shrimp) contributes only 30% of blood cholesterol levels. Most (70%) is contributed by dietary saturated FAT.

4. **a.** Key concept: at lower intensities, the proportion of fat to total energy production is greater. Therefore, a more logical approach to fat control is more frequent low-grade exercises, such as walking, particularly after meals.

5. **c.** Key concept: fruit between meals accomplishes three key objectives: (1) Its "clean" calories help to maintain a high metabolic rate and energy level while controlling hunger; (2) They provide an excellent source of fiber to keep us "regular"; (3) They are an excellent water source.

6. b. Key concept: water with meals dilutes digestive juices. Rather, opt for fermented drinks, such as wine.

7. a. Key concept: our bodies are constantly losing water, usually two–three liters per day. In a 70 kg person, 42 kg (60%) are water. Five percent of that amount equals 2+ liters. A loss greater than that, without replacement, will result in impairment of both physical and psychological performance.

8. True. The *first* thing to do if total cholesterol is > 200 mg/dl is to get BF% < 20% and re-check.

9. These are the calorie/gram values for each food type. Note how calorifically dense alcohol is.

10. *False.* Snacking intelligently (fruits) maintains a high metabolic rate, burns calories, and promotes weight loss.

11. *False.* Overcooking foods makes more work in extracting nutrients for the digestive tract.

12. *False.* Fatigue after meals could be a sign that imprudent food combinations were consumed.

13. *False.* Regarding acid production in the stomach, butter is a *fat*, cheese is a *protein*.

14. *False.* One cell type (muscle) cannot be transformed into another cell type (fat). What happens when you become more inactive is that the metabolic rate drops, and excess calories are deposited as fat.

15.

Eggs = P.	Pasta = S.	Butter = F.
Cheese = P.	Soy = P.	Banana = S.
Oil = F.	Nuts = F.	Bread = S.
Potato = S.	Meat = P.	Rice = S.

3

STAYING FIT IN PREPARATION FOR CHANGE

"When you realize to what extent physical activity is part of your *solution*, you will stop finding excuses not to do it!"

TO EXERCISE OR NOT TO EXERCISE: THAT'S *NOT* THE QUESTION!

Day Two: Wednesday afternoon

Back at my desk in the hospital library, I sat musing quietly to my, self about the whole issue of physical exercise. I was eager to present my theory on exercise and motivation to the good doctor (and the other patients) and gather his views, which, up to now had been free of dogmatism and disappointment.

I felt quite strongly that, over the years, exercise had gone from being something moderately pleasurable to being an obligate nuisance. It all started after one of my check-ups five years ago, when I was told by Dr Blum, in an off-the-cuff kind of way, that I should take more exercise, but I could not *feel* the need.

His medical argument, though intelligent and intelligible, was just a bit too abstract to be convincing. This was, I hasten to assure you, all quite independent of the fact that the good Dr Blum was himself no paradigm of fitness brimming over. He looked as though his commitment to physical fitness continually lagged behind his obvious enjoyment of life's corporeal pleasures.

In an effort to get to the root of all the collective confusion and guilt as to why exactly exercise (as presently imported and packaged by so-called fitness gurus and scientists), was not for me, I spent a Saturday morning in my garden researching the literature, medical and otherwise. My impressive findings, some stretching back many centuries before the Exercise Revolution, were as follows:

> Bodily exercise profiteth little.
> *The Bible: I Timothy 4 v 8*

> Exercise is bunk. If you are healthy, you don't need it; if you are ill, you shouldn't take it. *Henry Ford*

> The popular belief in athletics is grounded upon the theory that violent exercise makes for bodily health and that bodily health is necessary for mental vigor. Both halves of this theory are highly dubious. Athletes, as a class, are not above the normal in health, but below it. *HL Mencken (1951)*

I have never taken any exercise, except for sleeping and resting
and I never intend to take any. Exercise is loathsome.

Mark Twain

I get my exercise acting as a pallbearer to those who exercise.

Chauncey Depew (aged 94)

The only reason I would take up jogging again is so I could
hear heavy breathing again.   *Erma Brombeck*

Exercise? I get it on the golf course. When I see my friends
collapse, I run for the paramedics.   *Red Skelton*

I mean that's just how cynical I had become towards physical exercise. Then several months prior to my hospitalization, I had come
across in my readings a very intriguing group of people who were
reputed for their longevity and vigour, despite their apparent life of
material impoverishment. These groups were from hardship moun-
tainous areas: the Abkhazia district in the Caucasian Mountains; the
Vilcabamba area of Ecuador in the Andes Mountains; and the
Hunza Province of Pakistan in the Karakoran Mountains.

These communities have been extensively studied in recent
decades to determine the "common denominator" for their long-
lived hardiness. All three communities were characterized by:

1. A high level of *physical activity and vitality* (walking about, til-
   ling and gardening the land, chopping wood, animal husbandry).
2. *Virtual absence of obesity* and diseases related to obesity (such as
   diabetes).
3. Though the use of *alcohol and tobacco* was common, their use was
   quite moderate and limited as part of the ritual of conviviality.
4. *A high level of integration* into the community: no retirement nor
   isolation. All members had a well-defined and appreciated role in
   the running of their community's affairs.

I had always known that some form or another of physical activity
was indispensable for mental and physical health. My case was not
one of being lazy or exceedingly pressed for time (I have time for
whatever I want or think is genuinely important). I knew, and my
discussions about the genetic heritage with Dr Charles confirmed
this, the body craves some form or another of physical activity. You
would have to be a fool to not see that. Good gracious, on the eve
before my bypass surgery, I better have gotten that much straight.

But so many questions were left unanswered:

- Why do some people seem to get no exercise and still live to a ripe old age?
- How much is enough? Is there too much?
- Is there a *minimum* possible for good health for those of us who cannot run marathons?
- Why do we hear nothing of the *pleasure* of exercise? Has any scientist addressed that critical issue?
- What about exercise after angioplasty? Or after my bypass? Is that safe?
- Is it not true that, when being motivated to do something like sport (or, for that matter, anything) pleasure is an important factor, if not *the* most important factor? What is it about exercise that makes it so distasteful to me as such?

RETURN TO OUR HUNTER ROOTS

Then, after much soul-searching and in-the-field "observation and research," combined with the evolutionary perspectives that I had generated with Dr Charles, I felt that I had some very useful insights into the matter, just like a *real* social scientist. According to the medical anthropologists, it was really quite simple: if you look at the human species, as it turns out, we have spent our time something like this:

Years spent . . .	. . . doing this . . .
2,500,000+	Hunting and gathering
12,000+	Farming
300+	Office work
50+	Number crunching

According to these scientists, our genetic code (DNA) has spent most of its time hunting. In recent years, we have been able to survive on the material plane by merely thinking, as though the sole function of the body was to transport the intellect; as if the body were a mere accessory to the brain. That's how we get into health problems in the first place.

Looking back to our history throughout evolution, we are all descendants from various tribal forebears and, as such, we all had roles: some of our forebears were group hunters, some were lone hunters, some were gatherers, some were planners, and some of them were care givers. Everybody had a role that best suited their personality and body habitus.

The exact position of each person on this grid was a function of two innate characteristics: **physical energy level** (how much energy people actually feel on the physical plane) and **sociability** (just how much one likes to spend time with others).

In recent years, we have been able to survive on the material plane by merely thinking, as though the sole function of the body was to transport the intellect; as if the body were a mere accessory to the brain.

In a sense, each quadrant had a certain "personality". Nearly everybody could, from a motivation point of view, locate themselves and their perfect activity somewhere on this grid.

My "theory" was that if people could honestly try to find where they are on the grid, they would no longer feel guilty about activity. Considering their position on the grid, they could find the activity that suited their disposition, gave them pleasure and actually did their mental and physical health some good. Quite pleased with my theory, I drew the grid on the blackboard and awaited Dr Charles's arrival. (See below)

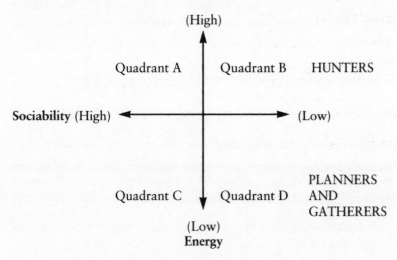

Quadrant A   Quadrant B   HUNTERS

Sociability (High) ←→ (Low)

Quadrant C   Quadrant D   PLANNERS AND GATHERERS

(Low)
Energy

Matching physical activity with personality type

Just after I finished drawing my grid complete with arrows and legends, I turned around and saw Dr Charles standing there with his hands on his hips, smiling.

"Are you trying to put me out of a job. Your're getting to be quite the teacher. Glad to see it" he said. "But I'm not planning any early retirement."

"Yes, well, I have a special interest in this subject. I'd like your view on this theory which is more sociologic than physiologic. It comes down really to a personality issue. What one *enjoys* is the key."

"Sure, shoot." He sat in my place and as he and some of the other patients listened, I explained my theory and went on to elaborate.

"Take the **Quadrant A** folks," I explained, "high energy, high sociability. You know them, of course, because these people are quite energetic, generally trim, quick-footed and, when true to their real Nature, quite pleasant to be around. They will organize the sporting activities at picnics and play with the offspring of other people after the victuals and wine, while we can nap peacefully. Their energy seems boundless.

"From an evolutionary point of view, these are the direct descendants, perhaps, of the group hunters in the tribal hierarchy of old. These are people who, as group hunters, need physical exercise to dissipate energy through the chase (running) and the kill (aiming and scoring). Just look at what activities are best suited to these people." I posed the question as much to the other patients present as to Dr Charles.

"Their favourite activities are those regular and spontaneous physical exercises that involve social interaction: activity for them is just another pretext to be with others, sacrificing personal identity and glory for the success of the *team*. Their success comes through the team's success. They appreciate group activities as a way to be part of an extended family', the group hunt, the team. That's why they engage in activity gleefully, team sports or group activities: football, soccer, volleyball, basketball, baseball, dancing, softball, doubles tennis or badminton and so on. They get dysfunctional (sad, constipated, irritable) when they cannot express their energy through exercise. For them, physical activity is a real joy to savour, a pretext to interact with others.

It's quite easy to understand from that point of view. We can no longer be real hunters, so we sublimate those hunting urges into more socially acceptable activities: sport. The underlying instincts are still there: chasing (running) and killing (aiming and scoring).

These people, by the way, can 'hunt' alone but really prefer the group hunt.

"Let's do the same exercise with the **Quadrant B** folks," I said, jotting down their characteristics. "High energy, low sociability. We find members of this group to be loners, the direct descendants of the lone hunters, who also need a high level of physical exercise to dissipate their energy. Because they prefer to avoid crowds, they prefer the *solitary* 'hunt.' Preferred activities include skiing, jogging, chopping wood, rowing, cycling, swimming, long-distance biking, wrestling, judo, martial arts, singles tennis, weight training, archery, Ping-Pong, skating (ice or roller) and so on. Here the hunt is no longer kill-oriented but goal or objective-oriented, such as beating one's time or speed or weight, while running or skiing or lifting. Here the issue at the heart of the matter is self-mastery, rather than group interaction.

I continued: "Now, take **Quadrant C** folks. At the other extreme of the energy spectrum we find a distinctive group whose *mental* energy levels are possibly high, but this energy does not necessarily translate to energy on the *physical* plane. These are the planners or gatherers. They are, on the physical level, rather slow moving and sloth-like. No matter. They are every bit as essential to the survival of the community as the hunters. Because they prefer crowds, pre-ferred activities are *low energy, but group oriented*, such as house work with the family, horseshoes, pétanque, bowling, ballroom dancing, hiking."

I concluded: "Last, but by no means least, take the **Quadrant D** folks. These people may still have hunting instincts but now rather than doing the chasing and killing themselves they are doing it either as spectators (hence, the outrageous popularity of televised spectator sports) or as 'hunters' in a different arena (business, legal, medical, professions).

"Maybe these are people who have dissipated their instincts to chase and kill in the business arena (chasing a client and killing an objective) and who have precious little left for team or solo sports. They are happy, well-adjusted and gravitate towards those activities that recharge their batteries. Moreover, they are also not the most social of sorts, likening exercise instead to a morning constitution. We use exercise, not specifically to condition the heart, but to condition the *soul*. In short, my body was simply not meant to move violently and certainly not in the vicinity of others! The Quadrant D folks, you see, abhor group exercise or group activity. For these people, aerobic classes in leotards are more an embarrassing display of collective neuroses than anything else. Perhaps, in the old days at university, they would play an odd game of tennis to channel out the libidinous overflow, but not something in a group like that.

"Favourite physical activities are: yoga, Tai Chi, long walks in the woods or by the seaside, golf, walking, badminton and, on a good day, some doubles tennis."

One of the other patients then posed an interesting question that stumped me: "How do you know if you have misplaced yourself on the grid?"

"Well . . . uuhhhh, Dr Charles what do you think about that one?" I asked, hoping he could bail me out.

"Well," he started slowly, "if you added another psychological dimension to the social and evolutionary, you may have your answer. As you do become more active, your attitude towards a whole series of life events changes and you actually get more energy from connecting with more people. That is, as you become more active, confidence changes and the first thing you notice is that your energy and sociability increase and you may even change from Quadrant D to Quadrant A. That's not really the point. The point is to enjoy the activity and not allow anyone to dictate certain activities that are against your real nature.

> *As you become more active, confidence changes and the first thing you notice is that your energy and sociability increase*

"Up to now, you cannot know, genetically, from what forebears you came in the tribal hierarchy but you can generally tell by how much you can forget yourself during an activity."

PEOPLE'S MOTIVATION FOR EXERCISING: PRIMARY vs SECONDARY GAIN

Dr Charles continued to speak: "Start by asking yourself two critical questions:

1. Do you feel guilty or bored during the activity? In brief, is exercise a chore for you?
2. Are you frequently injured, despite feeling 'at home' with that activity?

A 'yes' to either query indicates that you are, perhaps, a gatherer or planner instead of a group or lone hunter.

"You see, to really get long-term benefit from physical activity, you have to do it for its intrinsic value, not for secondary gain. For example, what are some of the aspects of exercise that have real value, by themselves? These are the motivators that bring us together, make us feel better to be part of the human condition." He jotted them down as people recited them off:

INTRINSIC VALUE
- Feeling good or peaceful
- Better mental health (less depressive episodes)
- Better physical health (decreased body fat, blood pressure)
- Feeling more energy or feeling lighter
- Playfulness or communion with Nature/others
- Preparing the body (the "temple") for medittion
- Distraction from daily affairs
- Loss of loneliness
- Spiritual awakening
- Increased sexual satisfaction

I paused at the last entry, "Excuse me, Doc, how does that work, exercise and sexuality?" I figured that something as central and vital as sexuality was as good as any motivator.

"That's pretty simple when you think about it and you really don't need fancy research to prove the connection between being physically and mentally fit and an enhanced sex life," he started. "Although sexual expression is obviously a complex, highly personal, and individualized affair, essentially what is happening is that we are using the body to connect with our partners, to lose our separation: an emotional and physical meltdown. To enhance this experience, it helps to have a body that can manage its way through the act of physical intimacy. So, exercise can increase your endurance and optimize your body fat so that a pleasurable experience lasts even longer and is more intense. That's because of the effect of regular aerobic exercise on the reproductive and cardiovascular systems. Muscles are better toned and conditioned, arteries supplying the sexual organs are open and delivering oxygen and glucose to the penis better, men have higher testosterone in the blood. All those effects are important in maintaining erections.

"In a word, better arousal to sexual stimulus and more reliable sexual function correlates very well with higher levels of aerobic fitness. Psychologically, a toned body also provides the necessary confidence and self-esteem to allow you to let the body 'do its thing' without a lot of neurotic interference. I apologise for the cut-and-dry scientific approach to something as delicious as sexual expression."

He continued, "And then we have all the **Secondary Gain Motivators.** These are motivators that we see all too commonly these days and which increase the illusion of separateness in the world, increase the feeling of isolation and only succeed in making physical activity boring." He jotted down the following:

- Guilt (by family or friends)
- Peer pressure: impressing others
- better "pecs", abdos, 25" arms
- "Winning" just for winning
- Just looking good
- Competition: being number 1

Dr Charles added, "There you have the proof of what our distinguished 'visiting professor' here was talking about: feeling good is a more powerful motivator than some abstract idea of simply trying to do something good for yourself. The benefits of activity will come quite naturally if you are truly enjoying yourself.

Speaking more generally, movement of the body is a celebration of life. It's the harmony of the body, mind and soul and, as such, a movement towards wholeness. It's a moment when we respect this temple in which something beautiful and eternal resides. Therefore, make sure you smile when you move the body."

"Smile?!" one of the participants joked, "I am usually either in so much discomfort or so bored that I can barely breathe well. I really like the after-effects of exercise, but not the actual exercise."

"Then you are doing the wrong activity and, more importantly, you're doing it for the wrong reasons: some secondary gain." Then he jotted a saying on the board that I will always carry with me:

Better a happy walker than an angry athlete.

Dr Charles concluded: "Though many of our guilt-motivated species have gone thankfully extinct, usually due to carbon monoxide poisoning, you can still see them along the motorways and city streets, slamming the cement with a vengeance as though they were going through some form of exorcism ritual and their facial expression seems to confirm their 'pain of purification.' And for what? Injury and discouragement. That's a *real* shame. Many people who need activity have been turned off exercise because they got confused about who they were and what their expectations were. Some of them ended up tearing or breaking something, coming into the office, limping like democracy's soldiers." After some small talk with several participants, I stayed a little later to chat with Dr Charles.

"That was really enjoyable. Congratulations," he said, with a voice and handshake of a colleague. "You came on very strong at the end as though you had something invested in it."

"Well, I'm going through a major heart operation tomorrow morning and I want to do things in my life that start to have meaning to me. Tie up all my loose ends. Serve my people. I think, as a businessman, I can get through to these people. They are my breed. We think alike. I understand them, their minds and their reward systems."

"Listen, it's been a really interesting couple of days spent with you. You have really been transformed. You learn quickly," said Dr Charles. I wasn't ready for this compliment.

"I was really sleeping my way through life and I had a lot of catching up to do. Thanks to you, I'm getting back on track, slowly, but surely."

"Just don't lose your way. I have to run around the hospital now. I'll come by tomorrow morning before your operation to wish you luck." Then he disappeared down the hospital corridor. Would I see him again? I felt so.

Feeling pleased with my new theory and its potential widespread applications, I sat down and read the chapter on Physical Fitness in 'The Book of Solutions.'

PHYSICAL FITNESS

I. GENERAL GUIDELINES ON EXERCISE PLANNING: ATTITUDE FIRST

The Natural Laws governing our bodies, minds and spirits

When you realize, exactly and concretely, to what extent exercise is part of your solution to your everyday problems, you will stop trying to find excuses *not* to engage in some. To get over the initial inertia or laziness, decide ahead of time that you are going to really enjoy this activity. You *alone* are responsible for the state and performance of your body: it's *your* temple.

> *Written on your tombstone will be the distillation of all your life's decisions. Some decisions are tougher than others. One body, one mind, one lifetime. You decide.*

Your body can be conditioned to not only avoid the major diseases already discussed, but also to enable you to tend to your personal and professional tasks with ease. Whether or not your body is in its optimal condition is dependent on whether you are living your life in accordance with the Natural Laws that govern you. It's really that simple: your body, like any other physical entity, operates under the governance of Natural Laws and either you adhere to them or not.

Those **Natural Laws** are:

1. The BODY functions best when adequately nourished, exercised and rested.
2. The MIND functions best when adequately disciplined, stimulated and rested.
3. The SPIRIT is in harmony when it is regularly purified, respected and loved.

Mother Nature will impose heavy fines on most people who violate her laws by eating the wrong foods, failing to get enough sleep or exercise, failing to get enough affection and love. When any of these needs is not met (for trivial issues like position, fame, fortune), the natural harmony of this triad is disrupted and life becomes a living hell.

The purpose of this session on *physical* fitness is to provide a set of simple and practical rules so that you may weave regular physical activity into your daily life. There is too much needless confusion and injury from people participating in regular exercise regimens. Examined below are the simple Golden Rules needed to keep you safe while accomplishing your health goals. Regular physical activity should be the keystone of any weight-control program.

The Problem

Sedentary people (people who have no or irregular physical activity in their lives) are roughly twice as likely to die from a heart attack as their more active counterparts. Moreover, a sedentary lifestyle carries the statistical equivalent of smoking a packet of cigarettes every day or having 20% extra body fat.

The Solution

A recent five-year study of more than 1,400 men (aged 40–60) showed that the more physically active men (who spent roughly 2.2 hours per week walking, jogging, swimming) had 60% less heart attacks than less active men.

The benefits of increased activity

The benefits to be gained from increased physical activity are both physical and psychological:

Physical
1. Increased work capacity
2. Lowered total cholesterol, Triglycerides(fats)
3. Increased HDL cholesterol
4. Lowered body fat: increased lean mass
5. Lowered blood pressure
6. Better lung function and gas exchange
7. Better joint flexibility, range of motion and bone mass
8. Better strength and co-ordination
9. Increased energy and stamina
10. Better fat and sugar control

Psychological
1. Improved self-confidence
2. Less loneliness, better socialisation skills
3. Less anxiety
4. Improved sexual expression
5. Less symptoms of depression
6. Better sleep
7. Healthy distraction from "affairs"
8. Better preparedness for change
9. Increased energy and stamina

The Golden Rules of Physical Exercise

Rule # I: keep in mind the importance of good equipment and hydration

Do not allow the system to overheat. As someone on a regular exercise program, you will need the cooling effects of fresh water: for each hour of exercise = one half liter of fresh water and a cup of orange juice (for the potassium), 30 minutes *before* beginning the exercise. Dehydration, deliberate (by wearing rubberized clothing or excessive use of saunas) or accidental, is not recommended. The resultant weight loss is temporary and will be regained through proper rehydration. Salt tablets are not necessary.

Rule # 2: prepare your body properly for exertion

Warming up the muscles improves circulation by decreasing the viscosity (thickness) of the blood, making it flow more smoothly through arteries and veins. A proper warm-up and cool-down is important for two reasons. First, it can improve performance up to 10% by decreasing muscle stiffness and soreness. Secondly, and more importantly, it helps to avoid irregular heart beats that abrupt physical exercise can precipitate. The best warm-up is a slow motion version of the activity we will be practicing. For example, if you are a runner, walk briskly for three–five minutes and then break into a jog, then run.

The same is true of cooling down *after* exercise. Five minutes of warm-up and cool-down is sufficient. In either case, brisk walking is ideal, as it prevents "pooling" of blood in the legs. Proper cooling-down allows proper circulation to recovering muscles to help clear metabolic waste products like lactic acid.

Rule # 3: find people you like to exercise with and set realistic goals

There are many forms of exercise to choose from, but you should find an activity you enjoy enough to participate in regularly.

Rule # 4: if pain (any type) starts, you STOP!

Again, pay attention to the signal coming from the body so as to avoid fatal accidents. Pain is Nature's way of telling you to slow down.

Rule # 5: regularity is the key

Being a strictly "weekend athlete" only invites accidents that will discourage a real chance of achieving lasting cardiovascular conditioning.

Rule # 6: watch heatstroke

The combination of severe heat, humidity and exercise can result in markedly compromized performance and even illness if not properly prepared for: never underestimate the devastating potential of this combination.

Preparation:

1. First of all, if at all possible, *exercise in the cooler hours* of early morning or in the evening. Not only will the heat be less oppressive, but the amount of carbon monoxide and ozone will be less as most cars will be off the road.
2. *Hydration.* In severe circumstances, we can sweat up to two liters/hour of exercise. That's a significant loss! Just weigh yourself before and after a run or jog and see the difference: that's all water loss. Solution: drink as much as possible 30 minutes prior to exercise (don't worry, water empties from the stomach instantaneously). Then, throughout the exercise, drink 30 ml (a large glass) of fresh water every 30 minutes. Tip: monitor the spittle production – it should be clear, not white.
3. *Clothing.* Wear loose fitting cotton clothing that is light coloured (reflects the heat better).

Rule # 7: watch Athlete's Foot and Crotch

Fungal infections are very common among athletes, especially in areas of the body where it is moist, dark and warm. Your feet and groin area are perfect for fungal overgrowth, especially if the area involved is kept warm, dark, and moist by wearing clothing that does not "breathe."

In general:

1. *Decrease exposure* to the locker room fungal colony: wear rubber sandals in the shower.
2. *Clothing.* Cotton, cotton, cotton! Always wear underwear and socks.
3. *Try topical cream or talc.* If itching or redness persists, consult your generalist or podiatrist.

4. *Keep affected area dry,* particularly after a shower.
5. *Try a vinegar soak on the feet:* 1 part vinegar and 10 parts water twice a day to dry the area.

Rule # 8: determine, with your doctor's assistance, if regular exercise is safe for you

Although these conditions are relatively uncommon in the general population, in fact, there are some physical conditions for which exercise is contra-indicated. They include:

Heart problems
- Malignant or accelerated hypertension
- Unstable angina or acute heart attack
- Unstable heart failure or valvular problems
- Unstable rhythms
- Aortic aneurysm or dissection

Lung problems
- Embolism
- Unstable asthma
- Pulmonary hypertension

Other
- Unstable pregnancy
- Unstable diabetes or thyroid disease

Intelligently and effectively preparing the body for change

LIFETIME FIT PROGRAM

When it comes to physical activity, it is important that you choose something that you'll enjoy. It does not matter what the exercise is – jogging or swimming are fine, but so is brisk walking, skipping rope, or chopping wood, as long as you get more pleasure out of it than just doing something good for your body.

Regardless of your choice of exercise, to be of optimal effectiveness an exercise prescription for cardiovascular conditioning must adhere to these FIT guidelines:

F = *Frequency:* optimal frequency is three sessions/week or every other day.

I = *Intensity:* the training heart rate (THR), the steady state heart beat.

T = *Time:* the duration of the exercise. Optimal = W~–30 minutes/ session.

Steps to calculate your training heart rate (THR)

Your THR is a "steady state" level of intensity that is both safe and effective in conditioning your heart.

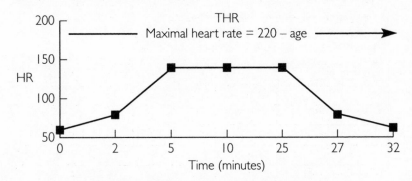

Preparing the body for change: training heart rate

It is a percentage (65% would, for example, be expressed as 0.65) of your maximal heart rate, calculated by the formula below:

THR = [(22O – age – resting heart rate (RHR)) × intensity level] + RHR

Step # 1: enter your figures into the blank spaces:

[(220 – age _____ – RHR _____)]

(a) age = _____ years of age as of your last birthday.
(b) resting heart rate (RHR) = _____ beats/minute just after awakening in the morning.

Step # 2: the intensity level is a function of your cardio-fitness rating.

(a) To determine your overall cardio-fitness level, you will need to perform the Step Test:

- make a step (newspapers or telephone books will do nicely) 30 cm (12") high;
- set a metronome at 96;
- step up and down on the step for three minutes at the rhythms dictated by the metronome. After three minutes of stepping, sit and find pulse within five seconds;
- now carefully take your recuperating pulse for a full minute after stepping.
  Note here _____ beats: first minute;
- find the percentage corresponding to the level you achieved.
  For example, if you are 46 and counted 124 beats in the first minute of recuperation, your level is "Below average." Your **intensity** will be, therefore, 0.65.

Level (Intensity)	Age 18–25	26–35	36–45	46–55	56–65	65–99
Olympic (0.85)	up to 65	70	75	80	85	85
Athletic (0.80)	up to 75	80	85	90	95	100
Above Average (0.75)	up to 90	95	95	100	110	115
Average (0.70)	up to 105	110	115	120	125	130
Below Avg. (0.65)	up to 125	130	135	140	145	150
Fair (0.60)	up to 150	160	140	160	170	175
Poor (0.55)	> 180	> 185	> 165	> 185	> 190	> 201

Step # 3: plug in all the variables in the formula. For example, a 46-year-old man, with a RHR of 72, intensity level of 0.65, would have a THR of:

THR = [(220 – 46 – 72) × 0.65] + 72 = 138 beats per minute

That is, whatever activity this man has decided to do, to avail himself of the conditioning effects on the heart and mind, he should do that exercise for three sessions of 20 to 30 minutes a week at 138 beats/ minute or 34 beats/15" . Optimally, start your exercise for about five minutes, stop and check your pulse. If your measured THR is faster than the ideal, you're working too hard. If your pulse is slower than the ideal, pick up the pace until you reach your THR. range.

Once you have begun a conditioning program to *strengthen* the heart, you can move rather smoothly through the *conditioning* stages in a few weeks. Here's how to progress safely.

As you work out regularly at your THR three times a week for 30 minutes per session, you will notice an improvement in the efficacy of your heart. Now you can monitor your progress yourself. No more working out "in the dark!" Every week, your resting heart rate and your Step Test results will show the increasing efficiency of the cardiovascular system. For example, if your Step Test (described on page 142–43) was 135 and your resting heart rate was 80, your trends will look something like this:

Week	Step Test result	Resting heart rate
1	135	80
5	130	75
10	125	70
0	115	60
30	105	50+

Note: as the THR calculation is dependent on results from the Step Test and resting heart rate, as overall cardio-fitness improves, these will go *down*, while your training heart rate will go *up*!

Exercise for blood pressure improvement: special note

With regard to BP, moderate aerobics activity (55% to 70% of a person's predicted MHR performed 30–40 minutes five days a week) is the recommended level of physical activity to control BP. This differs from the recommendation for improving aerobic capacity which is more intense aerobics activity (80–85% MHR). At higher intensities, BP in HTN people does not decrease.

THE FOUR-MINUTE WORK-OUT

This highly effective work-out is designed to increase strength, endurance and stamina without a heavy investment in time.

Upper body

1. Time required: three minutes, five–six times a week, every morning before work.
2. Methods:

(a) *Push-ups*: either knee-bent or straight-legged, flat on ground or at 45°, perform the maximal number of push-ups (counting aloud), possible in one minute (no more). Rest in the up position only, while breathing out on elevation.

Push-ups

(b) *Curl-ups* (the "Crunch"): lift head and shoulders off the ground about 15–20°, while sliding your hands along the floor towards your knees. Perform the maximal number of curl-ups (counting aloud), possible in one minute (no more). Rest in the up position only, while breathing out on elevation.

Curl-ups

Abdominal Snap: there is a great 30 second morning work-out for the tonicity abdominal muscles that will also help to keep the intestine regular. It's called the "Abdominal Snap." Breathing calmly and deeply, stand, knees slightly bent with the feet at the width of the shoulders, with the palms of the hands on the thighs, just above the knees. Slowly expel all the air from your lungs and then suck in your gut as far as possible. While still holding the breath gently, snap out the gut and repeat three times for that inhaled breath. This can tone the abdominal muscles while giving a "wake-up call" to otherwise lethargic intestines.

(c) *Chair dips:* using a chair (or any solid object of comparable height), keep body straight and lower your buttocks to the ground, without resting them there, forming a right angle. Repeat for a one-minute count (no more).

Chair dips

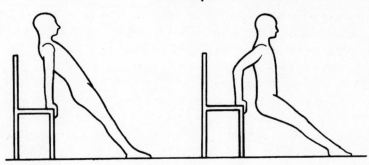

Lower body

It is important to improve muscular endurance and strength of the legs and buttocks. As the legs help return blood to the heart, they represent a "second heart." Invest in them.

1. Time required: one minute, five–six times a week, every morning before work.
2. Methods:
(a) *Squats:* with feet spread as far apart as your shoulders, perform the maximal number of squats (going down to a semi-seated position, while breathing out on ascent), possible in one minute (no more). Rest in down position only.

Squats

Practical application

For those times when you are "on the road," travelling around the world, unable to get in the work-out necessary to condition your heart, we propose a quick, but intense, four-minute work-out to be done every morning before going to work. This mini-work-out is not meant as a replacement for the Lifetime FIT Program, but as a supplement to help you to get your blood oxygenated in the morning to build up your endurance in preparation for the day's stresses ahead of you. Perform one minute of each exercise as shown above. Enter overleaf (with date) and add one per day.

FLEXIBILITY TRAINING

Later in life, you may not want to run a marathon, but you will want to bend over and tie your shoe or hold your grandchild. Yoga is the prime example of this type of training.

Benefits of stretching

The main benefits of stretching are as follows:

1. increased flexibility and improved circulation;
2. better breathing control and resultant greater mental equanimity;
3. greater mind/body harmony;
4. no special equipment.

To improve flexibility of the muscle groups of the back.

Time required: three minutes, three times a week.

Provisos:
(a) Time is critical here. While you may be adhering to a stretching or yoga class in the fitness club, maintain your progress by doing it just prior to retiring every night.
(b) It is important to remember *never bounce* when you stretch. Bouncing leads to small tears in your muscles. Just feel a gentle pull and maintain that position for 30 seconds.
(c) The duration is much more important than the intensity of the stretch.

	Push-ups	Curl-ups	Squats	Chair dips
Week One				
Monday				
Tuesday				
Wednesday				
Thursday				
Friday				
Saturday				
Sunday				
Week Two				
Monday				
Tuesday				
Wednesday				
Thursday				
Friday				
Saturday				
Sunday				
Week Three				
Monday				
Tuesday				
Wednesday				
Thursday				
Friday				
Saturday				
Sunday				
Week Four				
Monday				
Tuesday				
Wednesday				
Thursday				
Friday				
Saturday				
Sunday				

Methods:

(a) Seated on a mat, legs spread at 90°, gently lean forward as far as you can comfortably, and hold it for 30 seconds (count aloud).

(b) Do this same exercise to your left (only 30 seconds for the first several times) and to your right.

(c) Gain extra benefits (especially with regard to stress management) by following your breaths, in and out, for the entire 30 second count. Concentrate on them instead of on the muscles.

STRENGTH TRAINING

Recent research has shown that strength training has numerous benefits:

1. *Safely improves your metabolic rate.* This is vitally important for weight control (see Human Nutrition chapter). As you age, your fat compartment grows and your lean compartment (muscles and bones) shrinks. Muscle mass, a part of your lean mass compartment, is a very active tissue, burning up to 100 calories per kilogram *daily*! Therefore, increases in the muscle mass compartment = increases in metabolic rate.

2. *Increases your energy and stamina.* A better conditioned musculoskeletal system enables you to go about your daily chores without nagging episodes of fatigue.

3. *Improves overall musculoskeletal co-ordination and balance.* Weight training in the older groups improves walking velocity, balance, strength and stamina.

4. *Increases the mass of bones.* This helps ward off osteoporosis, a major cause of morbidity in older age groups.

5. *Improves self-image* and, possibly, self-confidence.

Provisos:

Several provisos are in order with regard to muscular endurance training:

(a) In terms of sequencing, always perform muscular training exercises *after* an aerobic session because such exercises prior to an aerobic session create an oxygen debt (causing premature fatigue).

(b) The American College of Sports Medicine warns that strength (weight) training *can* raise blood pressure, work on the heart and overall oxygen requirements. Heavy lifts can cause fainting (due to decreased venous return and decreased blood flow to the heart and brain). Exhalation on effort should be encouraged.

When to:
Strength training should always come after aerobic exercise, such as jogging. This is because strength training can help you to incur an oxygen debt, leading to fatigue later on.

How to:
To minimize injuries and improve overall performance, every muscle group should be exercised. The two major muscle groups to be exercised on alternate days are:
(a) **Upper body:** chest, abdominals, arms (biceps and triceps), shoulders and back.
(b) **Lower body:** abdominals, thighs, buttocks, calves.

Terms:
(a) **Reps (Repetitions):** the number of times that the exercise is to be performed sequentially; for example, doing ten reps of biceps curls means doing that exercise ten times without stopping.
(b) **Sets:** groups of reps; for example, doing three sets of 15 reps of biceps curls means doing the above exercise twice with a pre-determined break between.

Objectives:
(a) **Increasing strength:** accomplished by doing many reps with lighter weights.
(b) **Increasing mass:** accomplished by doing many reps with heavier weights. Use either free weights (barbell or dumb-bells) or resistance machines, according to your liking.

Getting ready:
(a) **Hydration and warm-up:** as for FIT, plus some loose stretching to limber up.
(b) **Nutrition:** shift the bulk of daily calories from carbohydrates to proteins for muscle reparation.

General movements:
(a) Rest 45–60 seconds between sets: stretch the muscles between sets.
(b) Instead of using rhythm or momentum to move the weight, be deliberate and take about two–three seconds for a complete

movement, such as a squat or curl; you should feel the muscle fibers pulling gently, almost burning.

(c) At the "top" of each movement, squeeze the muscle (contract it hard) for extra mass.

Days 1, 3, 5

Upper body	Reps	Sets	Weight (men/women)
1. Chest:			
(a) Lateral wings	10	2–3	10 kg/5 kg
2. Biceps:			
(a) Dumb-bell curl lateral wings	15	2–3	5 kg/3 kg
(b) Preacher curl	10	2–3	5 kg/3 kg
3. Triceps:			
(a) Push-ups (see 4 minute work-out)	10	2–3	–
(b) Chair-dips (see 4 minute work-out)	10	2–3	–
4. Shoulders:			
Lateral elevations	10	2–3	5 kg/3 kg

Lateral wings

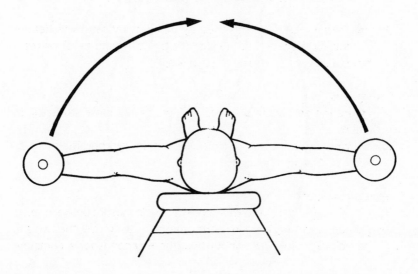

Preacher curl

Lateral elevations

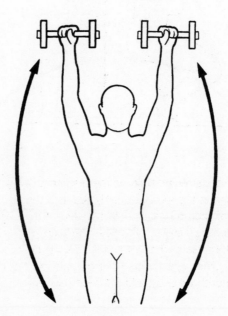

Days 2, 4, 6

Mid-lower body	Reps	Sets	Weight (men/ women)
(a) Abdominal Crunches (see 4 minute work-out)	10	2–3	–
(b) Thigh squats	10	2–3	–

Thigh squats

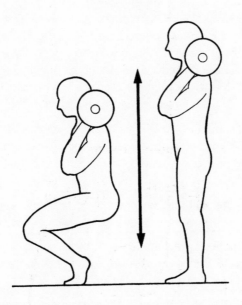

Progression:
To benefit fully from strength training, the resistance (weights) must regularly be increased as the muscles quickly adapt to the lower weights.

A good rule of thumb is: start with two sets at the beginning. When the recommended reps are easily achieved, add an extra set, for a maximal number of three sets. Then when that routine becomes easy to do, add 5% weight. Once again, when the muscles get used to this new load (within a month or two), add 5% more weight and continue until you have achieved the maximal **strength** (gauged by the weight you can lift) or **mass** (gauged by measuring circumferences).

POWER WALKING

Many people simply cannot find a sport, individual or team, that suits their dispositions and liking. Almost everybody likes to walk. Walking at a pace that increases the metabolic rate and heart rate (usually about one left + right cycle per second) is called power walking, as opposed to strolling. Recent research has shown that power walking has numerous benefits:

1. **Disease prevention.** People who participate in weekly walking for up to five hours are *half* as likely to have elevated body fat and cholesterol. In practice, power walking 30 minutes per day several days a week can dramatically reduce the risk (in men and women) of heart disease and cardiac death by 30% because of normalization of blood pressure, body fat, triglycerides and increased HDL cholesterol.

2. **Increasing bone mass.** Power walking is a weight-bearing exercise (swimming is *not*). As such, power walking increases bone mass by laying down new bone, thereby slowing the onset and severity of osteoporosis.

3. **Increases in stamina.** Instead of a coffee break, go on an "energy break:" power walking and two glasses of water or fresh fruit juice.

4. **Better mental fitness.** A natural result of communing with Nature, conversing with friends and feeling the silence. Walking is one of the best activities for "burnout."

5. **High accessibility.** No changing into sports wear and easy access to beginners make this "everybody's sport." Best of all, it doesn't cost any money!

The wheres and whens of power walking

Let's face it: power walking is all right for those cool days along the Hudson or Thames rivers, but a power walk at noon in Singapore or Kuala Lumpur or in December in Geneva is *tough* going. Think creatively!

Where:

When the pollution gets too much and the heat and humidity start soaring, take to the biggest walk-in refrigerators around: the malls. For those of you in hot climates, the first step is to find the closest shopping mall that is climate controlled.

Check the hours during which the mall is open and not so crowded. Start on the ground floor and walk briskly (taking short strides and swinging arms) from one end of the mall to the other. Jog up the stairways or escalator and repeat on the next floor until you come to the top. Now turn around and come down.

When:

The best time for power walking is after your largest meal (see Nutrition chapter). Lunchtime is the best from a practical standpoint as you need not leave the home at night.

HAVING A HEALTHY PAIN-FREE BACK

The mere mention of lower back pain at a management seminar or cocktail party will open the floodgates of "war stories" on lower back pain, complete with vivid re-enactments. The common folklore is that bad backs are reserved for those who make a living moving pianos, hoisting bricks, or playing rugby.

Nothing could be further from the truth. It is estimated that more than 80% of people in industrialized countries will be debilitated by this problem some time in their adult lives. In fact, the more sedentary you are, the greater your risk for developing severe back problems. That makes most of us at high risk to develop back pain that will limit mobility, both on the tennis court and at work.

Moreover, back pain means a major loss of money to an employee's company due to days off work. In the USA alone, back ailments, as the second leading cause for hospitalization (after pregnancy), cost industry $14 billion per year, including 93 million lost work days.

A brief review of the back anatomy reveals both problems and solutions.

The vertebral bodies are the bony building blocks, 33 in all, stacked interlocked one atop another. Between these vertebrae are rubbery, fluid-filled, discs, which cushion the weight of the upper body. Then there are muscles (roughly 140) and ligaments, like the stays of a sailboat mast, which hold the spine erect in a natural flattened S-curve, the optimal configuration for flexibility, weight bearing and shock absorption. In the upright position, the spinal cord and the sensitive nerves run just behind these discs in such a way as to be pinched by the compressed disc pushing backwards when you bend forward.

As long as the concave curve in the lower back is preserved, the disc, in most circumstances, tolerates the compression that comes from the pressure of the body's weight. Problems begin when you eliminate that inward curve of the lower back by habitually bending forward, thus compressing, and possibly heniating, the disc backwards.

To complicate matters further, enter the major technological advances of this century: the TV, telephone, computer and automobile and you have the worse activity possible for the back – **long-term sitting**. Though you may be committed to a livelihood that requires a lot of time on your backside, you need not fall into the 80% category of back sufferers cited above. The following table gives some of the common causes of back pain.

Problem	Cause(s)	Comments
Slipped (herniated) disc/Muscle strain	1. Accidents or trauma 2. Poor posture/bending 3. Obesity 4. Poor abdominal tone 5. Twisting while lifting 6. Falling	1. Learn to lift and bend well: bend knees! 2. Improve abdominal muscle tone 3. Consider yoga
Osteoporosis	Demineralization of vertebral bodies in back due to: (a) Xs calcium loss due to Xs use of diuretics like caffeine and alcohol (b) Decreased intake of calcium or Vitamin D	1. Maintain bone mass through exercises such as walking or weight training and by adequate calcium intake 2. Decrease caffeine and alcohol intake 3. Get plenty of sunshine
Degenerative joint disease	Simple wear and tear: repeated trauma due to sports injuries or child bearing	Maintain back suppleness by yoga or stretching exercises
Ankylosing spondylitis	Heredity	

Before developing acute back pain

The key to remaining free from this scourge of the 20th century is to prevent development of back pain through the following measures:

1. *Regular aerobic exercise is crucial to maintain the strength of the back muscles.* Brisk walking is ideal. Complement these activities with some night-time stretching or yoga.

2. *Get rid of the potbelly and get the weight under control.* Added weight distributed up front will only put more strain on the back muscles. Moreover, the spine receives most of its mechanical support from the massive abdominal musculature, not the back muscles themselves. Tone up the abdominal muscles by flexing them while sitting on planes, lifting and driving.

   While driving on long hauls, keep the knees higher than the pelvis. Maintain the natural curve of your spine by placing a cushion or a rolled-up towel behind your lower back to lend support Do not twist in getting in and out of your car. Realign the back every hour or so of driving by standing, place hands in the lower back and bend backwards.

   Best single exercise for preventing back pain: the abdominal "Crunch": called the "Crunch" because you only come off the floor enough to lift your shoulder blades off the floor (about 10–15° – no more). This action selectively strengthens the rectus abdominus muscles (those abdominal muscles in front known by body builders as the "six-pack") and provides frontal support to the lower back. Do this slowly and completely until you feel the muscle "burn" and then do five more.

   As a variant to the above manoeuvre, tilt to the left and right side while coming up. This will strengthen the internal and external oblique muscle groups that act as a girdle to the side aspect of the abdomen.

3. *Lift objects properly.* Perform the "Marble Test" in the morning. Put a smart marble in your breast pocket during a normal work day, at home or at the office. During the day, if the marble rolls out of your pocket, that is because you bent over *at the waist*, instead of squatting to pick something up. Above all, do not bend over to pick something or someone up: let your legs do the bending. When lifting, keep the object very close to your body. Lift twice: once in your mind, visualizing the best way to do it and then in reality. This helps to avoid bending over to pick something up.

Moreover, bending your legs will build powerful leg muscles and this is important to your heart. When the heart pumps blood TO the lower body and legs, it does so with the help of gravity. Getting the blood BACK to the lungs requires more assistance as the blood flow is now going against gravity. Strong leg muscles can help by "milking" the blood in the veins upwards. Strong legs, therefore, can act not only to save the back but also as a second heart!

4. *While sitting in your car or at your desk, sit up and avoid stooping.* The natural contour of the back is that of an "S," not an "I" (too straight) and definitely not a "C" (stooping crushes the internal organs). During the day, tense your abdominal muscles to give them the strength they need to support your back. Be certain that your chair supports your lower back well.

5. *While travelling . . . .* Divide the weight of your bags evenly so as not to strain one side more than the other. Likewise, instead of carrying a mammoth single bag, consider carrying two lighter bags.

6. *Sleep the right way.* Ideal situation for the back: firm mattress or tatami, on your side with the top leg bent and bottom leg straight.

7. *Women beware.* High heels throw the back into an exaggerated position. Thought by some to be sexy but should come with traction devices.

Once you develop acute back pain

There is a whole array of therapeutic modalities (massage, hot water bottle, manipulation, acupuncture, ultrasound deep heat, traction, shoe inserts, surgery), none of which are 100% successful. In fact, most back pain subsides, regardless of approach, with bedrest, aspirin and the tincture of time. Otherwise, see your doctor for further investigation, particularly if accompanied by fever. With a little care and forethought, you will defy the adage:

"Once a back patient, always a back patient."

Back flexibility plan

I may not need to run a marathon at 60, but I will need to be flexible enough to tie my shoes   *1990s manager*

I. *Knee-to-chest chest:*
(a) Bring your thigh as close to your chest as you can.
Hold it for a count of 10. Repeat with other leg. Breathe.
(b) Bring both thighs as close to your chest as you can.
Hold for a count of 10. Breathe through.

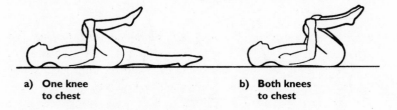

a) One knee **b) Both knees**
   to chest   **to chest**

2. *Stretch for lower back and hip:*
While lying, keep your hips and shoulders on the floor. Bring your left knee over your right thigh and *gently* press down with your hand on your bent knee toward the floor. Hold for a count of 15. Repeat with other leg.

3. *Sit with your right leg straight.* Bend your left leg and cross your left foot over your outstretched right leg. Then bend your right elbow and rest it on the outside of your left knee. Now with your left hand straightened behind you, slowly turn your head to look over your left shoulder and rotate your upper body in the same direction. To get a better stretch as you rotate your upper body to the left, *gently* push your left knee with your elbow to the right. Hold that position for 15 seconds. Repeat with other side. *Do not ever hold your breath. Breathe through.*

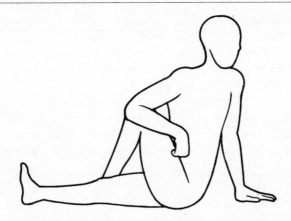

4. *Half-Cobra (Spine stretch).* Completely relax the spine. Raise up your head first, then raise the top part of your torso off the floor, using only the back muscles for lift. Keep the lower part of your abdomen on the floor and relax the neck and shoulder muscles. Keep breathing and smiling. Hold the Cobra position for a count of 20 seconds.

A YOGA SAMPLER:
PREPARE THE BODY AND MIND FOR LIFE'S CHANGES

Introduction

Yoga comes from the Sanskrit word that literally means "to unite with God." In practice, it refers to the mental and physical practice of directing one's focussed attention on a concrete or abstract object to gain control over natural forces, including one's body and mind. The original idea was to get the body supple and strong enough to sit for long hours, until the mind's restlessness was vanquished. It is not a religious or political movement, but a routine for mental and physical fitness.

The underlying principle is that through such exercise, we can quiet the mind long enough to see the illusory and hypnotic nature of our ego

(Latin for "I") and the world that our personality has created. It can be, for many of us, the first step in self-mastery. Incidentally, independent of all the philosophy behind yoga, these exercises are an excellent warm-up for such sports as running, golf, tennis, squash, badminton, swimming and skiing.

By no means is this brief overview meant as an exhaustive or scholarly treatise on the discipline of yoga, which dates back almost 5,000 years. Its purpose is to provide a glimpse into the Universe of Yoga, a sampling, if you will, so that participants can experience a little of the harmony generated by such a practice. Once you have had a little "taste" of yoga's offerings, you may wish to take a formal course, offered most everywhere, which will elaborate upon what is discussed here.

Consistent with this "tasting" approach to yoga, as no advanced positions are suggested, most of this routine is suitable for children, pregnant women, those of advanced years, highly sedentary people, those suffering from mild arthritis, unless otherwise noted (such as Salute to the Sun). Drawings accompany the text where necessary.

Getting ready

1. The practice of yoga should come naturally, *never* force it. This pertains specifically to your breathing: *never* hold your breath. Rather, breathe through every position, even when instructed to hold that position for several seconds. Do not try to progress too quickly: injury or disappointment will result. As you go through the movements, just breathe, relax and ∴ . observe.
2. Practice yoga because it makes sense to *you*, not for the promises of enlightenment (whatever that means), or any other result. You and others will eventually appreciate the exceedingly subtle changes brought about in your body and personality.
3. Wear loose fitting clothing and socking or bare feet. Remove any jewellery (watches and rings) that constrains free movement. Keep your watch on the side to keep track of time.
4. Start by practicing for 20-minute sessions, every day, preferably not within 90 minutes after eating.
5. Required materials:
   (a) a small cushion or folded towel for sitting positions;
   (b) a small carpet or exercise mat, if your floor is uncarpeted;
   (c) a candle and notepad (optional).

The practice: two basic routines, to be done on alternate days of the week

Each routine lasts less than 20 minutes and they are based on two starting positions: one standing and one sitting.

Routine # 1: Standing Postures – a great way to get energized in the morning

Start by getting out of bed and standing with your hands at your side and your feet spread slightly wider than the width of the shoulders.

Step # 1. The Triangle: a simple *lateral* stretch to make the torso, back, shoulders, more supple. Raise the right arm, reaching for the stars, and then bend slowly to your left, while sliding your left hand down your left leg as far as possible. While breathing normally, turn and look up at the raised hand, hold that position for about 15 seconds. While breathing normally, come up slowly and repeat with other side. Repeat cycle twice more slowly, each time increasing time spent in lower position (up to two minutes). Breathe, relax, and . . . observe.
Total time ~ 6–8 minutes.

The triangle

Step # 2. Chest Expansion: a simple *forward* stretch to make the torso, back, shoulders, more supple. Clasp your hands behind your back, slowly straighten your arms and lift them towards the ceiling while slowly bending forward.

Breathe through, do not strain. Hold position without straining for 15 seconds. Now, with hands still clasped together behind the back, bend back several centimeters. Hold position without straining for five seconds. Return to normal standing position. Breathe, relax, and . . . observe.

Total time ~ 4–6 minutes.

Chest expansion

Step # 3. Salute to the Sun: a slightly more advanced posture, which is a splendid combination of several postures. Note of Caution: if you (1) are in the second or third trimester of pregnancy, (2) suffer from severe back problems, headaches or high blood pressure, skip this posture. Remember, as with all yoga postures, *breathe, relax, and . . . observe.*

Getting to the floor: from the standing position, raise your arms up, far above your head, and then slowly bend forward, exhaling gently and slowly. Even if you must bend your knees, place the hands flat on the floor. Then, while inhaling with head erect, place the right foot as far back as possible. Still while breathing normally, allow the left leg to join the right leg, so that you are in the "push-up" position.

From the "push-up" position, bend first the knees, then the arms, and allow the head to "dive," so that the entire body performs a scooping motion. Your body ends up in the "salute" or cobra position, with head up, arms straight, back bent backwards and lower body touching the floor. Of course, you are still breathing normally. Relax there for 15 seconds. Breathe, relax, and . . . observe.

Getting off the floor: from the "salute" position, you will simply do the reverse of what you did to get you there, with one twist. Raise the buttocks off the floor, making an inverted "V" with your body. Slowly, bring up the right leg forward, then the left. Slowly, with palms flat on the floor, straighten the legs and resume the standing position. Breathe, relax, and . . . observe.

Repeat the entire Salute to the Sun three times. Total time ~ 4 minutes.

Salute to the sun

Routine # 2: Sitting Postures – an intelligent part of any travel work-out

This routine includes certain elements that you may add to enhance the holistic benefits of the routine: meditation with a mantra (explained in the next chapter) and meditation with a candle (demonstrated below). Both will markedly improve your memory and concentration.

Start by sitting on your bent knees, hands on your thighs and do a few head rolls. While breathing normally and with eyes open, gently roll your head in a 360° circle, first to the left and then to the right.

Step # 1. The Frog: still seated on bent knees, keep your toes touching and spread your knees to form an angle of about 90°. Then slide your hands out in front of you until your forehead touches the floor. Hold that position for 20 seconds while breathing normally. Return to seated position. Repeat five times. Breathe, relax, and . . . observe. Total time ~ 4 minutes.

The Frog

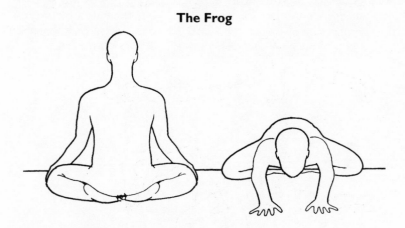

Step # 2. The Back Bend: still seated on bent knees, place your arms directly behind your shoulders Slowly, allow your hands to creep backwards, as an inchworm, until the arms are at a 90° angle to the torso. Now, lift your pelvis off your feet, as illustrated. Once again, while breathing normally, hold that position for 20 seconds. Return to seated position. Repeat three times. Now, slowly, in the bent knee position, roll the knees and hips to the left and the right several times before ending up seated on the floor. Breathe, relax, and . . . observe. Total time ~ 4 minutes.

Back Bend

Step # 3. The Butterfly: while seated on the floor, or folded towel, or pillow, grab your ankles and pull them gently towards your pelvis. While holding the ankles or feet there, use your elbows to press the knees to the floor, a position to be held for 20 seconds. Breathe, relax and . . . observe. Repeat three times. Total time ~ 4 minutes.

Step # 4. The Spinal Twist: seated with legs stretched out in front of you, place the left leg over the right knee on the floor. Then, slowly twist the arms and entire upper body to the LEFT, placing both hands, if possible, on the floor. Looking over your left shoulder, hold for ten seconds. Breathe, relax, and . . . observe. Repeat on right side. Total time ~ 2 minutes.

Spinal Twist

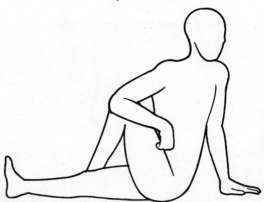

Step # 5. Sitting Meditation with Candle: after a few days or weeks of the two routines, your body will be supple enough and your mind will be calm enough for some extremely simple sitting meditation: the activity for which yoga was originally invented. With nothing scheduled, in a quiet room, try this meditation with a candle (or any simple object) to improve your powers of memory and concentration. Meditation with mantras is discussed in the next chapter.

Note of caution: There is no need for painful contortions in yoga. In the meantime, get a chair and practice that way until you are comfortable sitting on a cushion or towel.

So, sit on a cushion or folded towel, with legs folded comfortably in front of you. Place your wrist watch and notepad off to the side (to mark the progress and observations) and the candle 50 centimeters (about 20 inches) in front of you. Now, just sit there, your gaze fixed on the flame, with your hands on your knees, your head and spine in alignment, as, once again, you breathe, relax, and . . . observe. Just observe. Start by doing it for just five minutes, then ten minutes, then whatever your ego will tolerate.

Observe the thoughts as they arise and linger around seductively, feverishly at first. Then, as the mind and senses become more trained, the thoughts will still arise but do not linger or persist . . . like leaves on a river, they just pass by. As negative thoughts go by, do not struggle with them or even be provoked by them. Gently and smiling, bring your attention back to more worthy objects, the flame and your breathing.

Sitting meditation with candle

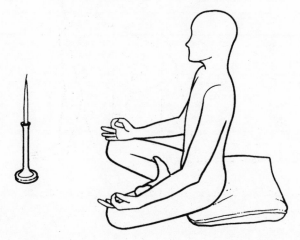

II. FITNESS ACTION PLAN: THE OBJECTIVE-ORIENTED APPROACH

I had now come to the last part of this interesting chapter on Physical Fitness – an objective-oriented approach.

Now, you are prepared either to make your own fitness program from the previous pages or choose one of the following menus according to your objectives.

Control Weight and Body Fat

M	T	W	Th	F	Sat	Sun
20' YOGA in AM + 15' Walk	4' Workout 15' Walk	20' YOGA in AM + 15' Walk	4' Work-out 15' Walk	20' YOGA in AM + 15' Walk	4' Work-out	Rest
No starch except breakfast 20' YOGA in PM +		No starch except breakfast 20' YOGA in PM		No starch except breakfast 20' YOGA in PM	No starch except breakfast	

Improve Strength, Energy and Stamina

M	T	W	Th	F	Sat	Sun
	4' Work-out	20' YOGA in AM	4' Work-out	20' YOGA in AM	4' Work-out	20' YOGA in AM
Strength training	FIT 20' YOGA in PM	Strength training 20' YOGA in PM		Strength training 20' YOGA in PM	FIT	20' YOGA in PM

The four Steps to High Stamina

1. *Snack between meals.* Out with the coffee break, in with the energy break: fresh or dried fruit and fresh water.
2. *Tune the Body.* Use your desk or sink, and do 25 quick push-ups and 25 "Crunches" (half sit-ups).
3. *Clean Up your Nutrition.* Eat only certain foods that are compatible: proteins with proteins. NO FAST FOODS!

4. *Oxygenate the Brain.* Find a quiet corner (office, taxi, toilet) and close your eyes and breathe deeply × 10. Visualize something peaceful, an evergreen forest or inland lake.

   (a) Lifetime FIT Program: as discussed, you can expect your recuperation rates and resting heart rates to begin to decrease nicely at the rate of approximately one beat per minute per week of training at your THR.

   (b) 4 minute work-out

   (c) 5 ' flexibility in PM.

   (d) Consider yoga or Tai Chi in AM.

Increase Cardio-fitness and Endurance

M	T	W	Th	F	Sat	Sun
4' Work-out	20' YOGA in AM	4' Work-out	20' YOGA in AM	4' Work-out	4' Work-out	20' YOGA in AM
FIT 20' YOGA in PM		FIT 20' YOGA in PM		FIT 20' YOGA in PM		

Have a Healthy Pain-Free Back

M	T	W	Th	F	Sat	Sun
3' Abdominal exercises	20' YOGA in AM	3' Abdominal exercises	20' YOGA in AM	3' Abdominal exercises	20' YOGA in AM	3' Abdominal exercises
Back exercises or 20' YOGA in PM	15' Walk	Back exercises or 20' YOGA in PM	15' Walk	Back exercises or 20' YOGA in PM	15' Walk	Back exercises or 20' YOGA in PM

Preserve Sanity and Inner

M	T	W	Th	F	Sat	Sun
20' YOGA in AM	20' YOGA in AM	20' YOGA in AM	20' YOGA in AM	20' YOGA in AM	Family activities	Family activities
	15' Walk	FIT	15' Walk	Back exercises	15' Walk	

4

STAYING SANE
AGAINST ALL ODDS

"If you fall off the fast track in the 1990s, you
risk more than falling down and hurting yourself.
You may actually die."
Senior Manager

THE BIG BALANCE: STAYING HAPPY IN THE FAST TRACK

Day Three: Thursday morning – The Countdown begins

By 7:45 a.m., on the second full day in the hospital (the morning of my bypass operation), I arrived at the door of the hospital library where I saw a handwritten Post-it sign: "Class is out till 8 a.m." I was especially interested in what insights I could generate with Dr Charles about the whole issue of stress. I had read so much about it (hard to avoid these days). While waiting, I pondered the whole issue of stress.

I honestly thought that I was not very stressed. After all, I wasn't screaming at anyone any more, nor anyone at me, I didn't feel desperate or particularly suicidal (though I knew that there were several colleagues close to me who had been depressed and had actually contemplated suicide last year). My habits of eating, drinking and smoking were under my firm control and I could, if I *really* wanted to, stop smoking and lose weight. My relationship with my wife and children, though far from perfect, was still workable and free of any public friction (we were sure not to expose this problematic aspect of our lives to our children). My job was as secure as anyone's and I enjoyed the respect of most of the colleagues I worked with. Above all, I lived for a good fight, I even thrived on all sorts of confrontation. In fact, my short temper and provocative personality were well known at the office and at home but I felt that I just didn't get stressed!

By 8:15 a.m., I was ready to settle down in the hospital library. I found, to my annoyance, that one of the other patients coming for the talks in the library, somewhat older than myself and also with a portable heart monitor, had squatted there. I had attempted the previous night to "reserve" *my* favorite reading place in the reading room with my bathrobe flung over the chair, and a note "Do not disturb" on my notes. What a nerve! As I felt my facial muscles getting a little tense, I fumbled for the sublingual nitroglycerin tablets that were dispensed to me in the event of any chest pain. Just then, the intruder looked up and with a feigned smile said, "Oh, I'm sorry. Did I take your place? It seemed to be the best seat in the house . . . , the view, the sun and all."

"No, no, *no*. Not to worry," I said, trying to hide my annoyance. *Why can I not assert myself without closing down? Why can I not learn the art of being gentle and firm in my demands?* The last thing I wanted to do was to get angry here, not so much for my heart's health, but so that someone whom I held in such high esteem as Dr Charles would not come in to find me upset over such a trivial issue. "I'll just sit over here," I offered, smiling, while I picked up my book, bathrobe and moved on. Finally, calmed down, my muscles relaxed, my skin cooled down, I settled down for some early morning reading. That was my first real proof of the effects of emotions on my health.

Dr Charles's lessons in his book continued in his unabashed style. Intent to read the entire Sanity chapter that morning, I flipped to the page that I had dog-eared and saw that it began with a bold quote:

"Life moves so much more rapidly now than it ever did before . . . the huge acceleration in the rate of growth of facts, of knowledge, of techniques, of inventions, of advances in technology . . . . We need a different type of human being . . . who is comfortable with change, who enjoys change, who is able to improvise, who is able to face with confidence, strength and courage a situation of which he has absolutely no forewarning . . . the society which can turn out such people will survive; the societies that cannot turn out such people will die."

Abraham Maslow, *Frontiers of Human Nature*

Life if nothing else, is change, glorious, chaotic, change, full of ups and downs: more like a roller coaster than anything else. We are just hanging in as best we can. Are you enjoying the ride?

Ultimately, to succeed personally and professionally (whatever that nebulous word means to you), all changes in life, however fundamental or unpredictable, must be balanced by newly developed personal abilities to deal with them effectively and creatively. This balance must be respected if we are to have any chance, as individuals or as a species, of survival (see opposite).

So your happiness is not the absence of change but the ability to effectively deal with it. Therefore, we should devote most of our energies and resources to upgrading our personal abilities to deal more effectively with change.

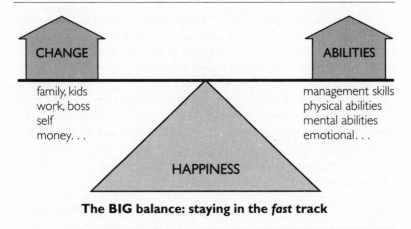

The BIG balance: staying in the *fast* track

By personal abilities, Dr Charles clearly meant our physical skills, mental, emotional and even, spiritual, skills. I became confused and irritated. Why not, I pondered, just arrange the environment optimally to *dampen* change, to staticize life a little? And where did the whole issue of stress come in? Already several pages into the chapter and the word **stress** hadn't even been mentioned.

Just then, Dr Charles walked briskly in the door, somewhat out of breath, looking first towards the window where I usually sat, and then over to where I was and smiled. "Oh, *there* you are. I just came from morning rounds in the ICU where the person at the Master Cardiac Monitor noticed that about five minutes ago your heart started going in and out of a very peculiar irregular rhythm. You got the whole ICU into a panic. Are you all right? What's up?"

As I explained the situation to him, he shook his head smiling, called up the ICU with the "false alarm" message and we started our one-on-one over a cup of warm herbal tea and honey.

"Well," I started, "I'm just starting reading the Sanity chapter and already I notice that you emphasize the whole idea of personal abilities and the changes of life. That's fine but what about engineering my immediate environment: this hostile world, my marriage, my job, my external life, making sure all the little pieces are falling into place. Surely, that's a good place to start." I said this, hoping that my last 15 years were at least somewhat well-spent. I thought about how much energy I had spent trying to control my environment, making certain that I wouldn't be caught off guard by unforeseen circumstances.

"Well, sure, we all try that approach but it will be effective only to a limited degree. Most of us exaggerate our abilities to influence and control external events. It feels good because there is lot of perceived change after we are finished thrashing about. That'll work fine until you become more fully aware, wide awake. After all, life is one big classroom: if it's completely free of failure, you're not taking enough risks. We have trouble distinguishing which events in life we can change and which we cannot. Surely you have heard this prayer:

> Let me have the strength to change the things that need changing.
> Let me have the patience to accept the things I cannot change.
> Let me have the wisdom to know the difference.

Most external events we cannot change and so the real change must come from *within* us, preferably in some proactive preparation for the inevitable change. Ghandi once said:

> For the person who is humble, there is no question of rejecting anything. He will reason (that) it is the imperfection of my own intellect that today's other stanzas seem to me inconsistent with these. In the course of time, I shall be able to see their consistency. So he will tell himself and others, and leave the matter there.

Anyway, let's just presume that the changes we just looked at are going to continue to increase in an inexorable kind of fashion. That much is supported even by the nuclear physicists who acknowledge that the Universe is continually sliding towards a state of increasing disorder. That is the whole principle of Entropy. And there is not really that much we can do about it all: life's that way. Whether you are aware of the Grand Design of it all is not important: it exists. The real fun comes from putting the bits of the puzzle together, using and deciphering life experiences, buffing and polishing until the Grand Design shines through. For now, though, don't question the methods of this madness, just enjoy the ride."

HIERARCHY OF NEEDS

Doctor Charles continued his theme: "But there's another very good reason to concentrate on change *within*, a more practical consideration, rather than one based on external events. If you are really interested in finding balance and happiness, it's much easier to change the way you look at things rather than the things themselves. If you cannot see how a particular piece fits into the mosaic, change your glasses. After all, you and I are seeing the world through the prisms of our **need systems** and as your needs change, so too your view of the world. This must be understood before we can understand our motivations, as our individual needs color everything. You want to change reality, change your need system.

"Because whether we realize it or not, we approach everything and everybody with an eye to using them to help us satisfy our particular needs. If this is done as a 'power play' or in a dishonest, manipulative ,way, we can create even more loneliness and separateness within ourselves and in the world."

"What kind of 'needs' are you talking about?," I asked.

"Let's borrow a basic idea of Hierarchy of Needs from the famous German psychologist, Abraham Maslow," he said as he drew a pyramid on the blackboard (see below).

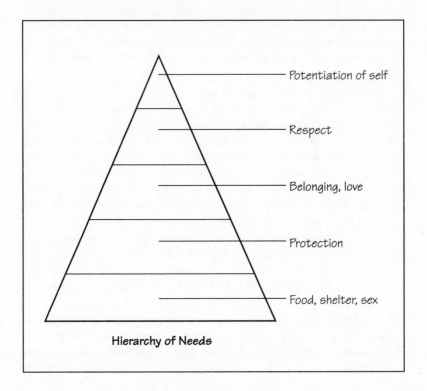

Potentiation of self

Respect

Belonging, love

Protection

Food, shelter, sex

Hierarchy of Needs

"Maslow organized the needs of the human being according to a certain system of *priorities*. Things start really basic, at the level of the body, at the level of physical survival." At this point Dr Charles drew my attention to 'The Book of Solutions' where the differing needs had been detailed."

Physiologic needs

On the lowest levels, you have the basis of physiologic survival: *homeostasis* (stability) of the internal environment or keeping the whole thing going on the strictly material level. You have a physical body that requires maintenance and so you eat, you drink, you defecate, urinate, make love, wash, and so on.

As the body detects an imbalance of some need (food, sleep, exercise, sex, sugar, fat, water, calcium, oxygen, nicotine, alcohol or whatever), it will set out to gratify that need in order to maintain the internal balances. Unless these basic needs are satisfied, we cannot, without considerable effort, move on to the next level. In a word, food nearly always takes priority over poetry, respect, love, belonging, or self-actualization.

It should be noted, however, that the primal gratification of these physiologic needs, say for example, hunger, can provide the relief from other needs on other levels, such as love or belonging. For example, highly anxious people who are seeking to satisfy the need for security or esteem (see following sections), will often exhibit "nervous eating" or nail biting as the next best (and certainly more accessible) thing. It is well recognized that obesity due to anxiety is a psychological or emotional problem, which later becomes a physiological problem. Remove or control the anxiety and the obesity disappears.

In most cultures and settings, even if we are farmers, we need something called money to satisfy these needs (i.e. to go shopping for food and drink). When children grow up without ready access to the means to gratify these primal needs of physiologic survival, it is possible that they will be so marked by the deficit that their whole life will be consumed by making sure that "there will always be enough," leading to overeating or hoarding. This is perhaps how some of us spend so much of our precious time just existing to survive and so little time actually living life fully.

Security needs

Once these most primordial needs are satisfied, a different constellation of needs arises: stability, protection, freedom from anxiety, structure, law, order, security from war, pestilence, shelter from the elements and natural disasters, and chaos. Failure to satisfy these needs can lead to all sorts of obsessive behavior, activity that tends to ensure that our social "lifeboat" has absolutely no "leaks." Our minds will impose a certain order and structure to the world.

Money plays a critical role at this level, enabling us to purchase a roof over our head and provide necessary mobility. It is also useful to prepare for unforeseen calamities. What is "enough" will always be a function of conditioning from parents and peers, amplified by cultural and personal variables, such as personal taste.

History is replete with examples of needs for security and order being so profound that, under certain circumstances, the people will choose tyrannical order (totalitarianism) over chaotic freedom.

Belonging and love needs

Once satisfied on the former two levels, a more sophisticated set of needs emerges: the need to belong, to give and to receive love and affection, the need for "emotion meltdown," being part of something much bigger than our physical or psychological selves. This is not quite the same as pure physiological sexual expression, but includes all ways of forgetting one's loneliness: forming groups on the ground of common values, a sense of camaraderie.

That is, as our consciousness expands, we are aware of our physical, social, and cosmic place in the Universe. At a certain point in our lives, we pull away from the warmth of the family, and we will feel alone: this causes pain and anxiety. To temporarily relieve the pain of loneliness and to gain a sturdier identity, we join groups: football or baseball fans, social clubs, gangs, hobby associations, drug groups, churches. Now, we *belong*. As goes the group, so go the group's members. Just witness the fans after a football match.

That is, once you begin early in life to feel "alone in the world" and that separation causes a certain anxiety and pain, we all seek to alleviate this through various ways of belonging.

Respect needs

For many of us, the satisfaction of the first three levels is insufficient for a completely healthy life, until we receive the respect and recognition we feel we deserve. Passing through the various stages of life should bring recognition in all cultures. We have participated in the "rites of passage": we have worked hard, occasionally drifted well outside our "comfort zone" into the dark forest of our fears, climbed mountains, killed our first meal, seen ghosts, had children, made sacrifices, buried our dead, and lived to talk about it. This earns the respect of peers.

Receiving this deserved esteem from peers and superiors will lead, in most circumstances, to a normal amount of self-confidence, while frustration of this need leads to a sense of inferiority and helplessness.

Having money, though indicative of the fact that we have been well compensated for our numerous battles, will not guarantee gratification at this level, at least, in all cultures. In fact, overdoing it at this level could make problems at the level of belonging needs.

Being able to purchase a home in an expensive area in an attempt to gather respect from peers or feel superior to them will only succeed in alienating us from our "extended family" and frustrate the more primal need of belonging. In warrior terms, overt victory creates anger. This explains why hyper-wealthy people often dress down or get fake tans to foster the impression that they are still connected to their primal roots. In fact, these people cannot really decide what is better: to belong to the family of humankind (with all its blemishes and warts) or to spend energy in a pretentious power play by creating the impression of being "above it all." This internal conflict often confuses and drains the energy of wealthy people which is one reason why they seem so sad and smile less most of the time.

Just study the "smile index" of various groups in whatever society: unless the financially endowed have made efforts to maintain their extended family and treat others less fortunate as "brothers," it is rare to see them smiling spontaneously. On the other hand, less financially privileged people, regardless of their culture or country, seem to always have a ready smile as they are connected, they "belong" to a larger family. This belonging carries more happiness than any amount of money.

The "self-actualization" needs

For many of us, satisfaction of the above-mentioned needs still leaves us restless because we are living our lives in such a way that we are in direct conflict with our true natures.

We all are born with a certain innate potential, which lies unrealized in us until we test ourselves to see what kind of person we really are: a "people" person (who loves being around people), a salesperson (who can sell anything to anybody), a studious person (who needs to be around problems and ideas to analyze), a "numbers" person, a surfer beach bum person (who just wants to take "one day at a time" and do no harm), a spiritual transcendental person (who is good at "showing the Way" by "living the Way"), a teacher at heart (who learns and then empowers by demonstrating), a children person (who needs to be around unspoiled innocence), an artist (who needs to show alternate insights), an athlete (who needs to show the beauty of discipline and persistence through mastery of the body) or whatever.

If we are, for example, by nature very friendly and honest, but feel as though these qualities are thwarted because of the type of livelihood we have chosen (perhaps with earlier hopes of satisfying other more basic needs), we will be deeply frustrated because it's "just not us."

This is most interesting because many of us will go into one or another walk of life because of secondary needs (security, money, respect), but altogether neglect the inner potential that aches for self-realization.

SIMPLIFYING LIFE

When I had finished reading, I mentioned to Dr Charles, "You know, when I see the needs laid out like that, it becomes a lot easier to get a handle on just why I've done certain things in my life. For example, in the current scheme of things in my life, why do I work as hard as I do, why do I voluntarily submit myself to the unrealistic deadlines, why do I travel through seven time zones, as my body lags (sometimes dangerously) behind, why do I isolate myself from my loved ones, why do I put my marriage at risk?"

"The answer is *simple*: because it definitely answers your needs at certain levels even if it paradoxically poses problems to your mental and physical health and other aspects of your life. Otherwise, you wouldn't do it. Let's take a look." Dr Charles made two columns on the blackboard. "Here are your 'Needs,' as you perceive them, see if your lifestyle, as you have arranged it, answers those needs."

Need	Answered by lifestyle
1. Physiological: food, sex	→ Yes
2. Security: shelter, protection	→ Yes
3. Belonging: loving	→ Yes from some (colleagues) No from others (family)
4. Respect: status	→ Yes from some (colleagues), No from others (family)
5. Self-potentiation	→ Possibly yes or possibly no

"At the end of the day, you must ask one of the most fundamental questions: '**What do I really need to get by in this world?**' For example, towards the end of his life, Ghandi needed next to nothing, a loincloth, a walking staff and his spectacles. Other great spiritual leaders such as Jesus Christ, Mohammed, Buddha, Krishna, Moses, Lao Tzu and others showed us that for complete and enduring happiness we must: first, be true to ourselves when it comes to why we are really doing something; second, not allow ourselves to become too attached to our respective need systems; and thirdly, never use others as means or objects by which to gratify those needs."

Dr Charles continued: "At the other end of the spectrum, some psychotic and pathologic people need to control, hurt or even kill others to survive, to break even. Imagine that, needing to kill (physically or emotionally) to break even. These are the Hitlers, Stalins and other megalomaniacs. We are between these two extremes somewhere, arranging our lives as best we can.

"To survive today, for example, we all need, or at least think we need, all sorts of trappings of the 'good life;' it is up to each individual to decide how much they want and how quickly they hope to get it. What you will notice is that almost all of us are occupied all of our lives with the very basics of physical survival, the first couple of levels of the Hierarchy of Needs. We get stuck there, spinning our

> *To survive today, for example, we all need, or at least think we need, all sorts of trappings of the "good life"*

tires, just flitting back and forth between the sensations of needs grat-ification and boredom. The point is not to imitate Ghandi (that was his role at that time and place and, anyway, his type of person comes along every *century* at most), but to try to be aware of what *your* real needs are to be happy. Above all, one wants to be certain that to sat-isfy one's needs, we don't use others as objects of desire, because then, from a spiritual point of view, we move on that spectrum in the wrong direction. With each and every act of need gratification, however minute or hidden, we can shift our position on this spectrum one way or another, either towards spiritual liberation or entrapment."

Suddenly I felt very weighty, full of needs; even dominated by them. "Where do we begin, then?"

"The solution is to simplify. Don't become a victim of your own desires."

> **Desires are like our children: the more we yield to them, the more they become unmanageable.**
>
> *Chinese proverb*

"To maximize happiness, one must maximize satisfaction while keeping needs and desires to a minimum. You could express it this way," he scribbled this on a blackboard:

Happiness = Satisfaction/Needs

"In other words, real happiness will increase as our *satisfaction* with life increases and that's largely up to our perceptual skills. Happiness will also increase as our *needs* decrease, and this is definitely under our direct control. Either way, happiness is ours to enjoy. Otherwise, we are spending our time chasing our tails. To get stuck here spells only boredom and many of us are involved in the repetitive tasks satisfying basic desires, resulting in overkill at this most basic level. In simple terms, most of us spend too much time surviving and too little time actually living and enjoying life. Then it's over. That's a shame."

INTERPERSONAL RELATIONSHIPS AS ENDS IN THEMSELVES

I was keen to continue our conversation and addressed Dr Charles again: "But aren't there going to be many situations in life where people actually want to satisfy each other's needs, such as marriage?" I knew I was opening up a real can of worms, but I felt that this was one area where I needed some insight.

"Of course," he started, " there will always be great potential for what we call symbiosis or mutual co-operation. Most relationships, personal or commercial, begin in the spirit of 'how can we benefit each other?' Promises are made, people in, say a marriage, view themselves in a collective co-dependent way. Lovers get locked in an emotional, some would say a hormonally-directed, love trance: the egoism of two. Vaulted adolescent expectations pave the way for inevitable disappointments. Physiologic and some of the security needs are gratified and everyone is 'happy.'

"Then after the courtship ritual has worn off, as the routine and gravity's effects set in, the *power play* begins. Manipulation, control and scapegoating become key words of this stage. There will always be a winner and a loser, but the real loser is the collective unit: the couple and children. This is where most relationships fail to get on a solid footing. Instead of perceiving our mates as someone to construct with, we perceive them as someone who interferes with our need for extra-marital meanderings (through new sex needs or needs for a macho-oriented respect through multiple conquests). That is, the need to impress and acquire power on one level (security needs) prevails over, and often conflicts with, the need to preserve the microcosmic unit of society, the family (belonging needs). Moreover, something very important is put at risk: trust, the very lifeblood of *all* relationships.

"Should the couple be able to ride out the (hormonal) storm," he said, "the rewards are significant: renewed trust of each other, trust of self and independence. The couple become co-conspirators in a relationship that is principle-driven, not convenience-driven The couple become committed to honesty because they no longer fear disappointment. That is the first step to becoming soulmates that can now act as hardened flints upon which the light of truth can be ignited."

"I must say, Doc, that in the course of my relationship with my wife, whom I love dearly, I've been through some of those tough moments of doubt and mistrust," I admitted, "and it wasn't easy to find our way clear."

"What was it like," he probed, "during those stages of the relationship?"

"At times, very lonely and, frankly, very sad. There would be times after long business trips that I would return home bone tired and really inconsiderate of Jane's needs. Since she had been stuck at home for so long, I would feel obliged to take her out for a nice dinner, in an effort to smooth over the rough areas. Well, those dinners were often quite painful. Nice restaurant and all, both of us just sitting there without really much to say, looking past one another, as if we were both waiting for the whole thing to pass. Totally humorless and devoid of any real intimacy. Something was lost, at least temporarily."

"And now, where are you both?" he asked.

"Well, like I say, I'm not even sure that we *have* found our way clear yet. I've left some loose ends dangling. I spoke to her, and she was there for me, but we have a long way to go . . . . When, that is *if*, I get through this thing, I'm going to start to open the dialog up again, to reintroduce the electricity into our relationship, the humor and the laughter."

I continued. "I suspect Jane wants to go back to work once the children are in university. I was never really aware of her personal and professional needs as you described them just now. She seemed to agree to the whole thing, probably never realizing what her decisions entailed. She's been such a great soldier in so many of my battles in life. I really just want to get back on life's path with her as soon as possible while we are both young and well."

"It sounds as if you are beginning to appreciate the distinction between the Hollywood version of 'falling in love' and the active process of deciding to love someone, regardless of the consequences," he noted.

"You know, up until we met and discussed this I would have said that my relations, particularly with my wife, were the most stressful in my life. Now I am beginning to see why."

THE EFFECT OF LIFE CHANGES ON HEALTH

I was a little confused by the term "change." "You mentioned at the beginning of our discussion, that we all must strike a balance between our abilities and the changes of life, but what changes are we talking about here, Dr Charles?" I asked.

He prefaced his reply with a quote:

> **Fortune changes like the swish of the horse's tail.**
> *Buddha*

"Just look around a little bit. The world is in a state of complete flux. As a species and a civilization, we create the change, we are the agents: it is our doing and that is fine the way it is. If we fail to adapt ourselves to the new models of the world that we ourselves have created, we will go the way of the dinosaurs. We will get sick and die."

I thought of my own "species" of the professional manager and my own life. We help to create the "fast track" that we are really no longer able to run in.

"You know these changes as well as I do," he said. "The primary risk factors that we have been talking about for the past two days, blood pressure, smoking, cholesterol and physical inactivity, only really account for about half of heart disease. There is another 50% or so that we must account for. Additional key factors are operating."

As Dr Charles spoke, I thought of several of my non-smoking colleagues who had been well known at the office for their obsessive attention to their blood pressure, cholesterol and exercise programs yet who had died suddenly from a heart attack.

"Doc, I remembered way back that you said that 'disease begins in the mind.' Is that what you mean? Is there any hard data to prove that?"

"What I meant is that in 50% of cases of coronary heart disease, and this is well-documented, there are very strong behavioral components to the traditional risk factors (cholesterol, diabetes, smoking, blood pressure, overfat) on a **worldwide** basis."

I was stunned. "You mean that my mind can increase or, rather, has been increasing my blood pressure, my cholesterol, my blood sugar and so on?"

"Very possibly. It has been shown in experiments with individuals in very stressful jobs like accountants during budget time or fighter pilots that cholesterol levels are dramatically increased over less challenged colleagues. The same, of course, is true of blood pressure.

"With regard to smoking, people don't begin to smoke or continue smoking because of some *physiologic* innate addiction, but, rather, for *psychological* reasons like peer pressure or performance anxiety. Those who quit always find it easier once they find a technique of providing for the mind the same things that smoking does, only less dangerously. Obesity, excess body fat, is, *without a doubt*, related to the nervous eating and sedentary living that comes with our separation anxiety. Even diabetes can be traced to disruptive effects of chronically elevated adrenaline and cortisone levels during uncompensated crises.

"Throughout history, stories abound of people dying suddenly in the throes of extremely strong emotions: anger, hostility, fear, grief and even joy. Look at this scale," he said as he referred me to a page in 'The Book of Solutions.' "It's called the Holmes-Rahe Scale, a tool to gauge the direct relationship between the magnitude of life changes and the effect of these changes on the health on a larger scale."

> *Throughout history, stories abound of people dying suddenly in the throes of extremely strong emotions: anger, hostility, fear, grief and even joy.*

The Holmes-Rahe Scale

Instructions

This is a Life Event Survey (LES). Please indicate which, if any, of the following stresses of life you have experienced within the last 24 months and then calculate your score.

Event	Rating
☐ Death of a spouse	100
☐ Divorce	73
☐ Marital separation	65
☐ Jail term	63
☐ Death of a close family member	63
☐ Personal illness or injury	53
☐ Getting married	50
☐ Fired at work	47
☐ Marital reconciliation	45
☐ Retirement	45
☐ Change in health of family member	44
☐ Pregnancy	40
☐ Sexual difficulties	39
☐ Gain in new family member	39
☐ Business readjustment	39
☐ Change in financial status	38
☐ Death of close friend	37
☐ Change in type of work	36
☐ Arguments with spouse	35

☐	High mortgage	31
☐	Foreclosure of a loan	30
☐	Change in responsibilities at work	29
☐	Child leaving home	29
☐	Trouble with in-laws	29
☐	Outstanding personal achievement	28
☐	Spouse begins or stops work	28
☐	Begin or end education	26
☐	Change in living conditions	25
☐	Change in personal habits	24
☐	Trouble with boss	23
☐	Change in work conditions	20
☐	Expatriation/Repatriation	20
☐	Changes in place of education	20
☐	Change in recreation	19
☐	Change in church activities	19
☐	Change in social activities	18
☐	Change in sleeping habits	16
☐	Change in number of family meetings	15
☐	Change in eating habits	15
☐	Vacation	13
☐	Minor violations of the law	11

Total: _____

Total up your LES score

Doctor Charles explained. "For those whose changes came too fast or too severe, such as that group who scored more than 300, the chance of developing an illness in the near future (within a three-month period) was about 80%, 51% in those who scored between 150 and 299, and 37% in those who scored less than 150. The severity of the illness corresponded to the score. Those diseases ranged from serious diseases like heart diseases, ulcer disease, diabetes, alcoholism, cancers, depression, suicide, and certain infections, to less life-threatening annoyances, such as the common cold and indigestion.

"When you look at this research what is the first thing about the events that you notice?" he finally asked me.

"Well, two things really. The first comment is that there is really no such thing as positive and negative experience as much as there are positive and negative perceptions of experiences. All experiences either involve **loss** or **change** of some type, but all are potential growth experiences. For example, death of a spouse is loss of a soulmate, being fired is loss of a familiar structure, a job and all that goes along with it (a steady paycheck, respectability, a self-image), sexual difficulty is the loss of an image of ourselves as virile and responsive and so on. I understand that intellectually, but on the emotional level, it's more difficult."

"Yes, very good. That's because these life events pass through the filter of our emotions and are therein amplified and exaggerated. And that strikes at the very heart of our natures. You see, as physical beings, we are an extremely acquisitive need-based species: we acquire things to create and reinforce the illusion of more security. We are conscious of our struggle for physical survival and try desperately to enhance the chances of the survivability of our genes. But, in fact, in the money chase, we lose track of our mission here on Earth until we are snapped back to attention by a loss of some kind. We are building our castles on sand. After all, loss, including death, is always going to be an inherent part of the life cycle, it gives the whole process of life meaning.

"Undoubtedly you have heard of Dr Elisabeth Kübler-Ross, who has written of the five stages of death and dying." He wrote the following list on the blackboard:

1. Denial and isolation
2. Anger
3. Bargaining
4. Depression
5. Acceptance

"We can see some or all of these stages in each of our profound losses. How quickly we go from denial to acceptance is up to our attitudes. Are we embracing change as the agent of learning or merely spending all of our time and energy preventing loss and the growth that comes with it.

"We surround ourselves with creature comforts to the point of contradicting our genetic code. We're back to that. Our bodies and minds are simply not made to be overly pampered. You know what they say: a little material success is good, a lot is dangerous. Too much material success and the maintenance thereof, can seriously distract us from our real mission in life. A little success is the most difficult thing in the world to have: we always want for more and we tend to overdo it. We then get soft, mentally or physically, and we get sick. It's as simple as that," he said. "What was the other point that you noticed?"

"The other more subtle point is a question: what happens to the groups that don't get sick, for example, the 20% in the group whose life events scored more than 300? It seems that 20% actually have found a way to thrive on the whole issue of change. There must be, in life, some factors that help to compensate these events. What do you think they are, Doc? What types of strategies, concretely speaking, are feasible for allowing ourselves to embrace change?"

"Well, I've been in practice for 25 years and working here in the library and ambulance service during semi-retirement for another six years, since my bypass. I've seen all types of people come and go. Some get the message, some don't. In a perverse kind of way, some people coming through here actually need to have a heart attack bypass and all that goes with it to realize what life can offer them. That's their wake-up call. That's one helluva dangerous wake-up call."

In a perverse kind of way, some people coming through here actually need to have a heart attack bypass and all that goes with it to realize what life can offer them.

THE CONNECTION BETWEEN CHANGE AND GROWTH

At this point I was reminded of a detail which had earlier confused me. "By the way, speaking of stress, why, during the course of our discussions and in the first several pages in your chapter on Sanity, did you never mention the term stress? Do you realize that in business life we use the term virtually every day."

He said, "It is simply one no longer suited for a discussion of human sanity in the 1990s. It was a fine term for the embryonic discussions in the 1960s, but the term really has been overworked and perpetuates misunderstandings of the real issue. For the second millennium, we should do better."

After all, how could a term that was borrowed from the testing of metals possibly apply to the human condition? His view, one that I had grown to seek over the past two days, was that the semantics of the word "stress" had actually contributed to shroud the whole issue in confusion and folklore. The result is a lot of negativity attached to change and antiquated tools for dealing with it. It had gotten to the point where people actually were beginning to follow the common advice to "avoid stressful situations," and that could mean walking away from opportunities. The point is not "What is Stress?" That's a **trap**. The point is "What is Life and where are the opportunities of learning from it?"

"People are simply allowing themselves to be ripped off," he said, "in the sense that they don't know that they are losing a precious opportunity for personal and professional growth, something that gives this crazy world real meaning, when they try to avoid something challenging. Most people, I believe, know it deep down."

Deep down, I could see that in my own life. As a professional, I had spent much of my youth jumping through hoops, getting diplomas and degrees so that I could arrive at a certain mythical "plateau," an Olympus for professionals, where life was problem-free, secure and static. Like some deposed dictator in exile, I had actually become a pampered prisoner complete with "golden handcuffs." I had to admit that as life had become more predictable and secure, it had also become a bit more boring and rather stale. Moreover, *that security was so precarious*.

"Take a look at this," he said as he drew a simple graph on the chalkboard showing the relationship between growth (personal and professional) and life changes (see overleaf).

"You see," he explained, "there is a direct linear relationship between the experiences of life and our growth. The more we are challenged, the smarter we get, the more we grow, the better equipped we become and we move on, ready for the next experience. We can see this with our children.

"Think of your most challenging and difficult experience. For me personally, the year spent as an hospital intern, away from my family, alone, working 100+ hours a week or doing a stint in a war refugee camp or working on a children's cancer ward or in an hospital for mentally handicapped people, the death of my father, whatever. I can see the direct impact of those profound experiences on my growth. Those experiences have created rooms on my soul, dimensions that

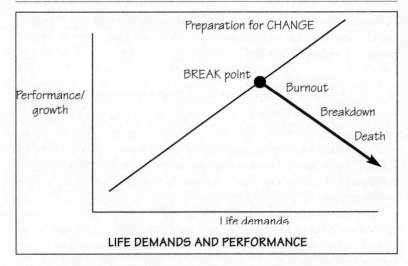

LIFE DEMANDS AND PERFORMANCE

have truly enriched my life experience. I wouldn't trade them for any other, no matter how painful they were at the time."

> **When the ego cries at what it has lost,**
> **The spirit smiles at what it has gained.**

"But how soon we forget these simple lessons. Trying to make life more *secure*, we make life more *static*. Experiences get a little more challenging as we get older, we get overwhelmed and start to move towards the 'Break point' that you see here on the graph. Our bodies and minds warn us as we approach this point, but generally we do not listen. The result for the majority of us who cannot listen to the signals is the slippery slide towards burnout, breakdown and illness, and death. For these unprepared people, changes of life go from the exciting 'spice of life' to the dreaded 'kiss of death.' This is because we are failing to follow the Natural Laws that govern the body and mind, especially when it comes to nutrition, sleep, thought control and exercise. These are the aspects that would better prepare us for change.

"Only a small percentage are really thriving on these life changes," he said as he pointed to the continuation of the line climbing up. "They are ready for change and prepare for it. For them, the changes of life are the 'spice of life.' These people are the ultimate survivors and they are smiling through every experience, thankful for the lessons. These people know that you cannot make good porcelain without a hot fire."

> **Expect the unexpected and your expectations will be realized**

It was true, as much as I found some resistance inside of me to some of these ideas (because they meant that I would have to work on myself), I could hear the voice inside of me acknowledging the common sense of it all.

"In the end, after all," said Dr Charles, "in exchange for the pain caused us by certain crises, comes valuable lessons. The Chinese, whose culture has thrived on change, have a character for the concept of CRISIS.

Within this character are two separate, though intertwined characters for (1) danger and (2) hidden opportunity. That's the mindset to work towards. Obviously, it's a good idea to recognize the inherent danger in change and to protect yourself from the imminent and real dangers (as opposed to the imagined sort) while keeping a keen eye on whatever hidden opportunity might be within."

> **Do not fear the winds of adversity.**
> **A kite rises against the wind, rather than with it.**

"Basically, to stay 'steep on the growth curve' that we just looked at, two types of engineering are necessary: mental engineering and physical engineering. Control of the mind must come first because the mind controls the body, as we've seen and it is in the mind where the balance between heart and head happens."

During the next five minutes or so, Dr Charles and I discussed together how we may be working with antiquated role models and reward systems. Values and paradigms that were working for our fathers are not necessarily valid for us any longer.

"In my father's day (he was a lawyer)," he said, "a university education was enough to guarantee success; that is, physical and emotional survival. Nowadays, an unemployed PhD or medical doctor is by no means unheard of. Schools, that are presently teaching some of the next century's leaders, can teach the basic mechanics of life – business, physics, medicine – but not how to develop self-trust and creativity that will help us to improvise as the needs arise."

We proceeded to make a list of elements that could help make a difference in our worldview. Under the heading of "Mental engineering," he wrote one word:

Courage

"Thoreau wrote once that we live out our lives 'in quiet desperation,' a life of smothered hopes. Turning that sad situation around starts with this Catch-22: the successful resolution to a tough, fearful situation involves courage (that 'can do' attitude), a bit of a psychological leap of faith, and a little discipline. Of course, if you had the courage lacking, it would not be a desperate situation. But simply muttering to yourself, 'I am going to be courageous,' will not work. Courage is based on trust. You *must* be able to trust that your resources and allies are in place. We always come back to our ability to trust, at *all* levels.

"The first step of all, to *dare to dare*, is a real leap of faith that requires a trust in the madness or grand design of the world, trust in others (otherwise delegation of tasks is impossible), confidence in our personal (physical, psychological and spiritual) abilities to rise to whatever occasion and so on. Also, a little self-discipline is required to help us live in accordance with the Laws of Nature which guide us all to the internal knowledge within ourselves. Discipline provides the self-confidence and lucidity to jump into whatever action the circumstances demand."

Dr Charles continued, "In the words of a great thinker, 'Had ye but faith, ye could move mountains.' Because if you cannot muster the courage to participate in your own evolution, there's not really much sense in talking about the rest of it all. After all, if we are not going to change here," he said, pointing to his head, "we really do not have the right to expect that things will change *here*," as he placed his hand over his heart.

"You must *want* to evolve in a new way and then go for it. That's very hard because we are all deeply attached to our need systems, however reactive and antiquated, it's *ours* right or wrong. The first

> *You must* **want** *to evolve in a new way and then go for it.*

step is to give up the natural tendency in all of us of wanting to win popularity contests, of gaining approval, of getting affection.

"But often, if we allow it to happen, feeling stuck with our need system, we are led blindly by our desires, senses, and passions to the point of constant restlessness. Next, trouble follows and we start to feel impotent and alienated. Then we make the fatal mistake of losing trust. Without trust, in our abilities, our minds, our bodies, our spouses, our God, we have no hope of sanity in this world. Without trust, panic is the *only* option. Therein lies some real hope. Paradoxically, when life becomes too complicated and the resultant desperation becomes severe enough, it can provide the impetus and motivation for going from mere physical survival to personal psychological and spiritual evolution, like the phoenix rising from the ashes." He glimpsed at his watch.

"Oh my! I am late for mid-morning teaching rounds on the Medicine Floor. And your 'procedure' is at 3 p.m.," he said as he started for the door. He had a way of nimbly going from one state of mind to another.

"I'll tell you what: look over the rest of the Sanity chapter and we'll take this up a little later. Could you keep an eye on the library for me, answer any questions that other patients may have. You know: 'see one, do one, teach one.' The keys are behind the desk and lock up if you leave. Thanks a lot." And he was off, leaving me in the quiet of the reading room with the manual. The section we had been discussing finished with an invitation to learn the fine art of daring:

> Two roads diverged in a wood and I –
> I took the one less travelled by
> And that has made all the difference.
> **Robert Frost:** *The Road Not Taken*

The idea that one could worry effectively intrigued me. Smiling inwardly, I sighed deeply, as though allowing the soothing lessons to seep in like spring rains and flipped the page to read on.

II. PREPARE YOURSELF FOR CHANGE: ART OF EFFECTIVE WORRYING

Many of us set concrete objectives for our business life, market share, profit margins and so on. Perhaps, as a concrete personal objective, now is as good a time as ever for learning calm management of your mind through the art of effective worrying.

Let's face it: as long as we are human beings, as long as bosses, peers and children exist, it will be our destiny to worry. The only question remaining is, will we do so effectively, with an eye to actually solving the *real* problems of life or will we spend sleepless nights in a cold sweat, fretting over *imaginary* ones? Nothing is ever solved by emotional hand-wringing. Most problems in life that cause us worry end up on the floor of the editing room of life.

But what is effective worrying? How would I recognize it? By checking the signs and symptoms, you will be able to answer for yourself: Where do you spend most of your "worry time"? (see below).

	Effective worrying	Fretting	Panic
Subjective feelings	Satisfaction	Constant anxiety, rushed	Extreme anxiety/depression
Objective symptoms and signs	None	high blood pressure ... sweaty hands ...	Heart attacks, strokes ... Chest pains, blackouts ...

I spend most of my "worry time" _____

To worry effectively then, first of all, do so at *your* rhythm, don't be rushed! Effective worrying is an active natural process of methodically sculpting irritating situations into real growth experiences. It, therefore, involves the anticipation of and preparation for problems, that we realistically know are part of the territory of life. It should even be a happy experience: a chance to actually learn something about life if you can allow it, without wasting time on fretting.

The following strategies are tried and true and they will help to stave off the common little neuroses that plague daily life. Things like general insecurity, inferiority complexes, mild bouts of depression that waste the precious little time we have with our loved ones. These strategies also provide friends, colleagues and family with a sorely needed role model for sanity in the "fast track."

III. FIVE EFFECTIVE STRATEGIES FOR STAYING SANE AND MINIMIZING REGRET

Strategy # 1:
Know and simplify your real needs in life

The Truth waits for eyes unclouded by longing.

While traveling, away from the family and all things familiar, sit on the edge of your bed one night and ask yourself what you really need in life. Make a real list. Where, on Maslow's Hierarchy of Needs, do you spend most of your time? You may find a little voice inside of you saying, "Yes, well, I may not really need it, but I want it to make life more interesting, fun , livable, whatever." That's OK, too. For the sake of discussion, let's group all wants, desires, whims, under the rubric "Needs," wherever they fit into Maslow's Hierarchy.

Then (and this is the hard part), decide whether you are satisfying those needs at the expense of your sanity, your health (that's a paradox!), or the wellbeing of someone else. Don't wait for the signals that you are missing before you respond. Material happiness is found somewhere in that tension between uncertainty and complete satisfaction.

> **To be without some of the things you want is an indispensable part of happiness.** *Bertrand Russell*

Some solutions

1. *Appreciate what you have by "going without" for a while:* if you have doubts about what you really need, set up a time when you can arrange to do without satisfying that need. Take coffee, shopping, tobacco, drugs or sex for example. Just observe your reaction to an

electricity blackout after a storm. Without the conveniences of the music, the lights, the heating, the cooking, how do you react?

2. *Simplify your life:* it's not difficult to see why our culture has been struggling to survive in recent decades: we are all too wrapped up in the more basic needs of material survival and too little occupied in the needs of the soul. Our supermarkets and malls have become a metaphor for our modern existence: they have become dehumanized and are hygienically plasticated and sterile. We don't get dirty any more. We've exchanged, on the material level, the problems of too little for the entrapments of too much. At least with the problems of too little, we rushed into the company of others and made music. With too much, we protect our wealth by pushing others away.

Take a free weekend or better, a week (steal one, if necessary!) and go on a retreat in the forest, in the mountains or near the sea. Practice silence. Learn to meditate, to pray or talk to yourself again. Rediscover the simple pleasures of cooking with the family.

Learn to live like your ancestors without the modern conveniences of electricity, washing machines, hairdryers, electric this and that. Light some candles and a fire in the fireplace. Read Thoreau Walden or the Bible or any literature that will refresh you spiritually.

> It is easier for a camel to go through the eye of a needle, than for a rich man to enter into the kingdom of God.   *Matthew 19:24*

Strategy # 2:
Face the facts and then, get into action!

When problems arise, spend the first five minutes gathering all the facts of the matter. Then, ask "What can be done?" or try to get the resolution of the affair under way; then go on to something else. Never worry for more than 15 minutes about an affair of money, fame, power, pride or other earthly trivialities

"There are no problems, just opportunities." That should be your mantra. In most situations, however, when confronted by life events, we lose our cool heads, panic and get emotional, "Whose fault is this, anyway?" Approaching the problem that way limits and hides what may well be obvious solutions. Instead, get the facts of the matter, whatever they might be, in a cold-blooded fashion and start to work with them.

Write them down as you see them and then as the other "players" might see them and analyze them. Absolutely reject any tendency in your mind to arrive at any conclusion on the basis of conjecture. Stop torturing yourself by second guessing! Surrender yourself to reality. Fatalists will throw their arms in the air, waiting passively for God to deliver them, but God will help initially through prayer only as a sounding board for the sincere person who wants to help himself.

A lesson from the medical front: fortunately, long before a surgeon opens someone's abdomen or chest or cranium, he has gathered, in a calm fashion, all the facts on that patient (past medical history, medication use, allergies and so on) and would never allow supposition or guesswork to play a role. Do likewise! Emotions and ego aside, cold-bloodedly collect the data.

After careful and complete study of the circumstances, if you can do nothing further about the situation for the moment, let the cards play themselves out. Detach yourself. A little benign fatalism goes a long way: relax, go out for dinner with your spouse, have a nice bottle of red wine and go to a funny movie or show, have a nice massage. After all, you will sleep well knowing that the record will show that you have done your level best. The tempest will pass. Happy moments are precious: savour them instead of putting them off.

Strategy # 3:
Learn to trust the "others" in your life

> Water, water, everywhere, nor any drop to drink.
> Coleridge, *The Ancient Mariner II*

Our industrialized societies have a tendency to increase our feelings of solitude by materially rewarding the time-urgent and aggressive behaviour pattern. After all, it's a "dog-eat-dog world, son. You gotta be a bastard to get ahead in this game." But, in fact, no one is really a winner because the overall effect of this behavior is to de-ritualize life, making us automated robots, caught in a tense and unpredictable lockstep of mistrust.

Unfortunately, instead of developing a "conspiracy" or team with our immediate families, many people will go well outside their immediate "tribes" to where trust is impossible and problematic. The health risks are too great to be playing this game of Russian roulette, both physical (in terms of bringing some infectious disease back into the fold) or psychological (running the risk of losing the most precious commodity in your life: trust).

You may feel alone, but you are *not!* You have developed conspiracies in love and honesty with your God, with your spouse, with yourself. These people are the flints for the fire of truth. Occasionally going for a walk, while actually conversing with and soliciting advice from the great thinkers: Shakespeare, Krishnamurti, Goethe, Emerson, Thoreau, is great solace for the alienated soul. When that type of secular prayer fails, try the real thing. Either way, our destiny is to return to this Universal trust.

In our everyday life, we must stop separating, classifying and imposing judgment on people on the basis of *differences*. Love and allow yourself to be loved. When feeling "blue," avoid solitude as it will only succeed in making you anxious; come back into the network. Connect with someone: colleagues, friends, family, acquaintances, your Creator, as often as possible, even continually. Start on your next business trip to overcome that false timidity and self-doubt and initiate conversation with those right next to you to decrease that feeling of separateness.

Some solutions for learning to trust others in your life

Learn to listen

People are all around you. Share your experiences and listen to theirs. No matter how hard it is to restrain from commenting on everything, give them the greatest gift any human can give to another: an open heart, a listening mind, and a listening heart. Next time you meet someone again, connect your inner soul with theirs: look into their eyes as if to ask: "How are you doing in there? How does life look from your angle?"

Do not miss the precious opportunity of learning to listen carefully to others, without prepared answers. Don't think, don't act, don't suggest, just listen to the present moment shared with a fellow traveler. That's the best thing you can do for someone. Don't forget: only when you listen can you increase your knowledge base. Speaking only tests your new theories.

> *You have two ears and one mouth so that you listen twice as much as you speak.*

This is *especially* true of children and adolescents. In every situation with children, there will be a certain amount of real worrying that must be done to arrive at a solution. If we, as parents, are too quick to assume an inordinately large percentage of that worrying, the child automatically "under-worries" for himself. The only result will be a child who has been emotionally handicapped in terms of solving the challenges the world has sent him or her.

Therefore, as worrying for them short-cuts the learning process, simply provide a watchful eye and a friendly sounding board. That's usually all the "safety net" they want or need. Inspire self-confidence by allowing them to fight their own smaller battles now, in preparation for the bigger ones later.

This is perfectly evident in adolescent jargon. When you hear language like, "get a life," "chill out, Dad," "Mom, give me a break", "get out of my life" or any of the standard litany of adolescent verbal thrashing abouts, it generally is a signal to let *them* do some of the driving in their affairs. Properly deciphered, what they are trying to say is, "Trust me, Dad."

Happily, accepting these calls to trust only increases our credibility and accessibility for even more crucial times ahead. Sadly, evidence abounds that we, as parents, rarely have the generous confidence to accept such an invitation. In many instances, it will be the *last* time we are invited to trust them.

Avoid the folly of scapegoating

Waving your fist at your loved ones or at God serves only to show how desperately out of touch and insecure you are. An understandable psychological reflex that we all fall victim to is to point the finger when something goes wrong. The adolescent in us all comes out: how many times in an argument do we hear, "yeah, but *you* did this, *you* said that . . ." and so on. It must be *someone's* fault. Why do we need to ascribe fault every time something goes wrong? Because it takes the pressure off us to do some work on *ourselves*.

Beware of pointing a finger at someone, because when you do three fingers point back at you.

To err is human, it is part of the human condition. After all, life is falling down six times and getting up seven. Many of us are not afraid of erring, but we are deathly afraid of the loss of face that often comes with such human frailty. Then when our error is discovered, lies and cover-up, guilt and shame ensue and we weave a very tangled web of misrepresentations of the truth, all the time missing a unique opportunity to set up LIFE as a no-fault proposition.

Practice the art of skillful self-effacement

People want "justice" when something goes wrong. Get there first. When you proactively get to the source of the problem first – "Oh, I made a mistake. Sorry about that. Let's fix that up . . ." – you completely disarm the mob instinct for justice. Defuse a potentially explosive situation through calm, deliberate, analysis. Analyze the situation carefully and when the analysis shows that you may well have had a hand in the problem, admit it

Let's face it: when you make a mistake, your whole world (at work, at home, colleagues, spouses, children) is watching you to see how you deal with it. It's really *your* call. Cover it up and lie about it, you are labeled a coward and a liar. Do it right, you are a hero and children need that type of hero to counterbalance the false hero stuff that Hollywood inculcates them with.

One of the great benefits of this approach of recognizing your mistakes first is that people around you are impressed by the confidence that you exude and will actually start to emulate this self-confidence. In effect, by saying "I'm human and I made a mistake that I am not proud of, but not ashamed of either," you are not forced to eat humble pie, as it is you writing the menu.

Understanding intimacy

This is a tall order, because it means letting go. For some of us, the separation from our real family of man has gone so far that the only channels of intimacy left to us are sex and drugs, or alcohol. This is best seen in one of the commonest settings for loneliness: the "singles bar." Although construed and advertised as a way to engender intimacy, the noise, smoke and alcohol-induced falseness of these places leaves you with an even greater feeling of loneliness and frustration than before you entered.

Over the years, we have cut ourselves off from those activities that make us part of the larger human collectivity in the first place. There should not be any anxiety in physical love, just the joy of allowing your borders to melt together with those of another.

Beware of the power play in sexuality. Power-playing in sexual relations only serves to profane one of the most beautiful of human experiences. Unfortunately, in the goal-oriented West, the achievement of the male orgasm, at any cost, is usually the prime objective of the act of love-making.

What we learn from Oriental medicine is to prolong the male orgasm as long as possible, even deferring it to the next session of intimacy. Ideally, as we get older, if we want to preserve our energy and go easy on the prostate gland, men should experience ejaculation with less and less frequency, say, an average of two or three times per month. The experience is more intense and memorable and we conserve our sexual energy, making ourselves more sexually potent. When we speak of restricting something, we are speaking of ejaculation, not love-making! Love-making should take place as often as is feasible.

The reason why many of us feel isolated is that we are using physical intimacy in a power play to temporarily chase away our sensation of loneliness. Nothing is free and certainly when feelings are involved. In this power play where one party dominates another, someone pays in emotional terms, though in the heat of the moment you may not appreciate that fact. The sad result is that both parties are even more isolated and disconnected than before, accompanied by confusion and betrayal: an opportunity to rekindle trust is lost.

As in every aspect of life, if we manage to lose ourselves through sexual intimacy at the expense of someone else's isolation, we blemish the special nature of the experience: the *post-coital blues*. Many of us are so sad after love-making: after an intergalactic orgasm, we shrink our consciousness back to within the confines of our skin, all alone, again. By power-playing our partners, we are setting ourselves up for depression because the power play only succeeds in reinforcing the illusion of our (now aggrandized) self.

It's about forgetting yourself and your separateness and then coming "down" again into separate bodies. What better time to inject humour! After the climax, reach out and "get high" again on humor: laugh at your silly anxiety, laugh at your silly investment in isolation, get out a chilled bottle of champagne and some flowers (everyone loves surprises!) and keep the intimacy going, tell jokes about yourself. Laugh in your mind about how difficult it is to let go of the power play game of sex. Laugh together at the excessive seriousness that we attach to the human condition.

Transforming judgment to appreciation

Unless you change and become like little children you will never enter the kingdom of heaven.

Matthew 18:3

Liberate yourself from the *Angry Parent–Naughty Child Syndrome*. We are blessed (some might say cursed) with a mind that has as one of its central aspects, the tendency to see the dichotomy in everything: pain vs pleasure, black vs white, good vs bad, accepting and rejecting, fear vs joy and so on.

It was not always this way. We start out all right as children with a mind that just sees things as they are: amoral. There is no right or wrong until the "age of reason" (colloquially placed at seven years of age). What happens then?

That charming, fearless, carefree, knee-scraping, rough-and-tumble, risk-taking, amoral, child gets his or her first exposure to adult life, complete with a foreign (often competitive and hostile) value and reward system. Life goes from being present moment-oriented, soft and light, to being heavy and calculated, future-oriented. As the child is made aware of who the bad guys are, "the value of a dollar" and that "time is money," he learns to take fewer risks, becomes more conditioned, less spontaneous, fears all bad outcomes, hopes and works hard to strong-arm reality. In short, the child in all of us has been smothered and "grows up."

The child accomplishes this by incorporating everything his authority figures (parents, teachers, nannies) represent to him. This is very useful to his survival as now he doesn't need to have Daddy around to tell him not to touch the hot stove, not to stay out too late, not to drink too much alcohol and so on. In the process, there is also the risk of a negative side: the Angry Parent–Naughty Child Syndrome.

The major downside to this way of thinking is that when the child develops his or her own "mind talk," it is complete with a new inherited set of ideas of self-deprecation, worthlessness, lack of compassion and humorlessness. Life becomes hard. Imagine now with Daddy's (angry?) voice in his mind, a pendulum starts swinging between the *naughty boy* and the *angry Daddy*. This is the origin, I would argue, of the classic swinging pendulum between natural present-oriented spontaneity (the child) and future-oriented regret and guilt (the angry father).

I can imagine that some day we will regard our children not as creatures to manipulate or change but rather as messengers from a world we once deeply knew, but since we have long since forgotten, who can reveal to us more about the true secrets of life, than our parents were ever able to. *Alice Miller*

You can actually recognize this syndrome in everyday life all around you: at work and at home. After all, where do you think all those negative emotions come from in the first place? You are not born with them. Next time you are around some people, listen to how they play golf or tennis or cope with being stuck in traffic: "You fool!" You idiot!" I can't believe that you can be so stupid?" And this mindtalk, handicapping and disempowering, is the legacy we leave our children! Listen to the way children play, among themselves and alone.

The average adult then wrestles with this dichotomy all his adult life, swinging back and forth between the poles until these two "selves" can live harmoniously together. Often this schism is so taxing and painful that one half must "kill" (emotionally) the other to survive!

We see everyday phenomena as either "good" or "bad" for us through the *emotional* prisms or eyeglasses focussed on what our agenda is that day or that year. We are overjoyed by things going "our way" and dejected when things "go wrong:" Oscillating between euphoric mania and lachrymose depression, we allow ourselves to be buffeted around like puppets, victims of a capricious Universe. We totter precariously on the edge of insanity. Looking at more primitive societies, one could deduce that insanity (loosely defined as the state of being "out of touch with reality") is the product of civilization's preoccupation with worrying.

Start the healing by being gentle with your children. They are only in our trusteeship. Kahlil Gibran expressed this eloquently:

> **Your children are not your children. They are the sons and daughters of Life's longing for itself. They come through you but not from you . . . You may give them your love but not your thoughts, for they have their own thoughts . . . You may strive to be like them, but seek not to make them like you. For life goes not backwards nor tarries with yesterday.**
>
> **You are the bows from which your children as living arrows are sent forth. The Archer sees the mark upon the path of the infinite, and He bends you with His might that His arrows may go swift and far.**

Then, for ourselves, as parents, we must lighten up a bit. Try as you may, children are going to follow their own destiny. Therefore, love and feed them and watch them fly!

Try to avoid harmfully judgmental mind talk by easing up a bit. Laugh at things. Open up your heart. Live according to principles of fairness and dignity: "There but by the Grace of God go I." Free yourself of that destructive dichotomy. Give up acting the role of parent: just be a friend. Give up always being perfect and right and profitable for others. Once in a while, drop the mask. Be gentle and compassionate with yourself. Do the best you can and then let go of it.

Strategy # 4:
Learn to trust the grand design of life

Love life for its inconvenient chaos, its horrific beauty, its opportunity for self-discovery. There are no chance occurrences. We are all acting through, as best and sincerely as we are able, a role that has been written for us, as though actors in a great play. The only challenge is to do so with dignity. Do not fall into the intellectual trap of trying to PROVE the existence of a Grand Design to life. For personal transformation you only need to entertain the possibility of one.

Remember: life is the real career. Quick! Before going on, answer the following query, without reflecting too much: "*Are you winning in the game of life?*"

Some solutions for learning to trust the grand design of life

Learn to go with the "flow"

One of the biggest challenges for smart Type A people (who are very competitive) is to find out what experiences require an **active** "jump-in-with-both-feet approach" and what experiences require a **passive** "let-it-be" approach. The vital importance of not trying to overcontrol, of not straining, is illustrated in the physiology of your own body:

Natural bodily functions	Straining or excess control yields . . .
1. Eating	Indigestion, constipation, obesity
2. Defecation	Hemorrhoids, bleeding
3. Urination	Pain, burning
4. Childbirth	Severe complications, unnecessary pain
5. Sexual expression	Impotence, frigidity, isolation
6. Sleeping	Insomnia, chronic fatigue

Learning to go "with the flow" or "roll with the punches" would also enable us to gradually shift from the status of a victim of circumstance (here the attitude is judgmental) to the more open state of mere appreciation of life's mad methods; all the time keeping our sense of humour and confidence intact to live another day. Save your "big guns" for the really important issues. Practice serenity, it will come in handy some day.

Embrace and welcome every experience *as it is*. Then, determine your role, if any, in it. Quiet the automated activities and neurotic chatting of your mind through meditation, listen to the internal voice to find the clear path. Have confidence in this voice and be unafraid to deal with the lessons that the consequences have. Clinging to something or someone after the appropriate time has passed only creates terrible emotional suffering.

> He who binds to him a Joy,
> Doth that wingèd life Destroy.
> But he who kisses that Joy as it flies,
> Lives in Eternity's Sunrise.
> *William Blake*

Then, refuse to move on to the next experience without having extracted every bit of wisdom offered; it is there for the taking. The difference between wise living and foolish living lies therein. Do the best you can and then let go of it. Having done that, our role is complete and real understanding and wisdom can then seep in slowly. Remember, we all have different "loads" in life.

Realize that time is not the enemy

> As if you could kill time without injuring Eternity.
> *Henry David Thoreau*

Most of us waste our time off work by fretting about going back to work and then spend our time at work yearning for leisure time. We, therefore, lose the lessons served up to us by life experiences in the present and then wonder why life is passing us by. That's precious time foolishly spent.

> To everything there is a season, and a time to every purpose under
>   heaven:
> A time to be born, a time to die; a time to plant, and a time to
>   pluck up that which is planted;
> A time to kill, and a time to heal; a time to break down, and a time
>   to build up;

> A time to weep, and a time to laugh; a time to mourn and a time to dance;
> A time to cast away stones, and a time to gather stones together;
> A time to embrace, and a time to refrain from embracing;
> A time to get, and a time to lose; a time to keep, and a time to cast away;
> A time to rend, and a time to sew; a time to keep silence, and a time to speak;
> A time to love, and a time to hate; a time to war, and a time of peace.
>
> *Ecclesiastes 3:1-8, The Old Testament*

Are we spending our time well? Couldn't we be cramming even a little more into the time we have? Isn't there yet another ingenious way to cut finer and finer slivers of time? Are we unhappy when we cannot rush through things?

In case you have forgotten, things **do** actually take time to do properly. Some things can simply not be rushed; they have their own rhythm. Just go out into your garden and study it carefully. Nature will not be hurried into making roses bud or making the sky clear of clouds. Nature will, rather, make you synchronize yourself to her rhythm. The only way to know that rhythm is to study Nature (*people* are part of Nature) and realize that everybody has their own rhythm.

We go to great unnecessary lengths to become wise. What we do not always realize is that *all* the wisdom you will ever need to understand the life experience is within you already, just waiting to be discovered. By quieting the noise or internal chatter of the mind, through, say, regular meditation and prayer, the mind's eye can see clearly.

As we all have experienced, there is a sort of time lag between an actual life experience and wisdom. Do this mental exercise:

When some type of change or loss happens to you, how long is the time lag until you see the lesson within the experience (i.e. wisdom)?

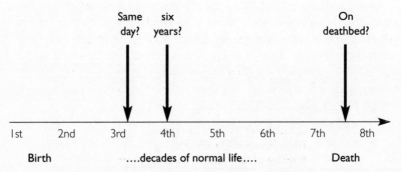

Shortening the time lag to wisdom

This lag, which for some can be several decades, is strictly a function of our **attitude**. Eventually, we all "get the lesson" of every experience, sometimes six months later, sometimes six decades later. Nearly everybody is full of wisdom on their deathbed, but can experience that same consciousness prior to that.

The key to a regret-free life is to become wise as early as possible by milking every experience for a lesson. When you make learning about life the career, all time becomes "your time."

IF I HAD MY LIFE TO LIVE OVER . . .

I'd like to make more mistakes next time. I'd relax. I would limber up. I'd be sillier than I have been on this trip. I would take fewer things seriously. I would take more chances. I would climb more mountains and swim more rivers. I would eat more ice cream and eat less beans. I would perhaps have more actual troubles, but I'd have fewer imaginary ones.

You see, I'm one of those people who live sensibly and sanely hour after hour, day after day. Oh, I've had my moments, and if I had it to do over again, I'd have more of them. In fact, I'd try to have nothing else. Just moments, one after another, instead of living so many years ahead of each day. I've been one of those persons who never goes anywhere without a thermometer, a hot water bottle, a raincoat, and a parachute. If I had to do it again, I would travel lighter than I have.

If I had my life to live over, I would start barefoot earlier in the spring and stay that way later in the fall. I would go to more dances. I would ride more merry-go-rounds. I would pick more daisies.

Nadine Stair, at 85 years of age

Discard the past: forgive and forget. After all, sour grapes make bitter wine.

As in Coleridge's timeless poem, *The Rhyme of the Ancient Mariner*, many of us have committed, in our youth and old age, careless transgressions against our enemies, our friends and our children. The crime hangs heavy around our neck and the waters and winds are so still that our "ship" is paralyzed. Only by looking within and finding the strength to forgive others are our own transgressions forgiven. Upon receiving the gift of forgiveness, our sails fill once more:

> O happy living things! No tongue
> Their beauty might declare;
> A spring of love gushed from my heart
> And I blessed them unaware;

The albatross of guilt

Sure my saint took pity on me
And I blessed them unaware.

The selfsame moment I could pray,
And from my neck so free
The Albatross slid off, and sank
Like lead into the sea.

In short, have a soul and a mind that are nimble enough to move on to the next moment without carrying a residue (a grudge) from the previous experience that will colour the present situation.

Two holy monks, one aged and one a novice, came to the edge of a river in their meandering. There they found a beautiful young girl stranded on the river bank, unable to proceed across the river. After a whispered discussion with the young girl, the older monk picked up the girl and carried her to the opposite bank of the river, where he placed her, ever so gently, before signaling to the novice to move on.

After an hour of silent surprise and consternation, the novice turned to the aged monk and said "I cannot believe that you actually carried that beautiful girl across the river back there.

"Oh, that. I maybe carried her physically for a few fleeting moments and then set her down. But I can see that you are still carrying her in your mind."

What experiences are you still carrying around with you? Get rid of the excess baggage. Be big enough to forgive.

Live the present: Carpe Diem! Do not put off happy moments because there is nothing in life more precious. Watch children play and emulate their spontaneity. Shakespeare had it right again "Out of the mouth of babes and sucklings comes the Truth."

Your mind has been rushing you through everything beautiful and fun for ages: meals, picnics, love-making, hobbies, sipping fine wine, gardening, swimming, jogging. It's all been slotted into a little box.

As you get older, time becomes more precious: each moment becomes the past, wasting or killing time becomes a profanity. Always walk into every situation (even usually "passive" activities like sleeping and TV watching), determined to spend that time well, in a productive fashion.

> **Do not occupy your precious time except with the most precious of things, and the most precious of human things is the state of being occupied between past and the future.**
> *Ahmad b. 'Îsâ al-Kharrâz*

Some of the practical advantages to living 100% in the present moment are as follows:

1. **You feel lighter.** People who carry the weighty baggage of old negative feelings of the past cannot help but frown at the burden. They are saddened by the psychological residue of anger, envy and fear. Dump that weight. Learn to smile more often.

2. **You have more mental energy.** Maintaining negative feelings about the past or fanciful projections about the future takes a great deal of mental energy. The result is chronic fatigue which leaves little left for the present moment's opportunities.

3. ***Your memory and concentration improve.*** By clearing the decks of old finished business, you are alert and ready to take whatever comes your way. Imagine your mind to be a camera, your eyes the lenses and your memory the film. By holding the camera still (living the present moment), the image can be registered on the film (the memory can register the event).

Next time you are introduced to someone, stay present, don't listen to the way that *your* name is presented (classic mistake). Listen to how your new acquaintance is introduced, so that you do not have to sheepishly walk up to him or her five minutes later asking, "What was your name again?"

Plan for, then forget, the future: take care of the present and the future will take care of itself. In managing time (as though you could), remember that we cannot control the *amount* of time we have in life or in business; we can only control *how we use it*. Therefore, use your common sense, and to manage your time start by *living fully today* in the world.

Reintroduce ritual into life

When we are young, we notice all the beautiful days, later we only notice two or three per year. The present moments slip through our hands, leaving us with pale memories of the real things. Some of us are wasting our lives by allowing the rhythm of our lives to move too fast: fast foods, business lunches, pitstops along the highway. Starting in the morning, we get the pace going real fast: our mind talk urging us on and out the door, wielding the sword, *"c'mon! c'mon! c'mon! move! move! move! let's go! let's go! let's go!"* until late at night we get home, bone tired. The voice of the slave-driver continues, *"who said you could stop?! Lots of things still to do, can't stop, go! go! go!"* Faster and faster and faster. Sadly, some of us have even outrun the fun of running.

Solutions for controlling your perception of time should be centered around **rituals**. Reintroduce the time-honored rituals that have gone from our lives: night-time bed stories, breakfast in bed on Sunday mornings, family hobbies and sports, prayer or silence before meals, once a week concerts or plays in the city. Start by trying to do something in *slow motion* every day to slow the lockstep juggernaut down: meditate, smell the flowers, notice a painting, read a story, write a poem. When the phone rings, take a deep breath and pick it up on the second or third ring.

Strategy # 5:
Learn to trust *yourself*

Upgrade your attitude

Start with the way you think and view life. You must understand one essential fact: our life is *not* as it really is, but how we *perceive* it. White light passing through a red filter appears red. Most people on the street would swear on the heads of their children that the sky is really blue, but just ask any astronaut what color the sky really is. Our senses are best handled with a healthy dose of mistrust.

Generally speaking, if our attitude is upbeat and positive (growth-oriented), every experience is met by calm poise and reflection: "aaah, yes, that's interesting." If our attitudes are negative, "why me?," the experience provokes irrational fretting and loss of confidence. It is ALL in the attitude. Life does, in fact, whether we recognize it or not, have a Grand Design to it, there can be no real hazards. Therefore, if we are rightfully selfish enough to place a premium on our own emotional and spiritual growth, we can greet *all* experiences with the question: "What's the lesson here for me?" Otherwise, we sit fretting, unable to direct our minds, waiting to be crushed by events.

IF

If you can dream – and not make dreams your master;
If you can think – and not make thoughts your aim;
If you can meet Triumph and Disaster
And treat those two impostors just the same;
If you can bear to hear the truth you've spoken
Twisted by knaves to make traps for fools . . .
If you can keep your head when all about you
Are losing theirs and blaming it on you . . . .
Yours is the Earth and everything that's in it.

Rudyard Kipling

Therefore, survey your own experiences. When you are confronted with change or loss, are you:

Positive and expansive	*or*	Cynical and close hearted
Rational: "get the facts"	*or*	Emotional and fretting
A learner: "what's the lesson here"	*or*	A loser: "why me?"
Adventuresome/Resilient	*or*	Stiff and spoiled by civilization

A meditator	*or*	Frantic, panicky
Self-effacing, big-hearted	*or*	Scapegoater, finger pointer
Self-reliant	*or*	Overly dependent
Living in present	*or*	Living in past/future
A warrior	*or*	A worrier

Refuse to indulge in the tendency of negative thinking: it's a luxury that you cannot afford. Life is rarely *all* bad news. Look to the good news that is embellished in the bad news. Nothing is *ever* all bad. Defoe's humble hero, Robinson Crusoe, in a chapter appropriately entitled "Salvage from the Wreck," coolly analyzes the situation:

> *Bad news:* I am washed ashore a desert island, alone.
> *Good news:* I am alive, full-limbed, while the rest of the crew were drowned.
> *Bad news:* I suffered a dreadful deliverance: no clothes, no food.
> *Good news:* This is a tropical island. The ship's reserves are still accessible.
> *Bad news:* There is no fresh water.
> *Good news:* I, to my great delight, found fresh water.
> *Bad news:* I am without weapon against hostile creatures.
> *Good news:* I was able to fashion a small stick into a knife.

And we all know how that story played itself out. By simply controlling a negative mind, Crusoe put together a simple life that stressed the positive aspects. Jealously protect your self-confidence. One effective way is to get to know and love yourself for what you are.

Take a moment here and write your own obituary:

Here lies _____

_____

_____

_____

Avoid activities that increase the illusion of your own loneliness

The more you perceive yourself as some satellite adrift in a cold, hostile, world, the more your activities will reflect that paranoia of your fellow humans. Instead of viewing them as fellow wayfarers, you may be perceiving them as threats to your need systems.

Therefore, watch very carefully the self-references when you think and speak. It has been demonstrated that people who are constantly referring to their own melodramas (me, me, me), have a higher incidence of heart diseases, probably due to the isolated mindset. A good first step is to drop the self-righteous act. In the final analysis, it's only your mind, in its inability to give up the addiction to always "being right," that "has done you wrong."

Do an experiment: in the course of a normal working day, count how many times you use the self-references: "I," "me," or "mine." Do the same thing on a day off. Think of yourself as a member of the collective family of man. Replace "why me?" with "how can I help?" Watch your daily activity: in your humor, are you making people laugh at the expense of someone else? Their gender, their race, their speech patterns? That's isolating you and you will pay eventually for that with anxiety and sorrow. What goes around, comes around.

Walk down the street of a crowded city and see yourself as just another drop of water in a large ocean of humanity. Are two drops of water that different really?

In the normal course of human activities, we have all had experiences when we forget our separateness and self-consciousness, melting in with the surroundings. Below are some activities which help you to "lose yourself." The only rule is to never make other people feel worse as a result of your feeling better. A (+) next to the activity means overall activities which are beneficial to the harmonization of the soul, mind, and body, while a (−) signifies a possible downside or negative side effect, such as addiction, a health problem or merely increasing other people's isolation.

1. Sexual intimacy (+)	* 7. Humour (+)
2. Drinking alcohol (+/−)	* 8. Prayer (+)
3. Drug use (−)	* 9. Chanting (+)
4. Downhill skiing (+)	*10. Reading, writing (+)
*5. Meditation (+)	*11. Singing, dancing (+)
6. Tobacco use (−)	*12. Go for a walk (+)

and the list goes on.

The techniques marked with a * are *perfectly* safe: you can always go back into the "golden prison" of the self.

> Write your favorite way to "lose yourself"
>
> _____
>
> _____

Control destructive mind talk through meditation

How to control negative emotions and destructive thinking? First, worry cold bloodedly, free of emotional overlay. Be philosophical about the whole affair. If you are saddened by it or angered by it, the result will be emotional hand-wringing. Put it off until you have had a good run in the park or at the gym. You'll be better suited for it. But how to control negative thoughts when they lay siege to our minds?

Try this quick experiment. Sit quietly in a comfortable position, feet flat, gently close your eyes and concentrate your attention on the wave-like action of your breathing: in and out, in and out and so on (yes, *this* is meditation). The mind's attention will drift to juicier thoughts which may be more pressing: what you need to do, what happened to you that day, and so on. Don't react violently to your mind's drifting: be gentle and firm, as a good parent to an errant son.

Soon you will hear a voice coming from within: this is your **mind talk**. Now identify the *tone* of your mind talk: is it cynical, is it angry, is it inquisitive, is it some "I-told-you-so" soothsayer, is it sarcastic, is it guilt-ridden, vengeful? Just identify the tone for now. That will be enough to start.

Recognition of a "negative" mindset is the first step to learning to develop a trustful mind. Don't react to whatever you have identified, just recognize. If you listen to the voice of doubt and fear, you are lost.

Some solutions for developing a trustful mind

Do this through three powerful and time-honored relaxation techniques:

1. Meditation
2. Deep breathing
3. Progressive muscular relaxation.

MEDITATION

First of all, what is meditation? Forget everything you have heard about it. Meditation is an effective and *portable* tool that will help you take control of the stressful lifestyle of today's managers. It is a simple way to find out what aspects of your personality are keeping you from developing your full potential. As such, meditation is a wonderful way to help liberate yourself from the prison of time.

Moreover, in order to keep our sanity in our lives and balance between work and home, it is vital to be able to detach ourselves from our environments and rediscover, through meditation, the privacy and the peace of our own *self*. Anybody can "get it all together" while vacationing with family or friends for three weeks at the beach or in the mountains: that's no challenge. Can you keep it all together amidst the hustle and bustle of everyday life, complete with deadlines, marital strain, difficult children and the rest? It is the ability to bring to bear, in ANY situation,

> *Meditation is a way to distinguish real problems from imaginary problems.*

a calm control of emotions, when all around you is going to hell, that is at stake here. It is finding, nimbly and quickly, your "eye of the hurricane." So, in summary:

Meditation *is*:
1. Thought control: being present to the moment.
2. Freedom from, thus, control of thoughts.
3. Regaining control of emotions.
4. A means *and* an end.
5. Awareness of your place in the world.

Meditation *is not*:
1. A state of sleep, stupor or drowsiness.
2. A loss of consciousness.
3. A loss of control.
4. An escape from problems.
5. Separation from life.

Meditation should not be some dreary chore or homework necessary to get high or to change reality. Nor is it an anesthetic to help avoid the drudgery that we have created for ourselves. It is simply *being* in the present moment, confronting life straight on. Need we nervously flit from past experience to some future projections, or can we simply enjoy the nectar of the present moment? Can you simply *be*, without the urgency to act on something? We need not be overly concerned: life will survive without you for ten minutes!

Keep in mind that improvement in meditation is cumulative and exceedingly subtle. That is, even if you think that nothing is happening and you are "getting nowhere," the daily effort is increasing your concentration and willpower and getting your mind used to the idea of being still. What you are doing is

> *You cannot save time, you only can spend time better in a more aware state.*

slowly building a "room on your soul" where you can retreat for peace and solace when the world gets rough or boring. When the mind is relaxed, it can do its best. Before getting started, keep one important fact in mind:

Meditation with a mantra

Historically, mantras were sacred terms or syllables which, when repeated or chanted, liberated the soul. They were used to shift the attention away from the petty day-to-day tribulations that beset us to the inner Self, the Atman. Practically speaking, the purpose of mantras is to free the mind from the grip of logical thinking.

A Harvard cardiologist and author of *The Relaxation Response*, Dr Herbert Benson, maintained, as recently as the 1970s, that meditating with a mantra (he used the mantra, "one") could help control high blood pressure, irregular heart beats, muscle tension, hard alcohol and cigarette use and drug abuse. As such, it represents a natural solution to these ailments.

It is important that the repeated tone is not, of itself, of significant complexity or meaning to distract the attention. The classic and most commonly used mantra since antiquity, still widely used today, is "AUM" ("OM"). Undoubtedly, those who have traveled to India, Nepal or any Eastern philosophy shop in London or New York have seen the symbol of OM.

This eternal word is the whole world.
The Past, present and future. All is OM.
The Mandukya Upanishad

The best way to employ this mantra is to inhale deeply and, in a tone comfortable to you, allow the inhaled air to simply flow out while lipping the mantra: OOOOOOOOOOOOOOO mmmmmmmmmmmm mmmmmmmmmm. The inhaled air should be exhaled over as long a period as possible, at least 30 seconds. With time this will extend to greater than 60 seconds. The longer the sound is drawn out, the more its intonation will impart a feeling of wholeness and serenity. In the exercises suggested below, the mantra can be silent, as to do an audible mantra in a crowded airport lounge would get the airport medics swarming around you!

A ten-minute meditation routine to get you started

The following exercise is a five–ten minutes relaxation session that you can perform in your office, in the airplane, in public transportation, wherever you find it appropriate. The best time to start meditation is during a low-grade stress situation, such as a mildly to moderately animated argument (such as with your spouse or adolescent), a bumpy airplane ride (the ten minutes just prior to landing is a perfect occasion).

Another perfect (you might say destined) occasion is during a traffic jam. When you feel yourself getting anxious and irritated because you are stuck at the airport, ask yourself if you are going to waste time getting angry or if you are going to use that free time to take control of the situation and to meditate. Smile gently, imperceptibly.

Now your mind is more calmed. You are going to be able to perform your tasks in a more productive way with a more positive attitude.

Note: you may wish to read the following instructions slowly into a tape recorder to play back while you relax.

If you are in your office, tell your secretary not to disturb you for the next ten minutes, no phone calls, no interruptions. Sit comfortably in your chair, feet flat on the floor, rest your hands on your knees, relax your neck and shoulder muscles. Hold your head and back straight but *relaxed*, close your eyes.

Overall objective = Focus your attention on your breathing.

Remember that the mind and breath are closely connected. By controlling your breath and making it very slow, you are calming down the noise of your mind.

Observe the rhythm of your breath for a few seconds. It should be unrushed, unforced, like waves on the beach, in and out, fully.

Now focus your attention on your face, relaxing your cheeks and forehead. As you relax your forehead, your scalp also relaxes. Concentrate on your throat. Swallow once or twice. Now relax your jaws, tongue, don't squeeze your teeth together, open your mouth slightly. Move your attention to your neck and shoulders and as you relax, feel any remaining tension from the neck and shoulders drain out through the upper arms, lower arms with hands and then out through the fingers . . . leaving your arms and shoulders comfortable and relaxed. Just let go . . . .

Now bring your attention to your spine. Starting from the neck, let your focus slowly travel down the entire length of the spine to the lowest vertebra. As you let go and relax, notice that your entire back is relaxing, that it is free of tension and feeling warm and comfortable.

Now that you feel relaxed, your blood is circulating more freely in your body and in your brain. If you wish, start now to use your mantra. If not, just exhale the breath while concentrating on its rhythm. Each time you exhale, visualize that you are exhaling all the tension of your body and your mind.

Viewing the movie of your life: don't pay attention to your thoughts bubbling in your mind. Every one of the thoughts and feelings "passing" on the screen in front of your mind's eye will have psychological "hooks" as part of them. As they pass in front of you, they will attempt to hook your attention away from your breathing. For a while, your mind will go with them: you will get pulled along by a thought or an image. No matter. Let these thoughts pass, like a movie passing on a screen in front of your eyes, without feeling concerned and go back *gently, but firmly,* to your breathing.

Detach yourself from your environment and look at yourself inside. Listen to your quiet breathing, your heartbeat is slowing down.

You are now exercising thought control, by quieting the noise of your mind. Each time you are distracted by a thought or a noise, let it go and give your undivided attention to your breathing. Gently, but firmly . . . .

As you begin to enter the silence of your being, you start feeling at peace with yourself. Your mantra gets softer and softer as you go on. It feels so good to quieten the noise of your thoughts for a few minutes. Be selfish for just a few minutes and enjoy that *special* moment. Ten minutes is enough, especially when you take that break several times a day.

Continue focussing your attention on your breathing. *Very slowly* with your eyes still closed, start moving your head slowly then your hands and feet. When you are ready, open your eyes slowly and put a smile on your face.

DEEP BREATHING

Air was your first food as a new born.

To get back to proper breathing, *pay attention to the depth of each breath*. These three breathing techniques will help you to combat the tensions of stress in your life. You can use them on the run, anywhere, anytime (without anyone knowing) to calm down your mind and relieve you of mental and physical tension.

Humming breathing

This is an excellent mantra-like technique ("hummmm" sound while exhaling) to use while driving your car or anywhere you can have a few minutes privacy:

(a) Sit comfortably with neck and shoulder muscles relaxed.
(b) Inhale deeply.
(c) *Exhale* slowly singing the word *hum* on one note.
(d) Hold the m sound as you continue to exhale.
(e) Try to keep the tone steady and resonant until complete exhalation.
(f) Then take another deep breath and start again. Repeat five times.

Note: choose a pitch that is comfortable for your voice. Try not to let the sound die down at the end in pushing a little harder to keep a resonant tone until complete exhalation.

Alternate nostril breathing

Another breathing technique that can help you clear up your mind and control the noise of your thoughts in just *two minutes*. Try it out in the following way :

(a) If you are in your office, tell your secretary not to disturb you for the next three minutes (always give yourself one or two minutes margin), no phone calls, no interruptions.

(b) Sit upright with your spine erect and your head straight but relaxed.

(c) Use your right hand for this exercise. Your thumb will control your right nostril and your index finger will control your left nostril.

(d) Close the right nostril with the thumb and inhale slowly and fully through the left nostril.

(e) Hold your breath for two or three seconds only, *no longer.*

(f) Close the left nostril with your index finger and exhale slowly through the right nostril.

(g) Inhale through the right nostril while the left nostril is still closed.

(h) Again hold your breath for a few seconds only.

(l) Close the right nostril and exhale through the left nostril. This completes one round. Complete three rounds and observe.

(j) When you are ready, open your eyes very slowly, stretch your neck, arms and hands.

(k) When you want, stand up and stretch your spine backwards very slowly, while resting your hands on your lower back. Now you are ready to continue your day with more positive energy.

Note: do not perform more than three rounds at a time at the beginning. Rounds may be increased as your system adjusts.

Purifying breathing

Complete breathing is an efficient tool that will relieve muscle tension and clear up your mind in a couple of minutes:

(a) Sit comfortably in your chair with neck and shoulder muscles relaxed, feet flat on the floor, hands resting on your thighs.

(b) Then, close the eyes while gently pushing ALL the air out of the lungs, using your rib cage and diaphragmatic muscles to push out the air until they are "empty."

(c) Now inhale *slowly* pushing your diaphragm out in order to fill the lower part of your lungs: watch the abdomen get pushed out as the base of the lungs fill.

(d) Expand your rib cage and raise your chest to fill the lower part of your lungs.

(e) Make sure that your neck and shoulder muscles are relaxed and that you do not force inhalation, proceed *slowly*.

(f) Keep the air in your lungs for ten seconds.

(g) Exhale very *slowly* and *fully*. Repeat five times.

PROGRESSIVE MUSCULAR RELAXATION (PMR)

The following relaxation session will help you to fall asleep with a clear and relaxed mind.

Lay down on your back and breathe normally for a few seconds. Then in order to relieve *all* the tension of your body, you are going to contract all the muscles of your body for 15 seconds. OK, are you ready? GO!

Now stop, breathe normally without forcing and close your eyes.

Focus your attention on your head, relax your facial muscles, your jaws. Do *not* squeeze your teeth together. Relax your mouth, your lips, open your mouth slightly. Relax your neck and shoulder muscles. Visualize while exhaling your breath that you are exhaling ALL the tension of your body. Relax your arms, your hands, your fingers. Let go all the tension like a wave movement. Relax your chest, your abdomen muscles, your buttocks. Now focus your attention on your legs, relax your thighs, your knees, your feet, ankles, toes. Just let go of it all . . . .

Now bring your attention to your spine. Starting from the neck, let your focus slowly travel down the entire length of the spine to the lowest vertebra. As you let go and relax, notice that your entire back is relaxing, that it is free of tension and feeling warm and comfortable.

▶

Now that your entire body is totally relaxed and free of tension, your blood can circulate more freely inside your relaxed body.

Focus your attention on your breathing and exhale all the remaining tension of your mind. Allow yourself to disengage, like taking your car out of gear. Disengage and listen to the silence of your mind.

Breathe in deeply, you relax, breathe out all the tension of your mind. Don't let your thoughts disturb your peaceful night, let them pass and allow yourself to switch off *completely.*

You are going to sleep deeply and free of all thoughts. You feel relaxed and serene. Visualize sleeping like a healing process. You are going to heal your body and your mind with a good night's sleep very well deserved . . . . A warm night is waiting for you . . . .

Just relax and let go . . . . Let go all the tension of your body and your mind . . . . Don't think, just let go and let yourself be pulled in by your dreams. Enter the fantasy world of your dreams in a total state of relaxation . . . .

Have a good night's sleep.

Now, in everyday life . . . coping with a stress attack in 15 seconds

As we have seen, when you want to avoid a heart attack, you do not start to do something about it when the chest pain starts. Despite your best efforts to prepare for the inevitable stress that comes with the ever-increasing demands of business life, there will always be moments when our abilities are overwhelmed by change or loss. These are "stress attacks" and they will try to pull you down.

The following three techniques will help you to disengage in a matter of seconds and give you the opportunity of controlling the situation better, with a refreshed mind and an upbeat attitude.

Ride out the storm. Visualize victory

When the world starts to fall apart, realize that you have reached the present limits of your mind's abilities to deal with life. No reason to be sad or angry! This is a unique opportunity to expand those limits to the next level. This is your time to grow, you have been chosen. Shrinking from the opportunity by hiding in a bottle of alcohol or pills or running away will only keep you from growing.

Visualize yourself as someone on the beach in a violent storm: waves pounding the beach, winds throwing things around. While under a "stress attack," regain control of yourself in a quick and efficient way, on the spot, just by watching the breathing. Sure, it's shallow and rushed. You are going to ride out the storm. You are in a storm of emotions. Ride it out. Focus your attention on the muscle tension of your body and on your breathing, then:

(a) Drop your shoulders
(b) Relax jaw and tongue
(c) Breathe slowly and fully for 15 seconds.

One minute breathing relaxation

This is an extension of the above exercise that can be used separately or in conjunction with meditation. When stress strikes and emotions get out of control, while working (you feel you are overwhelmed by projects, deadlines), or before an important event (a talk you are about to give, an important meeting, a drastic decision), stop what you are doing, drink a large glass of water and breathe deeply as follows for one minute:

(a) Inhale slowly pushing your belly out to fill the lower lungs.
(b) Expand the rib cage and raise your chest to fill the upper lungs.
(c) Keep the air in your lungs for three seconds.
(d) Exhale *very slowly* and completely; repeat twice.
Make sure your neck and shoulder muscles are *relaxed*.
Don't force, proceed *slowly*.

Five minutes meditation

When stress starts to impair your performance, you can't concentrate well, your mind is full of unproductive, noisy, thoughts, you feel you are not enjoying yourself any more, clear your mind by taking a three Minutes, Meditation Break in the following way:

(a) If you are in your office, tell your secretary not to disturb you for the next five minutes (to get a margin of two minutes).

(b) Sit comfortably in your chair, feet flat on the floor, hands resting on your thighs.

(c) Close your eyes and relax neck and shoulder muscles.

(d) While watching your breathing, observe the tone and flavour of your thoughts and view them like a movie passing on a screen in front of your eyes.

Do not feel concerned by your thoughts, detach yourself from your environment. Thought control: clear up your mind, quiet down the noise of your mind. Allow yourself to disengage for a few minutes. Open your eyes slowly, gently move your head from side to side. Now, smile at your new found power and get back into the fight!

Note: stay clear and focussed at all times. When you feel that you are not enjoying life any more, practice some of the above exercises.

Unlearn coronary-prone behavior

The primary risk factors for heart disease and strokes (high blood pressure, smoking, high blood cholesterol and inactivity) only account for 50% or so of heart diseases. What contributes to the other 50%? Recent results of meta-analysis of long-term medical research indicate a very strong behavioral component. The question now becomes: are you prone to heart disease on the basis of your behavior? Ask yourself:

1. Are you easily threatened? Can you let yourself take off the mask once in a while?
2. In conversations, are you using the self-reference "I" excessively?
3. Do you feel the need to dominate every conversation or can you listen to others' views?
4. Is temper or other facets of verbal violence a problem for you?
5. Do you regurgitate unpleasant moments or can you "bury the dead" and move on?
6. Can you forgive and forget or do you carry the weight of grudges around with you?
7. Can you allow your borders to melt in with the borders of others on different planes: physical, mental, ideological, spiritual?

This is learned behavior, it can be, therefore, *un*learned. Manage anger and hostility by noting the advice generated by thousands of highly effective managers:

1. It's OK to get angry once in a while.
2. Know trigger points for anger and hostility – traffic jams, fax.
3. Consider alternatives to anger: "it's not worth my health:" anger *will* kill you.
4. Communicate frustration before it smolders into hostility.
5. Humor: the best medicine: don't let being too serious ruin your life.
6. Living well is the best revenge: fine dining, wine-tasting . . . .
7. Unwind between work and home to prevent "Overflow."
8. Never eat/make love under tension.
9. Never go to bed angry: start healing ASAP.
10. Perceive anger as a tempest which will pass: count to ten.
11. Never make serious decisions while angry.
12. Do not allow people to provoke your anger. Violence begets violence. Do *not* engage!
13. Ask the question: why are you angry? Anger is a sign of a failed strategy.
14. Eventually, anger must no longer be an option: give it up!

A two-step exercise to help you to start to identify behavioral problems and arrange long-term priorities

Step 1: on a calm weekend morning upon arising, ask yourself how you would like to be remembered by your loved ones (caring, generous, loving, sharing . . .).
Write it here: _____
This is the "*desired* perception of self."

Step 2: under normal circumstances (not during or after an argument), walk around the house and survey your family members individually. Ask them honestly how they will remember you (caring, generous, loving, sharing . . .). Be prepared for some surprises!
Write that answer here: _____
This is the "*actual* perception of self."

When the desired and the actual perceptions of self are identical, your priorities are becoming well ordered and you are heading for a regret-free life.

Broaden one's definition of success

As experience will show, broadening your definition of success to include other vital aspects of life (besides financial security) can be difficult. The mere ease and accessibility of financial remuneration for most of us is so seductively tangible that using precious mental energy experimenting with less obvious milestones of success is scary.

Moreover, attention to the pecuniary aspects of life alone quickly leaves one with a feeling of frustrated emptiness and the feeling of having missed something else. There's no need to *forsake* the financial aspects of life; indeed, once ensured, we can move on to less vital ways of making life meaningful.

You know your definition of success is broad-based if you can answer "yes" to the following:

1. I can laugh heartily with my spouse on a regular basis.
2. My children consider me a "friend."
3. I am getting closer every day to my overall objectives in life (whatever they may be).
4. I am less afraid of death (and other uncertainties) than I used to be.
5. Learning to live with life's paradoxes is exciting.

Do not exchange precious years of your life, your marriage or your health for a perceived need for professional control or validation. In short, ask yourself in every stress situation,
"Is it worth getting sick for?"

Success is a game where we set goals, go for them and achieve what we set out to accomplish. Happiness is a state of mind, of being satisfied with what you end up with. Be altruistically selfish: write for yourself a LifePlan. An example of a LifePlan might be:

Nobody on his deathbed ever said that they wished they had spent more time at the office!

While I am still alive and well, I want to accomplish these things:

1. Get a pilot's license.
2. Learn a musical instrument.
3. Sail around the world.
4. Learn a martial art.
5. Learn how to cook Chinese.
6. Get to know my spouse/kids.
7. Learn how to juggle, learn a new language.

In this game, there are no magic weekends or vacations. Start *now*, because life itself is the real career and you don't want to die with regrets of having missed something important to you. You do not want to look back at your life and realize that you have missed the whole game of life because you were always absorbed by future projects: you fell "asleep at the wheel." Life is the *big* career. Be selfish.

> *In your mind, it's still an idea. On paper it becomes a plan.*

Rekindle humor and playfulness in your life and marriage

Humor leads to an open heart and love because it helps us to take ourselves and our melodrama less seriously: it lightens the load. Through humor we melt with others and humor helps us to realize that our plight is shared by all people. Laughter promotes mental and physical healing. Playfulness through sport brings you back to companionship with others, away from morose solitude, and rouses the child within.

A merry heart does good medicine, but a broken spirit drieth the bones.   ***Proverbs 17:22***

Don't be so stiff. Loosen up. Surprise them all and yourself as well. Crack the mold. Develop new dimensions to your soul. Once in a while, take a walk on the Wild Side. A little spontaneous chaos and silliness will keep the child inside of you alive. Even when you cannot escape becoming a victim of the blues, laugh at your getting stuck! It will all pass. Life is already serious enough without undue sadness.

Be downright silly at least once a day. Take off the mask. Tickle your spouse or kid until laughter flows uncontrollably. Imitate your favorite dancer. Do Karaoke in front of your family and friends: mystify and intrigue them by breaking out of old molds. Part of your predicament may be due to the fact that, in an effort to develop a reputation of sorts, you have allowed your friends and associates to put you in a box summarily labeled ("angry," "aggressive," "staid" or whatever) and stored on the shelf for safekeeping. If you feel stuck, get unstuck; get out of the "box" that people have put you in and enjoy, at least temporarily, an unknown territory.

A note of caution: do not use humor as a tool of ridicule, as a cynical attitude in disguise, as just another power play with "winners" and "losers." Long-term, this expression of bitterness will make you miserable.

Power-playing profanes. Never laugh at the expense of others: this increases separateness and sets back emotional and spiritual advancement. You cannot get bigger by chopping off someone else's head!

Develop a real sense of adventure in your life

Learn to appreciate life's adventure. We quietly complain to ourselves how stale and routine life has become: "Oh, God, just another day." The gray days just start melting into one another. We have it all figured out already: no surprises, but no adventures either! Don't blame the world for the hassle, thank the world for the adventure.

> An adventure is only an inconvenience rightly understood.
> An inconvenience is only an adventure wrongly considered.
> Chesterton, *On Running After One's Hat*

If your adventuresome self needs dusting off, start by reading the Lansing chronicle of Sir Ernest Shackleton's epic shipwreck and four-month drift in Antarctica (prior to the time of faxes and radios), entitled *Endurance*. Then go camping (*real* camping) for a week in the remote mountains with your teenage child or your spouse. That reading and trip will do wonders for your confidence to confront anxieties upon return to civilization, as well as for the bonding with your child.

To further awaken the warrior within, make a list of the most challenging moments of your life, good and bad. They are undoubtedly those moments when you, in a courageous mood, ventured well outside of the normally well-circumscribed "comfort zone." Do not allow the following narration to be a distillation of *your* life.

Henry James wrote about a man who had a nagging suspicion that something terrible was going to happen to him during his life . . . somewhere in his fifties, he figured out what that terrible thing was: the terrible thing was that *absolutely* NOTHING was going to happen to him. He was going to go through his entire life safely without adventure, without danger, without full participation. And by the time he figured that out, it was too late.

Edward Albee

In life experiences, most of us are not just afraid of the loss that comes from experiences, but are afraid of the fear of the loss involved with those experiences. The pain is caused by persistent clinging to fearful thoughts, by an inability to "bury the dead."

Daring is an attractive quality and a good one to engender. Don't make the fear of failure more devastating than the task itself. The only failure is **not** trying. Somebody fails when they cannot see that every experience is designed to put them in touch with some aspect of their personality that needs improvement. Life is perfectly designed that way, with your growth in mind.

If not me, then, who? If not now, then, when? If not here, then, where?

Let go, trust yourself and enjoy the ride. After going through the experience that you feared so much (that presentation before your colleagues, for example), look back at the few minutes just before when you were fretting and buying into the idea that you were going to fail. Act now and in the future as though you could not fail. That optimism will carry the day!

Allow the truth to set you free

Self-analyze and self-criticize in a gentle but firm way. The mind, once you begin to unravel the knot of its neuroses, may start to rebel through prevarication. Telling even "white lies" is symptomatic of an insecure ego that is excessively hungry for approval.

You are as sick as your secrets.
Dr M Scott Peck, MD

The best way to start being lighter is to be completely honest: as a human being, you are *perfect* in your imperfections that you are working on. Therefore, accept and love yourself as you are with all your blemishes and bumps. Living openly with those weaknesses will remove all the taboo aspects of being imperfect and is a good first step to moving on.

In every dealing, at every juncture, the truth will set you free from the need to constantly remember what tangled web you have woven this week. Fretting about being discovered can be a terrible source of stress. Let go. Strive to be transparent and light. Your integrity will increase as your anxiety decreases.

Practice effective fear management

> We have nothing to fear but fear itself.
> *Franklin Delano Roosevelt*

As long as we have physical bodies and delicate egos, we will have fears. These fears will limit our potential and dominate our life. If we study our daily activities, we can see various fears being acted out through our actions.

As children and adolescents, our fears limited us. Fear of the dark made us less inclined to explore uncertainty, fear of our parent screaming at us made taking risks less interesting, fear of an angry father or angry God made us lash out irrationally, perhaps hurting our health (such as cigarette, drug or excessive alcohol use), fear of being embarrassed by an overbearing and insensitive teacher in class stopped us from getting the education we deserved, fear of the "bad guys coming to get me" made us develop attitudes towards others that precluded synergistic relationships. Many of these fears are carried over to adulthood.

As adults, our fears still limit us. Fear of our children failing socially and professionally in life (which would bring into question our child-rearing and other abilities) makes us argue with them about their grades and friends they keep. Fear of growing old (alone) is exploited by unsavory and unscrupulous people who propose "helping you" to appear younger through facelifts, fake tans, liposuction, hair dyes. Fear of not having enough money makes us accept inappropriately heavy workloads. Fear of losing respectability makes us wear a heavy "persona" mask and, perhaps, assume a social position or job that puts us in direct conflict with inner principles. Fear of not gaining approval from others makes us laugh nervously when it's just not funny, and makes us say "yes" when we should say "no" or vice versa. And the list goes on.

Exercise

Spend three minutes calming the mind's chatter and answer as honestly as you possibly can the following questions:

1. The thing I fear the most is: _____

2. If this terrible thing I fear actually happened, I would _____

_____

The difference between someone who is courageous and someone who is fearful is not the presence or absence of the actual fear itself. Everybody has pretty much the same fears. The difference is that the courageous person realizes his or her place in the world; he has humbly subjugated himself to greater principles of love and service, to the will of the Creator, the most powerful ally. The coward has been arrogantly centering the world around himself and when the going gets tough, crumbles like clay.

When one peruses the vast contributions to humanity made by Eastern thought, one fact becomes clear: all fear stems from two classic and fatal mistakes:

1. the excessive attachment to transient things in life: money, beauty, youth, respectability, the dark, death; and
2. too little faith in your God.

Some would argue that fear is a key sign that your faith in the Grand Design is weak and faltering. Faith, simply put, is a reperception of your self (all that you identify with your ego and body) as a real part of the Self (the Force, Atman, Allah, God). Fears, therefore, are just a reminder that, perhaps, you are not as grand and infinite as you originally thought. As such, fears, if consciously handled, should represent an invitation to strengthen faith, to do internal battle with negative feelings or impulses. Fear could be the starting point of humility over arrogance.

Always keep some aces up your sleeve against fear. One effective fear-buster is the expression: "and so?" With a well developed sense of adventure, trust in yourself, you'll manage just fine. But they'll take my respectability, my spouse, my child, my hair, my youth. It will *all* be stripped away eventually.

Leave no loose ends

Some of us live as though we are going to live a million years. Big mistake. So, if you are afraid of losing your spouse or child, go right now and embrace them. Live as though you are living your last day. It may well be. Then if that fearful event comes to pass, you, at least, will not have the regret of having lost an opportunity of sharing love. Anticipate all eventualities and meditate on them. This realization will, of course, make you feel very vulnerable; that's all right, as the victories you enjoy will lead you on the path to lasting serenity.

Any negative emotion you might have is based in fear: fear of loss of something or someone, fear of success, fear of failure, fear of loneliness, fear of intimacy, fear of being judged and so on. Fears are perpetuated by allowing them to stay in the shadowy recesses of the mind. Ferret them out with prayer and meditation. Expose your fears by shining the light of consciousness on them. Laugh at them, at their irrational power over you and your family.

To do this, devote five minutes a day to disarming your fears. Fears evaporate when you defiantly hold your head up high with dignity and humility. Look Death square in the eye. John Donne, one of the greatest metaphysical poets, articulated this, in the 17th century, in his tenth *Holy Sonnet*:

> Death, be not proud, though some have called thee
> Mighty and Dreadful, for, thou art not so,
> For, those, whom thou think'st thou dost overthrow
> Die not, poor Death, nor yet canst thou kill me.
> Foe rest and sleep, which but thy pictures be,
> Much pleasure, then from thee, much more must flow,
> And soonest our best men with thee do go,
> Rest of their bones and soul's delivery.
> Thou art slave to Fate, Chance, kings and desperate men
> And doth with poison, war and sickness dwell,
> And poppy or charms can make us sleep as well,
> And better than thy stroke; why swell'st thou, then?
> One short sleep past, we wake eternally,
> And death shall be no more; death, thou shalt die.

Prepare the body for inevitable change

This is *not* one of those things you can delegate. Health is too important. To be able to worry effectively, you will have to know deep down that you did *everything* possible to preserve it, so that it is there when you need it.

Trouble starts because the human nervous and immunologic system evolves at a much slower rate than your technologically-driven lifestyle. The discordance between the genetic code, the DNA, that programs every aspect of our being, and our lifestyles has been the subject of considerable research recently in the field of medical anthropology.

It is estimated that while you are rushing headlong into the 21st century, your genetic code is lagging dramatically behind in cave-dwelling days. Consequently, the brain/mind orchestrates all systems of the body for a distinctly physical response: a flight or a fight which may never happen. You are left stewing in your own stress juices.

> *Your nervous system is still adapted to a time when survival required a physical response: fight or flight. That is the most compelling scientific evidence for why physical activity is a **non-negotiable** strategy for sanity management. Diseases hate moving targets!*

The human nervous system evolved during more primitive times when the major threats to survival were of a *physical* nature. Consequently, the brain/mind orchestrates all systems of the body for an appropriate *physical* response.

The nervous system, the cardiovascular system, and the hormonal system prepare the body for either a flight or a fight response: blood pressure, heart and respiratory rates rise (to meet increasing oxygen demand), lipids (blood fats) are elevated, platelets and other clotting factors responsible for the blood coagulation are activated making the blood thicker (in the event of potential blood loss due to injury), muscle tension increases (in preparation for a flight to safety or a fight) and sweating increases (as a cooling mechanism). The whole human physiology is in a state of alert. As discussed earlier, the only difference between now and ancient times is that the physical danger evokes a physical response, psychological threats demand a physical and mental response: that search for opportunity.

Physiology of alert

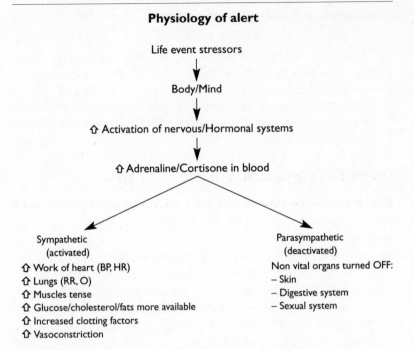

Life event stressors

↓

Body/Mind

↓

⇧ Activation of nervous/Hormonal systems

↓

⇧ Adrenaline/Cortisone in blood

Sympathetic
(activated)

⇧ Work of heart (BP, HR)
⇧ Lungs (RR, O)
⇧ Muscles tense
⇧ Glucose/cholesterol/fats more available
⇧ Increased clotting factors
⇧ Vasoconstriction

Parasympathetic
(deactivated)

Non vital organs turned OFF:
– Skin
– Digestive system
– Sexual system

Looking at this simplified schema of alert, what becomes immediately clear is that to defuse this potential pressure cooker, effective interventions are feasible at three points, as presented below:

1. *Minimize change in the environment: modify the cause of alert.* Be very careful here. As discussed, those life changes that cause "stress" are also promoting growth. Over-tampering with life changes, will create the illusion of making life "safe" while making it very boring and stale. Dampening change dampens growth. The result: an insipid life scarcely worth living.

   This type of intervention is the strategy that has been very much overvalued and its overuse, therefore, should be discouraged.

2. *Prepare the mind for inevitable change: appreciate the Grand Design.* Modify the way that we *perceive* life: no hassles, just lessons. As discussed above, this type of engineering on the mind is one of the most effective. Converting life experiences into wisdom is the essence of life.

   At first, to transform your perspective on life, you need only entertain the **possibility** of a Grand Design. Events will then start to fall right into place. Armed with this certitude that everything in life is for a reason, you will easily see the Design in every aspect of life.

3. **Prepare the body for inevitable change.** The so-called "stress cascade" seen above is the most compelling evidence that the body craves physical conditioning. If you want to stay in the fast track, develop a body that can stay there. The whole point is to develop a physical outcome to the challenges of life.

Upgrading physical abilities, step-by-step

Step # 1: damage assessment – the intrinsic value of symptoms

When your ability to respond efficiently to life's demands is overwhelmed, your body and mind send out distress signals. Being aware of how your body and mind are reacting to excessive stress in abnormal ways is already half the battle in steering clear of the long-term damage. Identify your "red flag" or alarm bells from the list of symptoms below (the * indicates the symptoms for which medication may be prescribed). Circle that symptom in pencil.

Now, as you begin to use the various tools offered, erase the symptoms as they clear up. That way, you know what really works for you. After all, *any* of the below symptoms may well indicate that your present system of sanity management is failing, at least, in part.

Physical symptoms

1. *Cardiovascular system:* *chest pain or pressure, rapid heart beat, palpitations, fainting, dizziness, *heart attacks, *strokes.

2. *Digestive system:* *ulcers, *gastritis, *maldigestion, *chronic nausea, "nervous eating," *diarrhea, anorexia, *heartburn, *upset stomach, *bloated stomach, *gas, *constipation, *hemorrhoids, loss of appetite, *irregular or painful bowel movement, foul breath and belches.

3. *Nervous system:* *"migraines," *headaches, *trembling, excessive sweating, *sleeplessness, tremors, ringing in the ears, dizziness, *restlessness.

4. *Immune system:* reduced resistance to infections and, possibly, *cancer.

5. *Respiratory system:* *shortness of breath, *asthmatic attacks, poor oxygenation.

6. *Musculoskeletal system:* *stiffness, *pain, *backaches, *headaches.

7. *General:* skin disorders (acne, psoriasis).

Psychological symptoms

1. ***Concentration and memory:*** thought disruption, reduced memory and concentration span.

2. ***Altered sleep patterns:*** sleeplessness, poor thought control, tendency to awake at unusual times, low energy and chronic fatigue.

3. ***Behavior:*** aggression, tension headaches, snapping, pent-up frustrations, behavior changes, depression, powerlessness, isolation, apathy, persecution complex, cannot smile, poor communication skills, excessive shyness, intolerance.

4. ***Cognition:*** problem-solving -decision-making, reduced ability to evaluate alternatives.

5. ***Emotions:*** crisis of confidence, tearful, apathy, depression, overall loss of interest, negative self-image, fear of future, preoccupation with past, problems relaxing, unexpected crying.

When you begin to pick up on these signals or cues that Mother Nature is sending, you may be initially annoyed by them, and present yourself to your doctor for some relief so that you can get on with your life. Say, for example, you present yourself to the doctor with the problem of an ulcer. What options do we, as physicians, provide for you: anti-ulcer medication? Fine. Do anti-ulcer medications cure the global cause of the ulcer (the separation anxiety that caused chronically elevated adrenaline levels that lead to uncontrolled gastric secretions)? No. The ulcer medication acts locally either by buffering or altogether decreasing stomach acid production or by altering microbial growth in the stomach. So the original problem remains. So Mother Nature knocks again. She sends you a sleep disorder.

You, once again, present yourself for a little relief from this global symptom of anxiety, "Can't sleep, Doc." Out comes the prescription pad: sleeping pills. These don't lower the adrenaline levels, so Mother Nature, in her efforts to save you from yourself, knocks yet again: your blood pressure goes up. Off to the doctor. Blood pressure medication in addition to the other two medications, all of which have secondary effects.

When you present yourself to the medical profession, you may or you may not find an ally or "coach" who can help you find proactive solutions to the real problems. This masking of symptoms is problematic because eventually your body will have to decompress and go for the cure: solving the original problem of anxiety.

The whole imposing edifice of modern medicine, for all its breathtaking successes, is, like the celebrated Tower of Pisa, slightly off balance. It's frightening how dependent on drugs we are all becoming and how easy it is for doctors to prescribe them as universal panaceas for our ills.

Prince Charles (1985)

We are living in the **Age of Anxiety**. An inability to deal effectively with the origins of our anxieties is a *failure* of your sanity management strategy. The most commonly prescribed medications in the past ten years are:

1. anti-blood pressure medications;
2. anti-ulcer medications;
3. anti-anxiety medications (tranquilizers).

Masking of valuable symptoms may be hazardous to your sanity and health. Think about it.

Start to decipher individual signs and symptoms, not as something to anesthetize, but as extremely valuable red flags or alarms warning of a potentially serious underlying problem. The signs and symptoms frequently reported to us by multinational executives include: high blood pressure, chronic fatigue, "nervous eating-drinking," sleeplessness, peptic ulcers, emotional lability, tension headaches, obesity and depression. One's reaction to a particular demand sends ripples through our mind and body, perceived as anxiety, sweaty hands, poor memory or concentration, poor sleeping habits and resultant chronic fatigue, anger, fear, "nervous eating" and so on. What are your "red flags?"

Step # 2: Developing reward systems that work

Your reaction to stress may be more dangerous to your life and health than the stress itself. How do you cope with stress? Do you cope in a way that brings about a "cure" or are you creating more problems (perhaps, more dangerous to your health than the original stress itself)?

Destructive strategies

	What you want . . .	What you get . . .
1. Drinking excess alcohol	Sedation	Depression
2. Drinking more coffee/colas	Stimulation	Fatigue
3. Smoking	Sedation	Illness
4. Tranquilizers/drug use	Sedation	Loss of lucidity
5. Taking aspirin/paracetamol	Pain relief	Masking of symptoms
6. Depression	Escape	Escape
7. Anxiety/Fretting	Solutions	Confusion
8. Anger/Emotion	Decompression	Time wasted

Constructive strategies

	What you want . . .	What you get . . .
1. Talking with someone	Understanding	Understanding
2. Return to breathing	Relaxation	Regained lucidity
3. Self-confidence	Calm deliberation	Calm deliberation
4. Humor	Decompression	Relief
5. Exercise	Decompression	Health
6. Meditation	Healthful tranquility without anesthesia	Healthful tranquility without anesthesia
7. Paying "sleeping debt"	Refreshment	Refreshment

Step # 3: Decompress the pressure cooker – enjoy *some* regular physical activity

Any activity will do as long as it satisfies two criteria:

1. you really enjoy it; and
2. it's reasonably good for the body and the mind.

Physical activity will help get oxygen into the system where it is needed. The one thing that the body and mind really need during the episode of alert is oxygen. Because you have forgotten to breathe properly, you are probably using your rib cage more as a corset than a bellows, precisely at the critical moment. Oxygen (O_2) produces energy and tranquility. Improper breathing can fail to deliver the sorely needed oxygen while trapping the waste products that the lungs were designed to clear (CO_2), which can increase your feeling of anxiety, shortness of breath and fatigue. The best way to get oxygen where it belongs is through aerobic exercise and deep breathing.

Step # 4: Pay your sleeping debt

Recent studies have inferred that inadequate sleep quality can reduce the effectiveness of your immune system, making you an easy target for colds and flu and, possibly, cancer long term.

A stressful job, family conflicts, traveling and living in hotels, ALL can have a major influence on the quality of your sleep.

The secret of sleep

For decades, sleep experts have been using clinical signs and electrical waves emited from the brain to discover the secret of sleep. They have found that a night's normal sleep consists of a 90–110 minute cycle, which repeats itself four or five times during the night, depending, of course, on how long you sleep.

The cycle is made up of alternating phases of sleep: the first phase is composed of stages of increasing depth of stupor, called **NREM (Non-Rapid Eye Movement) sleep**. NREM has four stages (stages 1, 2, 3, and 4). Stages 3 and 4 are the deepest stages of stupor during which we experience the strongest experience of subjective sleep, known as **slow wave sleep (SWS)**. Exercise, when optimally performed four hours before bedtime, can improve sleep quality.

Having the excuse that you are "too tired" to exercise may actually leave you more fatigued. Active people seem to sleep better and have more energy.

At the end of each set of NREM phase, there is a period of **Rapid Eye Movement (REM) sleep**. During REM muscles twitch, temperature and blood pressure fluctuate and dreams happen. REM is an extremely important and creative phase of sleep.

Note: avoid sleeping pills and alcohol prior to sleeping, they can cut out REM sleep.

Now let's go over a few measures that you could follow as you see fit:

I. *Before going to bed:*

(a) use your bedroom as your sanctuary: reserved for love and sleep;

(b) eat a light dinner and consume alcohol moderately. If you had a heavy business dinner, go for a 20 minute walk to start consuming the calories ingested. Lie on your right side (the side your stomach empties on);

(c) have a hot bath, drink warm milk with honey;

(d) distract yourself with a good book, a non-violent movie or a game (solitaire, chess . . .);

(e) have a glass of fresh water.

2. *Prior to sleeping:* try progressive muscular relaxation.

IV. SANITY MANAGEMENT STRATEGY

Commit to preparing your mind and body for change. Write a pledge to yourself.

I am going to begin forthwith to manage my sanity in earnest. This week, I will use the tools shown below. Then, I will grade the overall efficacy on the disappearance of symptoms.

Date: _____   Signature:_____

Your weekly schedule could look something like this:

M	T	W	Th	F	Sat	Sun
5' Meditation 4' Work-out	Yoga 10' 4' Work-out	5' Meditation 4' Work-out	Yoga 10' 4' Work-out	5' Meditation 4' Work-out	Yoga 10' 4' Work-out	Rest
Humming breathing 5'	FIT Evening meditation with mantra	Humming breathing 5'	FIT Evening meditation with mantra	Humming Breathing 5'	FIT Evening meditation with mantra	

Symptoms that I experience before beginning this program include:

1._____

2._____

3._____

4._____

Symptoms that I noticed were relieved *after* participating ____ weeks in this program include:

1._____

2._____

3._____

4._____

Useful insights learned from my interaction with this chapter include:

1. _____

2. _____

3. _____

4. _____

And smile as you go.

After finishing the chapter on Sanity, I sat there in what had become a place of real learning for me: a hospital library. While waiting for my procedure at 3 p.m., I sat quietly meditating on the movement of my breath, just calmly watching my thoughts go by like leaves on a woodland creek.

The time for my operation was approaching.

5

A NEW BEGINNING

"During the next 12 hours of my life, the distilled
lessons of 20 years' experience in this surgeon's
hands would help repair the result of my
excessive lifestyle . . . this was to be my
second chance."

THE BIGGEST CHALLENGE OF MY LIFE

Day Three: early Thursday afternoon – pre-op

It was now drawing close to the time of my operation. However, as fear started to enter my thoughts, I simply came back to my breath and could feel the corners of my mouth curling upwards. I was strangely at peace before the biggest challenge of my life and it felt really good!

It had all come down to this moment. It seemed so perfect: lots of fear and some tools to deal with it. No silly fretting, just dealing with it all in the present moment. How right Dr Charles was: when you are about to go through some change laden with uncertainty, traumatic like this surgery or not, you are very aware of every second's opportunity for growth.

I acknowledged the fears but did not let thoughts of them make me nervous. No chest pains at all right now. I knew that I was actually starting to heal myself even before my operation. I wondered how my room-mate, Ray, had done, but let even that thought drift by.

The ICU knew I was in the library and I hadn't any calls regarding "strange heart rhythms" from the Monitor Master. So, I thought, my heart must like the way my mind is handling all this.

As I sat there, looking at my body in a much more respectful and loving way than I had in all of the previous 47 years. I felt like caressing my body like the rider stroking the neck of a horse while on a stroll. I wondered just how my body would be changed as a result of this operation: for one, I was assured by Dr Lee, I would not have any more of the chest pain that had been nagging me over the years. I felt how smooth my breastbone was and how I would be stigmatized with the central scar of bypass surgery: member of the illustrious Zipper Club. Between that and the leg scars, I would really be a spectacle on the beach this coming holiday season.

During the next 12 hours of my life, the distilled lessons of 20 years' experience in this surgeon's skilled hands would help repair the result of my excessive lifestyle, my imbalances, my adolescent searching and groping and my silly seriousness. This was to be my second chance to respect this temple.

It takes a long time to become young
Picasso

My mind, which would usually be racing, buying into negative thoughts in a most uncontrolled way, stayed clear and calm. I reminisced about the reading I had done here while "captive in the classroom," the Ebenezer Scrooges, the King Lears, the Dr Faustuses, all themes throughout history of redemption and how opportunities were used or missed. I would arrange what was left of my life better than before.

Day Three: late Thursday afternoon – the operation

I made my way back to the step-down unit. As I washed myself, I could hear some muffled conversations at the door. I glanced reflexly at my watch as I slid it off my wrist: it was 13:30. *A bit early*, I thought. *Let's get on with it!* What had happened to my mind was that I could almost hear the voice of Dr Charles, adding little expressions to my mental phrases and, in doing so, saving me from drifting into negative angry thinking. I smiled in acknowledgement of my new way of thinking. I tested it again, *I only hope that I survive this operation so that I can use my new mindset to arrange my life. You will. Now it's automatic. Just trust yourself.* It was working well! I smiled broadly as I stepped out of the bathroom to meet two orderlies pushing a gurney.

"Good afternoon, sir. Are you ready?," asked one of the orderlies.

"Oh, is this for me? Well yes, just make sure that we are going to the operating block and not to the basement," I said with a wink of the eye. Keep your humor and rise above the storm, I thought. As I lay there on the gurney, the nurse from the operating room informed me that she was giving me a mild sedative through my IV port that would make me a little sleepy. The orderlies helped me slide over onto the gurney, pulled up the sheet over my chest, slipped on the cap, inserted the oxygen prongs into my nose, and we were off.

As we wheeled our way through the corridors, the orderlies carried on the conversation of their escapades the night before and I started counting the florescent lights passing overhead. Outside the operating chambers, were people huddled together, in vigil for their loved ones inside, as if around a primitive fire. Though no one could be there for me, I did not feel alone.

Crossing the threshold to the operating theatre, past the masked doctors scrubbing meticulously up to their elbows. Noticeably, the conversations of the personnel seemed to become more deliberate, both in tone and content. This was a serious place, indeed!

I was wheeled into Operating Room 12, a room completely dedicated to heart bypass surgery, where everyone was already wearing surgical masks, gowns and gloves. What a team full of energy, scurrying around like ants arranging and counting the silver instruments, tinkling like wind chimes!

As they slid me over onto the operating table, my last two sensations were my extreme thirst and someone squeezing my hand. As I looked up for one last time, I saw deep blue eyes behind a winking mask saying to me: "See you in a few hours. Have a good sleep." It was Dr Charles. I knew that I wasn't alone somehow. I smiled inwardly. As they placed the anesthesia mask over my mouth and nose, instructing me to breathe deeply, I drifted dreamily off. I was fading fast, hearing the words,

"Okay, we're ready. Let's do it . . . ."

Day Four: early Friday morning – post-op

When I finally awoke, I unglued my eyes long enough to discover that I was in a calm and darkened Surgical Recovery Room, Bed 4, at 10 o'clock in the morning. I recall the intense bittersweet sensation of depression and relief to find out I was really here. The first physical sensation was chest pain but this time it was a different type of pain, more on the surface, a pain due to having had my chest opened and my coronary arteries bypassed with a graft. I was alive!

The bellows-type of respirator machine that had been breathing and even sighing for me, had left my throat raw and painful. A tube was collecting urine for me, intravenous lines were "drinking" for me, *everything* was being done for me and I could not move at all. To add to this extremely irritating dependence, the lines and monitors hanging in the overhead light created the sensation of being in a cage: a prisoner of my previous lifestyle! This was not at all the kind of existence that I had envisaged for myself at this young age.

> *The lines and monitors hanging in the overhead light created the sensation of being in a cage: a prisoner of my previous lifestyle!*

I was able to raise my head high enough to see a figure in the corner of the room: I knew it was Dr Charles.

"How did I do?" I growled, with my eyes getting unstuck.

"Welcome back. By the looks of things," responded my guardian angel, "you did just fine."

"How did I manage that?" I asked. I was delirious.

"You've woken up the warrior in you. Not the angry, aggressive, person, but the serene person who loves and revels in change, the essence of life. Welcome back."

"Doc, I don't mind saying that I am a little scared, even a *lot* scared. Not so much about my condition, that's something I intend to take better care of now. But I'm afraid of what will happen to me when I go back into the so-called real world. I'm afraid that I will fail." I could feel a tear rolling down my cheek, but I didn't care with him. He understood.

"Just remember that whatever you're doing, wherever you are, you are not alone. Stoke the fire within. All you need do is *connect*. Stop isolating yourself. If someone is there, connect. If not, connect through meditation or prayer. Refuse to buy into the illusion of isolation and separation. That's what put you here. Just connect. You'll be all right.

"Listen, I'll talk to you a little later, Got to run just now, just wanted to be here when you woke up," he said as he slipped out the door.

"Yeah, see ya, Doc," as I fell off under the influence of the pain medications.

Day Four: late Friday night – post-op

Over the next 12 hours, I slept lightly in and out. That same evening, while dozing lightly, I could hear the medical team doing its rounds. As the group moved to the foot of my bed, I could hear the surgical resident reporting to Dr Lee, the Attending Physician.

"This gentleman is a 47-year-old status post 3-vessel CABG. No complications, good wound healing and pain control. Vital signs and ECG stable. Adequate hydration. Scheduled for the step-down unit in a couple of days . . . " and the surgical resident continued to meticulously report on every last detail of my case.

As the resident droned on, I slipped into reverie about my case and this highly gifted surgical team. Needless to say, my heart bypass (known in the medical trade as Coronary Artery Bypass Graft or CABG, pronounced "cabbage") for me was a saving grace and the wake-up call of a lifetime. It woke me to my senses, not just in how to better care for myself, but also how to start to appreciate the seemingly little things in life that I passed by so hurriedly every morning on the way to work. I had a second chance to live life fully, to grasp the moment with my loved ones.

I was on numerous medications: one to make my blood thinner (to flow better through the new graphs), an anti-arrhythmic (to control erratic rhythms of my heart), a blood pressure medication, and a slue of others.

As the team moved on to the next bed in the ICU, I thought of that glorious team of doctors and nurses who had clutched me from the jaws of death and nursed my heart and mind back to health. Many critical questions rolled through my head incessantly. Why did it take that to alert me to the dangers? What if . . . ?

It could well have been a nasty cancer or a stroke or anything else catastrophic. The big question for all of us who make a living with our minds is "What does it take to wake up and take better care of ourselves?" For me, it took a heart attack, coronary artery bypass graft, drastic change in lifestyle to refind the way, to awaken, to live life to the full.

And that was Dr Charles's lesson, or gift, I should say, to me. As I lay there inanimate, fed and drained of vital fluids by plastic tubes, poked, prodded, checked, wiped, caressed, I thought to myself how fortunate I had been, how sweet life is, how delicate a gift! I could feel a tear of joy streaming down my cheek and a gentle pain, a tolerable reminder, in my breastbone.

The *beep-beep-beep-beep* of the heart monitor, formerly a nerve-wracking annoyance, was now a gentle lullaby, a sign of life. Each *beep* represented a heart beat, a healthy heart whose muscles were now bathing in blood brought by new conduits. I drifted gently into the arms of Morpheus, still hearing the high pitched beeping in my dreams . . . .

Day Five: early Saturday morning – helluva wake-up call!

The next morning, even before I opened my sticky eyelids, I felt depressed that I would not be seeing Jane's face by my bedside that morning. I already sensed the brightness of the morning sun coming through the ICU curtains. It was much brighter than usual. Now the beeping was even louder and more rapid. The telephone at the nurses station rang . . . *someone* pick it up before it wakes up the whole ICU . . . the beeping, the phone. Then I unstuck my eyes.

What? This is not the St Andrew's ICU. Have they transferred me already? No! I was in my hotel room! My alarm clock was the angry beeping and the phone was ringing next to my head. While reaching for it, I knocked over the full ashtray on the night table. Are those mine? I felt like a different person than the one who had left those death sticks behind several hours before.

I picked up the phone.

"Good morning , sir, this is your 6:30 wake-up call."

"What?" I screamed back, "I mean . . ."

"I have you down for a 6:30 wake-up call, sir. You *did* ask for a wake-up call last night for 6:30. Well, it's 6:32 a.m. Is everything all right?"

"What day is it?" Hearing "It's Tuesday, sir," I bounded out of bed glancing at the wall mirror, no zipper scar on my chest! I ran to the bathroom, no pain! I was giddy with delight.

"Yippee!!!" I could barely muffle the cry of joy.

Still in my underwear, I ran to the hotel door, tore it open only to surprise the boy delivering faxes,

"Quick! Where am I? I mean, where are we? I mean, what city is this?" I asked.

"You're in Hong Kong, sir" he said, totally unfazed by my appearance.

I ran back to the bathroom, did a few push-ups on the sink. Then I stopped and realized that it had all been a dream, not a bad dream. Or was it a dream at all? Maybe this is the dream. I know, I'll call my wife!

I was trembling nervously as I dialled the numbers. *Please let this be real*, I prayed. The waiting was eternal and then finally, someone picked up the phone on the other end. It was Jane's voice.

Her "Hello?" was the sweetest music I had ever heard.

"Hello, Jane, dear? This is Peter!," I hollered. "How are you, my love?"

"Why, . . . I'm just *fine*. You don't have to scream, I can hear you perfectly well. How are you? Are you all right?" she asked groggily.

"Just wonderful. It's really *greeeat* to hear your voice after all this time! What did you do today?" I wanted to just hear her voice.

"Peter, it's 11:30 at night and we spoke two days ago. What have you been drinking, dear?" She had been awoken by her suspicions.

"Nothing at all, dear. Listen, uhh . . . uhhh . . . I am coming home early. I'm going to wrap up things at the office today and catch the red-eye flight tonight at midnight. I'll be home by early tomorrow morning. Buy yourself a pretty dress because we're going out on the town tomorrow tonight! I have some things I want to discuss over champagne with you. Got to run right now. Love and kisses. Bye!"

"Good-bye, dear," Jane said hesitantly. I doubt if she had heard such tenderness or energy in my voice since my earlier days as a graduate student. She must be wondering what is going on. That night, Jane would not be sleeping very well.

I slammed down the phone and caught my breath on the edge of my bed.

"Wow! I cannot believe this!" I said aloud to myself. "Wait a minute, I'll call the hospital! What was it now, St Andrew's Hospital here in town, I think. And Dr Charles. Surely that could not have been a dream!"

I dialled the operator, "Yes, operator, I'd like two numbers, one for St Andrew's Hospital and the other for Dr Richard Charles, MD I'll hold."

As I waited for the operator to look up those numbers, I noticed something bizarre on the nightstand: "The Book of Solutions!" It had a handwritten note on the cover.

> *I noticed something bizarre on the nightstand: "The Book of Solutions!"*

Dear Peter, Welcome back. You're on your own now. It was fun. When you get lost, just remember this expression: "when you were born, the world rejoiced while you cried. Live the rest of your life so that when you die, you rejoice while the world cries."

All the best.
Richard.

"Hello, sir?" It was the operator. I waited anxiously, almost knowing already what I was going to hear.

"Yes, have you got those numbers for me?" I asked.

"Sir, I've checked all spellings, but I show no listings, even on the private listing, for either a St Andrew's Hospital or a Dr Richard Charles. I'm sorry, sir."

"Well, thank you, anyway. Good-bye."

I was happy to get dressed quickly, feeling very fortunate to be tying my own tie and fastening my own cufflinks.

As I left the room, I noticed what a beautiful day it was, that the colors somehow seemed brighter. When a chambermaid caught me smelling the flowers in the lobby, I gently whispered a "Good Morning," looking for the smile and glimmer in her eye. I stopped at the bookshop to buy the morning paper, but bought a book of poetry instead, which I pored over gleefully while having my fruit salad in the hotel restaurant.

As I took in the sweet nectars through my eyes and mouth, I could not help but notice just how much things had changed. But it was me who had been changed. I had decided not to become just another tragic statistic. I was going to take charge, at last.

As I stepped out of the hotel, the familiar doorman asked me, "Taxi to your office as usual, sir?"

"No, thank you," I said, smiling. "I think I'll walk today, beautiful day and all." Waving high to the puzzled doorman in my wake, I leapt off the sidewalk, a first step in a thousand mile journey of discovery. Happy to be alive, I bounded down the bustling city street, disappeared into my new thoughts and into the Hong Kong crowds.

ONE YEAR LATER

Well the time had come full circle. I made an 11:30 a.m. appointment with Dr Blum for a follow-up of my medical exam two years previously.

"Well nice to see you," he started, "it's been a long time."

"Yes, it has indeed." I noticed that Dr Blum had put on a few kilos of weight and was moving a little more stiffly and slowly.

As he measured my pressure, body fat, etc. and examined my blood work, his bushy brows, instead of the usual frowning, were perking up. Dr Blum had difficulty holding back his bewilderment. He glanced at me above his glasses, smiling knowingly. He finished his notes and passed them over to me, asking, "Peter, could you *please* explain these findings for me?"

I took the notes and read:

History:
48 y.o. Male, senior manager, family history for heart disease and diabetes, here today for a routine check-up after many months. Active. Upbeat. High vitality.

No *meds*.

Physical exam: *trim, vibrant, male*
(1) *Blood pressure = 135/80 (last time it was ~ 165/95).*
(2) *Resting heart rate = 64 (last time it was ~ 84).*
(3) *Body fat = 23% (last check was 30%).*
(4) *Laboratory work: all optimal.*

Overall assessment
Health risk level: low.
Health age: 39.6 years of age.

Plan: *(amazing case: totally resolved Syndrome X!)*
#1. *Elevated BP: normalized with lifestyle.*
#2. *Excess weight: robust.*
#3. *Follow-up: no need for clinic return, except routine screenings for prostate exam and colonoscopy in 24 months.*

Blum, MD beeper # 413

Before I could begin to explain, he said, "I really don't know what to say. I see a complete turnabout in your rather dire situation of many months ago."

"Well, doctor, when we started working together several years ago, I found myself always attempting to improve myself from a *position of fear.* I was afraid of sickness, of death and that fear paralyzed me into inaction.

"Now, after what I've been through, I wanted to face all these issues of health and death and other fears that I may have squarely. I wanted to learn how to live. The result is that I found myself deciding health issues from a *position of strength.*"

Now I could see that Dr Blum was getting curious, "Peter, you are hiding something from me. What *happened* to you?"

"Well, the only way to even start to explain is to say that after some scary moments in Hong Kong, I guess that I finally woke up . . . yes, from a nightmare, and I started learning about myself. The first thing I learned is that, on the physical level, keeping my body fit and in good health is my duty, the prerequisite for a long, vital, journey. I alone am responsible for the care of my body and mind and no one, not even the best doctor (and doctors and nurses like I had were the best), can take as good a care of my body as I can. To prevent myself being buffeted about by the whims and caprices of the world, I grabbed my rudder and I composed this health strategy for myself." I pulled from my wallet a folded piece of paper showing what I had done over the past year.

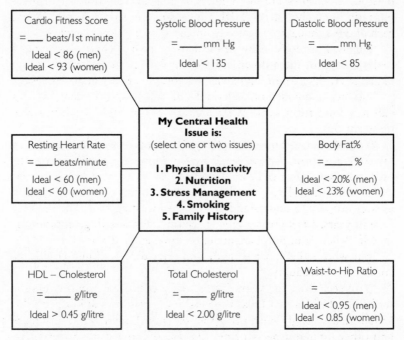

"You see, it's quite simple and I am living proof that it's effective. In fact, I call it the 'Lazy Person's Guide to Staying on Top.' The way I figure, there are only really five things in life and health that need fine-tuning.

I showed Dr Blum what I had jotted down on paper.

1. physical activity
2. nutrition
3. sanity control
4. family history; and
5. smoking.

"The way to use this chart is really simple," I explained.

"First, for the next six months only, identify the ONE issue that you know deep down needs attention. For me a year ago, it was physical activity. So, I circled that issue.

"Second, to determine just how this central issue, as I call it, is affecting my health, I fill in the blank spaces for systolic blood pressure, diastolic blood pressure, body fat percentage, cardio-fitness, waist-to-hip ratio, total cholesterol, HDL cholesterol and so on. As you know, each of those things are negatively impacted by physical inactivity.

"Finally, I just look below at the activity menu. I choose the things I really enjoy, jot them down and get on with it, at my speed, to my liking. It's really a lot of fun playing doctor. No offence intended, Doc."

"No, no, of course not. But surely, all this 'empowerment,' as you call it, comes from some *inner* attitude about life?" Dr Blum was quite curious.

"Yes, of course. You see, I always knew that I was, deep down at my core, a warrior. A year ago I went to Hong Kong with a bad attitude to life and a fear of death. I came home with a new faith in myself and in the Grand Design of life. I look at things differently, with a greater urgency to understand and to stop wasting time. For the first time in years, I feel greater inner harmony, and less fragmentation of myself. Believe it or not, I am actually enjoying life day-to-day."

"But who is this inner warrior you refer to?" Dr Blum could not contain his incredulity.

"You see, Doc, for years I was really confused. I had oversubscribed to the idea that I was the most important person in the world. I identified strongly with my appetites, my thoughts, and my fears and other limited aspects of my life. I had allowed my appetites to run rampant, creating havoc in my life. Now I realize that my fears and appetites (and they are many) are only there to be mastered as an exercise for me to strengthen my inner self, my inner warrior. What it comes down to, Doc, is who is really in charge in there," I said pointing to my chest, "and the fact of the matter is that to optimally enjoy this parade called life, a little self-discipline goes a long way." I could see that Dr Blum had stopped glancing at his watch and appointment pad and was with me, stride for stride.

> *"And the fact of the matter is that to optimally enjoy this parade called life, a little self-discipline goes a long way."*

"The funny thing is that I really didn't have to work very hard to get 'on the road,' I just started by letting my real self develop by cutting through all the outer layers of conditioning from my parents, teachers, society and so on. I feel as if I am witnessing the flowering of my new self. It's very strange and very refreshing." What was indeed strange was to be engaged in an equal conversation with Dr Blum, who, for so many years, had been a father figure for me.

"But how did you start this whole process of health improvement? I mean, your figures are so dramatically improved, beyond anything I could have done for you," he asked, in a searching tone.

"That's precisely my point. What I mean is that it's not really about an abstract set of medical figures, is it? They only really indicate some inner turmoil and imbalance anyway. What it is really about is the inner balance. The only *real* question I have from moment to moment is, in a given set of circumstances, when do I act and when do I observe. That is, when do I need to jump on a situation with two feet, so to speak, and when do I need to sit back and watch the cloud patterns go by."

"Just one quick question, Peter," asked the portly physician, "aside from all the inner mysticism, which, by the way, makes a lot of sense to a scientist like me, how did you manage to get rid of all that body fat?"

"Oh, that's an easy one. I just stopped trying so hard to crush my desire for rich foods and then just tried to train my body to enjoy without feeling guilty about it. I started by eliminating expressions from my vocabulary like:

> 'I love chips' or
> 'I adore spaghetti bolognaise' or
> 'I am lazy'
> 'I lack discipline'
> 'I cannot lose weight'
> 'I must do this . . . I must do that . . .'

or whatever. Those were impositions on a very limited and very vulnerable mortal ego, identity known as Peter, born 1947, died whenever. My ego perceived those impositions just as a child perceives the parental impositions that are crammed every day down his throat: with rebellion.

"I was building my castles on sand. All these references to myself, to me actually made me feel more and more lonely and perpetuated the illusion that I was the centre of the Universe. What Copernicus did for philosophy through astronomy, I needed psychologically.

"I've got a great story of an 'awakening,' of how I got a second chance to 'get it right,' that balance between heart and head, work and play, participation and observation. This is a story of how I transformed my personal and professional life from one where there were a lot of impossible 'shoulds' to a multitude of feasible 'coulds.' Now I think of my body as my horse. I would never deprive it of food unwillingly. But, now my body is under my control. My body is still attached to all the good things: rich foods, black Belgian chocolate, durian, foie gras, sex or whatever. The only real difference is that now, I am in control, not my appetites. And this is really just the beginning.

"Speaking of which, my body is hungry for something delicious. Come on, Doc, I'll invite you to lunch at my favourite French restaurant. By the way, do you like foie gras frais aux raisins? Maybe a little glass of Montrachet or Pauillac to go with. Or maybe a nice Australian white, they've been doing good things with wine these days. Watch the white bread, Doc: nutritional slap in the face. By the way, don't schedule anything right after lunch, we'll go for a walk . . . ."

POSTSCRIPT:
THE URBAN WARRIOR
STAYS ALIVE

The story of this patient is a *true* one, not of just one warrior, but a *mosaic* of many thousands of urban warriors, based on interviews and private consultations and compiled into one epic transformation: from "Mr Time-bomb" to the Urban Warrior. It is the story of many managers and professionals that needs to be told and listened to if we, as medical professionals, hope to have any chance of stopping the wave of "diseases of affluence." Patients on their deathbed become extremely lucid and aware. Their priorities are clear, they have little time to waste. Nobody on their deathbed ever wishes that they had spent more time at the office.

Throughout the centuries, paradoxical though it may seem, virtually all spiritual and secular cultures have used the analogy of war to signify the greatest of battles. History is replete with excellent examples of the warrior spirit.

Whether one studies Judaism, Christianity (the Crusades), Hinduism (the *Bhagavad Gita*) or Islam (the *Jihad*), the concept of "holy war" and warriors abounds. Over two thousand years ago, Sun Tzu compiled the *Art of War* which sprang from the great spiritual tradition of Taoism. The Japanese developed and idealized the whole concept of samurai and, in fact, warriors ruled Japan for seven tumultuous centuries starting in the late 12th century and lasting until 1868. Native American Indians, revered around the world for their noble spiritual traditions, had a warrior tradition. Even nowadays, everywhere you look, the warrior mindset is revived. These are warrior types for whom the battle is on the outside, out *there*, in the world. But what, indeed, is the nature of a *true* warrior who knows where the real battles are taking place? On this issue, above all others, we *must* get it right.

Throughout the years, we have all been taught that the war is "out there." We have to just face it. Life is war: an invigorating and prolonged conflict, composed of a constant series of battles, not just for power, money, land, food, water, but also in preservation of happiness, lofty principles, love. Territory is gained and territory is lost and you revel in the game. Sure we all take some tough "hits" now and again in the process which may temporarily send us into a tailspin, but that will never deter us, only spur us on.

In the material world of business, the generation of new ideas, and bringing them to reality and getting them exposed in the market alongside (or in front of) those of the competition is a real satisfaction to be savored. The "enemies" are well identified and the battle lines are drawn clearly in the sand. Any self-respecting professional, either in the academic context or out there "on the front line" will admit to the thrill of engaging one's talents and skills in pursuit of something meaningful, particularly if competition is involved. And you, as the modern descendants of these ancient warriors, all love it that way.

You can divide the world into two basic types of people: warriors and worriers. The warriors prepare themselves for the battles, while the worriers, crippled by self-doubt, spend precious resources fretting over a self-fulfilling prophecy. War has been part of the human experience from time immemorial. As modern corporate warriors, we have all had flashes of strategic brilliance on Life's battlefields. As it turns out, the greatest of all battles will be the internal battles against all sorts of devils: fear of being ourselves, hatred for our brothers and sisters, choice of the "easy" way instead of the "right" way, self-deprecation, self-doubt and feelings of unworthiness.

The Urban Warrior, realizing this has extended the playing field to include the greatest battlefield of all: *within*. You are the modern counterparts of the warriors of old, with a slight twist. That warrior within is the immutable, unspoiled and original essence of a human being prior to all the conditioning – a flame that can never be extinguished.

The *Bhagavad Gita*, one of Hinduism's great epic poems, suggests that the real battle has nothing to do with oppression of, or violence towards, others. Despite the obvious setting in the Gita of armed kinsmen pitched against one another on a tense, smoking, battlefield, it really has more to do with the internal battle of right choices and self-mastery than with bloodshed and violence. The battle within the human body is for the high moral ground between "opposing moral tendencies," as Ghandi called them. The real battle in life is within us constantly raging between the forces of **good** (truth, kindness, generosity, authenticity, impeccability, sincerity, justice, hope, humor, patience, and especially, love) and **evil** (greed, humorlessness, cynicism, intolerance, selfishness, laziness, ignorance, mediocrity, meanness, and especially, fear).

Thomas Merton, a man of peace and a Trappist monk, commented incisively on the Gita and the internal spiritual struggles of the protagonist, Arjuna:

> . . . the *Gita* presents a problem to some who read it in the present context of violence and war which mark the crisis of the West. The Gita appears to accept and to justify war. Arjuna is exhorted to submit his will to Krishna by going to war against his enemies, who are also his own kin, because war is his duty as a prince and as a warrior . . . .
>
> . . . The *Gita* is not a justification of war, nor does it propound a war-making mystique . . . Arjuna has an instinctive repugnance for war and that is the chief reason why war is chosen as the example of the most repellent kind of duty. The *Gita* is saying that even in what appears to be most "unspiritual" one can act with pure intentions . . . . This consciousness itself will impose the most strict limitations on one's use of violence because that use will not be directed by one's own selfish interests, still less by cruelty, sadism and blood-lust.
>
> from *The Asian Journals of Thomas Merton*

Another erudite interpretation is offered by a learned student of the *Upanishads*, Eknath Easwaran:

> First, we are neither body nor mind; these simply make up the vehicle with which we travel through life. Second, there is a purpose to the mind. It is not supposed to lounge around emoting and desiring; its job is to guide the senses, pulling them up when they start to run after something pleasant instead of going where we want to go. And the intellect is not supposed to sit in an ivory tower and classify things that do not matter.

In this metaphor, nothing is served by the stoic renunciation wherein our horses (the senses) are subjugated to a severe puritanical mindset. More intelligently, the sense and our desires (which give us life energy) should be trained and channeled to achieve our objectives in life, to get us where we want to go. That way, there are no regrets because we stay on the chosen route.

So many of us have failed to forge the balance between our head and our heart. Often, our head (the intellect or driver of the chariot, above) dominates the senses and desires and we have no driving passion in life because the horses are too dominated and crushed to get us through.

At the other end of the spectrum, the desires or senses are too strong (uncontrolled horses) and our ability to decide the best way becomes veiled in longing. Enduring happiness comes from achieving mastery of the desires and the intellect in a dynamic tension. This can be accomplished through meditation.

In our workaday world, we use certain "cues" to orient ourselves ("Oh, yeah, I'm a father, husband, manager: it's Monday, it's time to get up, use the toilet, drink some coffee and get to work"). Rarely in the course of a professional business career are we afforded the opportunity to ask the question: "Why are we doing this? Are we seeking parental ambition, peer approval, at any cost."

In blindly seeking to satisfy the approval of bosses, peers, spouses or parents, we may be setting ourselves up for profound disappointment. There are several things that actually make the inner warrior sleep.

Things that make the inner warrior fall asleep

1. Excessive talking, failure to develop a quiet mind.
2. Complacency/routine caused by excessive wealth, power or beauty, fame or fear of survival.
3. Peer pressure and approval hunger.
4. Excessive sensory bombardment.
5. Self-doubt, preoccupation with the ego, the limited self.
6. Excessive seriousness.
7. Excessive absorption with the *past*, projection too much on the *future*.
8. Bad wine, without ritual.

Things that make the inner warrior awaken

1. Reading (the classics), poetry and listening to others.
2. Developing a sense of adventure: fearlessness and daring to dare.
3. Independence, honesty and re-evaluation of priorities.
4. A quiet, disciplined mind: meditation and prayer.
5. Trust in self as part of Self.
6. Humor, playfulness and spontaneity.
7. Living the PRESENT being present to lessons at hand, living life ALIVE.
8. Fine (red) wine to celebrate a victory.

Instead of falling into the stale routine view of things, try to view events in your life afresh with the benefit of another perspective. So, in the so-called *real* world, fellow warrior, when you awake every morning and rediscover the same old physical, materialistic, world, pulling you in, seducing and distracting you, remember a few tips that will help keep the inner warrior alive.

There are forces acting within us, each tempting us to invest in them. At every juncture and in *every* decision, however trivial (from saying "Good morning" to the cleaning lady in the hotel to serious ethical decisions at work), these forces within us are constantly in opposition, in conflict. Both sides of this classic dichotomy are *essential* halves of the whole human experience. The "fire" of the conflict between good and evil forces provides not just the heat, but also the light necessary for personal growth. The true urban warrior is aware of that and he is undaunted by the battle – "We're always going to take some hits, but we'll come through in the end." There is no backing down from the "battle" because it is the essential human experience, waiting for you at every juncture, every instant.

The warrior knows that there are many things in life that can "go wrong," that, quite often, horrible things happen to very good people, but he is undaunted by the task. He is not paralyzed by his vulnerabilities because he knows how to handle certain mental, physical or spiritual turbulence that ultimately stems from identification with transitory aspects of life. The warrior is not easily frightened by thunderstorms, nor deluded by false idols.

In the course of life, everybody goes through certain times when, often quite by chance when we least expect it, we experience an awakening, a flash of the real fragility of life. This comes to us through some special experience, such as the illness of a child, a near fatal car accident, a dead bird in our driveway, glancing through the obituaries and noticing the death of a contemporary or close friend. With death only right around the corner, life goes from a chore or penance to something delicate.

We then try to put the whole thing into a new focus that gives back meaning to this experience called *life*. Once we succeed in developing this fresh perspective on things, we also succeed in arousing within a sleeping self that longing for real understanding of seemingly unrelated phenomena.

Lying in a hospital bed recuperating from heart surgery, "wired for sound," completely dependent on strangers and uncertain of your fate does indeed have definite benefits. You are thrown back upon yourself, you are afforded a reluctant pause for reflection to take stock of your life. Questions come up like:

- *Am I really doing what I want to do?*
- *At every juncture of life, am I making conscious decisions to do "the right thing," to pursue the "right path?"*
- *Am I honouring those with whom I am in daily contact (children, spouse, colleagues) by giving them undivided attention?*
- *Am I winning this game called "life?"*
- *Am I respecting my body, the temple of my soul?*
- *Am I keeping the smile on my face by keeping the flame in my heart?*
- *Am I honouring my life by living it to the fullest?*

A last word of encouragement

The key to awakening the urban warrior within is to start from where you are because, above all, to be an urban warrior you need to be completely unafraid of who you really are. There is no other place to start.

The good news is that once "awakened," the warrior cannot be crushed, or smothered or turned back. And it is impossible to stay "lost." Whether on the golf course, in the conference room or resting quietly at night, just quiet the chatter and you will find him.

So, potential fellow warriors, never fret. We are all on the path to becoming warriors: some of us are further along that path, some getting there faster and some are just better actors. No matter. Never be discouraged. If you don't get there now, it will be later. Sooner or later, we will *all* arrive. Just keep on trying and enjoy the ride.

APPENDICES

APPENDIX 1: SPECIAL TOPICS

This appendix is intended to provide a distilled version of important issues that, although they may not *directly* threaten your life, will, if not properly balanced, compromize your performance, as well as compromize your quality of life.

The topics are presented, therefore, in a concise easy-to-read encapsulation of what you *really* need to know.

WOMEN'S HEALTH I: OSTEOPOROSIS

It has long been called "the silent epidemic" because it sneaks up on 25% of all post-menopausal women without any real symptoms or warning. For many women, it is not the loss of menses (and all that comes with it) that scares them, as much as the very real possibility that they will be inevitably "bent in two." In this decade, getting osteoporosis is quickly becoming a matter of choice.

When oestrogen is no longer produced to keep calcium in the bones, the bones become brittle, porous, hence the name, "osteoporosis," and are a set-up for fractures. According to the Osteoporosis Foundation in Washington, DC (USA), osteoporosis is responsible for 1.3 million bone fractures every year. A full third of American women older than 65 will have a spinal fracture and about 15% will suffer a hip fracture. The Foundation estimates that the annual cost of treating osteoporosis is about US$10 billion, out of which US$7 billion is due to fractures.

Who's at risk?

At highest risk for "brittle bone disease" are white women who are thin, with a history of the disease in the family, women with a history of hysterectomy (with removal of the ovaries), women with insufficient exercise, a diet poor in calcium but high in alcohol, caffeine, and phosphate, women who are sedentary and who smoke.

Prevention of osteoporosis

Once the ovaries stop producing oestrogen, the calcium starts to rapidly "escape" from the bones. Some estimates show that women may actually lose up to 30% of total bone mass. Therefore prevention should begin well before the onset of menopause.

Calcium in your diet

The NIH (the National Institute of Health – USA) recommends that women get 1,000 – 1,500 mg of calcium each day (dairy and soy products, green vegetables, beans, fish, yoghurt). There are several easy ways to facilitate the absorption of the calcium mineral from foods. Here are some of them:

1. *get plenty of sunshine* (our main source of vitamin D – which facilitates calcium absorption); not hours, just 10 to 15 minutes/day while you walk to work;
2. *avoid excesses of caffeine and cola drinks*, which impair the kidneys' ability to reabsorb (conserve) calcium; if you cannot avoid these beverages, compensate by drinking a cup of skimmed milk for every two cups of coffee;
3. *don't overdo the fibre dose:* fibre contains phytate, which binds calcium and blocks its absorption. Compensate these losses by using calcium supplements;
4. *salt increases the amount of calcium lost by the kidneys:* shake the habit;
5. *medications* like aluminium-containing antacids, laxatives, steroids and diuretics may impair calcium absorption: compensate with calcium supplements.

Oestrogen Replacement Therapy (ORT)

In a special study convened by the NIH, ORT was found to be a highly effective method of curbing bone loss and fractures. Given the protective effects on the heart and bones, it is estimated that 80% of modern women would benefit from ORT without increased risk. Combining this approach with calcium supplements (1,500 mg of calcium lactate) and weight-bearing exercise (like walking) may help to make osteoporosis a disease of the past.

One critical proviso: all benefits in preventing bone fractures in older post-menopausal women are cancelled for women who smoke, according to a study in a recent issue of the *Annals of Internal Medicine* (USA).

Weight-bearing exercises

The best exercises to increase the bone mass are those that carry your own weight: walking, jogging, cycling, hiking and so on. Swimming does not bear your weight.

WOMEN'S HEALTH II: BREAST HYGIENE

Preventing breast cancer

There are several factors in our lifestyle that can cut our risk of getting breast cancer. The first step is to examine your **diet**.

1. Some experts believe that consuming too much *fat* may increase your risk for breast cancer. Fat could become a vital link in the development of breast cancers and other cancers of the reproductive tract.
2. Another factor concerns the formation of *free radicals* (unstable compounds that are formed in our body in response to some foods, pollution, cigarette smoke, radiation and like compounds). These unstable compounds, which lead to premature ageing, cancers and atherosclerosis, can be "scavenged" by a group of vitamins called anti-oxidants (vitamins C, E, beta-carotene, selenium) in appropriate dosages. For example, in New Zealand, where the soil is poor in selenium, women have one of the highest rates of breast cancer in the world. The excessive use of selenium can be toxic.
3. Studies performed at the National Cancer Institute (USA) concluded that women who consumed moderate (more than three drinks per day) amounts of *alcohol* ran a 50% higher risk of developing breast cancer.
4. *Exercise* seems to have a beneficial effect as studies at Harvard showed that non-athletic women have twice the risk of breast cancer than athletic women

Detection of breast cancer

Self-examination is the first step, and should be performed by every woman **each month** but not during your menstrual period. There is no excuse for not examining your breasts regularly. So, if you are too squeamish to do it, find a doctor or nurse to do it for you.

Recommendations

- The American Cancer Society recommends that women between the ages 20–40 years have a thorough breast exam by a qualified doctor every three years.

- The American College of Radiology recommends that by the ages 35–40 years all women should have a "baseline" mammogram (with which future mammograms, repeated every two years until age 50 can be compared, until normal). The advantage of mammography is that it can detect breast cancer about two years before it is detectable to the touch.
- Women should have their breasts examined by their doctor every year and a mammogram every one–two years until they are normal, at which point they should have mammograms every year.
- If you have a first degree relative (sister, mother or daughter) who has had breast cancer, your mammogram surveillance should begin ten years before their cancer was detected, when possible.

WATER

Water is the only drink for a wise man.
Thoreau: *Walden II*, "Higher Laws"

Some 200 to 300 million years ago, animals crawled up onto the land to have a look around. Our amphibious ancestors looked around, found life more interesting on the dry land, adapted and stayed "topside", while the predecessors of other mammals (such as the whales and dolphins) returned to the more stable environment of the seas.

Since that epoch, while living on the desiccated surface of our planet, we have become like "leaky" vessels, constantly losing vital fluids.

We must therefore, carry our oceans with us.

The human body is mostly water

Blood   90% ⎫
Kidneys   82% ⎪
Muscles   75% ⎬ H_2O
Brain   74% ⎪
Liver   69% ⎭

Functions: only oxygen is more essential

a. Dissolving and transporting nutrients;
b. Temperature regulation (especially during exercise);
c. Digestion and assimilation of foods (as component of saliva and gastric secretions);
d. Lubrication of intestines (to prevent constipation);

e. Metabolism and elimination (helps carry away waste products in urine);

f. Compensation of acid-base imbalances.

Losses

In general, your water needs increase as you become more active. A simple rule of thumb is: for every calorie you burn, you will use 1 milliliter of water. That is, an active person, burning 2,000 to 3,000 calories per day needs two to three liters/day, either as pure water, juices or fruit and vegetables. The losses are from the following sources:

a. *Perspiration:* up to one liter a day for inactive people and up to three or even four liters for active people living in hot, humid, conditions;

b. *Tears, saliva and breathing:* up to 0.5 liters (every time you exhale, you breathe out water and carbon dioxide as by-products of glucose metabolism);

c. *Urine and faeces* (normal conditions): 1.5–2 liters.

Check your water requirements by weighing yourself before and after you exercise (the premise being that all acute weight loss during exercise is due to water loss). If you lost a kilogram of weight, that's a liter of water that you lost and must replace!

Needs

If not replaced? With a smaller volume than normal due to: (1) *inadequate intake,* or (2) *inappropriate losses* (through excess coffee or alcohol use), the heart must work harder to complete the "circuit." A total body water loss of 10–15% can be fatal. The water supplied can be in the form of fresh water or fruits and vegetables, which, of course, are mostly water.

Symptoms of dehydration

These range from mild increases in heart rate, fatigue (both due to low blood volume), nausea and vomiting (exacerbating fluid and mineral losses) and constipation to cerebral impairment. Best sign of adequate hydration is a pale, straw-coloured, urine. Also, watch your spittle while exercising: is it white? If so, you are dehydrated! The sensation of thirst and a rapid resting heart rate are not reliable signs of dehydration!

Tap or bottled water?

Simple to determine: have your tap water analysed for nitrates and lead contamination.

Best consumed . . .

Between meals is the best time. With meals, water can dilute digestive secretions and impair digestion. Best temperature: at room temperature or slightly warmer. Ice cold drinks can shock the stomach lining and cause cramps.

CAFFEINE

Caffeine, the active ingredient in coffee and some teas, is methylxanthine, a derivative used worldwide for centuries for its stimulating effects. Its half life of $T_{1/2}$ ($T_{1/2}$ is the amount of time that it takes the body to clear one half the original concentration) is about five hours. That means that if you consume a coffee at 5 p.m., one half the original concentration is still present at 10 p.m.

Evidence

Attempts to sort out the debate regarding caffeine use have led to the conclusion that, in moderate doses (200 to 300 mgs), caffeine poses no definite health risk to **most people**. In excess of 300 mgs, sleep and REM is reduced, setting up a potentially vicious cycle of caffeine-induced insomnia combated unwittingly by more caffeine for arousal the next day.

Sources

One cup = 150 ml	*Average caffeine content (mg)*
Percolated, ground	83
Instant	59
Decaffeinated	3
Cocoa	6–42
Colas	15/cup
Chocolate	40

(*Source*: British National Formulary. London: BMA & Royal Pharmaceutical Society, 1992)

Effects

Possible effects on you include:

1. increases in blood pressure, heart rate, respiration;
2. diuresis of body fluids: stimulates water plus mineral loss;
3. temporarily relieves fatigue: at what price? The whole issue of caffeine as an ergogenic agent (performance enhancer) is still a much heated debate;

4. excess (300–1000 mgs), caffeine causes irritability, anxiety, insomnia, excess gastric secretion (possibly, predisposing to ulcers), irregular heart beats, dehydration and mineral *deficiencies*.

What to do?

1. Be moderate. Watch the aforementioned symptoms of caffeine excess and moderate accordingly.
2. Always compensate water and mineral losses with fresh water and fresh fruit.
3. Heart (may provoke erratic heart rhythms) and epileptic (caffeine lowers seizure threshold) patients and pregnant (excessive doses may lead to spontaneous abortions and growth retardation) or breastfeeding women, should avoid caffeine-containing beverages.

ALCOHOL

> It provokes the desire, but takes away the performance.
> Therefore, much drink may be said to be an equivocator of lechery.
> *Shakespeare*

Alcohol that we drink, ethanol or ethyl alcohol, is only one of many members of the chemical family known as alcohol. Ethanol is a small compound (just a 2-carbon fragment C-C-OH) that can be metabolized at the rate of roughly one drink per hour by the action of the liver enzyme, alcohol dehydrogenase, to water and carbon dioxide. If the enzyme system is overwhelmed by excessive alcohol intake, the process produces acetaldehyde, a toxin.

Though it is well-known to induce stupor and sleep, when the initial effect wears off, a heightened arousal period can occur, which can disturb sleep and REM (Rapid Eye Movement).

Physiology

1. Alcohol is a brain depressant and a toxin to the muscle of the heart.
2. Alcohol causes marked water and mineral losses.
3. Alcohol can worsen elevated blood pressure, increasing risks for stroke.
4. Alcohol is calorifically-dense: 7.2 call gram.
5. Because of its small molecular size, 25% is directly absorbed through the stomach wall.
6. Alcohol can cause or worsen snoring.

7. Research shows that two–three glasses of red wine/day decreases the risk of dying from ALL causes, especially heart diseases by increasing the good cholesterol, HDL.

Can alcohol make you fat?

Recent Swiss studies suggest that it is not just the "empty calories" in alcohol that makes it fattening: it is the way that alcohol suppresses the body's normal system of fat disposal.

Getting ready for a "heavy night"

1. Never drink alcohol on an empty stomach: buffer with water, juice, snacks. Make the first drink fruit juice.
2. Always compensate water and mineral losses with fresh water and fresh fruit. Hydrate well before cocktail parties.
3. Make every other drink a fruit juice a standard practice.
4. Watch the old "1-2-3 punch:" chips, fatty snacks and alcohol.
5. Pay your "fluid debt" before retiring: two–three glasses of water.

Preventing a hangover

A "hangover" is a euphemism for a severely dehydrated (low blood volume), hypoglycemic (low sugar), hypokalemic (low potassium) state wherein you have irritated the covering of the brain (the meninges).

So all right, you've had your big night, you feel tipsy, you are a little slow and muddled and you've forgotten the aforementioned tips. Anyway, you've found your way home. Prior to crashing, note these tips on how not to pay too dearly the next morning for the indulgences of the evening:

1. A glass of water for every drink you had, for the dehydrative effects of alcohol. Don't worry, your body will keep every drop as it's parched.
2. A banana or two, for the nice potassium and fruit sugar.
3. A 500 mg aspirin, for the inflammation and anesthetic. Don't worry, the bananas will prevent stomach irritation from the aspirin.

Then go to sleep smiling on your *right* side. This is the side on which the stomach empties itself so that the above can get downstream to be absorbed. Bon Nuit!

Am I drinking too much, Doctor?

First you take a drink, the drink takes a drink, then the drink takes you.

F. Scott Fitzgerald

If you suspect that you are drinking too much alcohol, stop drinking for a week and take careful notes on withdrawal symptoms, if any, such as: irritability, sleeplessness, anxiety, or tremors.

On a lighter note, you drink too much if:

1. you cry/laugh too much when you drink;
2. everything seems "just right" during a heavy night.

Best consumed . . .

With meals, with friends, toasting to something special. On an empty stomach, alcohol can break down the auto-protective mucus layer in the stomach (that prevents "auto-digestion"). This breakdown leads to gastritis and ulcers. Have a little natural snack like peanuts, olives or carrot sticks.

BUILDING STAMINA

There's one complaint seen regularly in clinics around the world: " . . . just not enough energy to get everything done, Doc." Inability to find energy to deal with your personal and professional agenda will cause you added stress. Having enough will cut you an added advantage and make life more fun.

There are essentially two global causes for low stamina: *organic* (disease states: heart disease, anemia, diabetes, cancer, sluggish thyroid, viral syndromes, flu, and so on) and *functional* causes (the way you are organizing your daily life). In this section, attention will be paid mostly to the latter.

Functional causes and remedies for low stamina states

Cause	Remedy
1. Low blood oxygen	Proper breathing exercise Stop smoking Improve posture
2. Low blood volume	Increase water intake Watch alcohol use Watch caffeine use
3. Low blood sugar	Watch refined sugar intake Eat fruits
4. Uncompensated stress	Stress Management And Relaxation Techniques (SMART)

▶

5. Inadequate sleep quality	Thought control Regular exercise Watch caffeine Optimize ambience Improve sleep
6. Excessive exercise	Relax and get some sleep
7. Carrying excess fat	Get rid of excess fat

The overall strategy for combating fatigue would be:

1. Examine the above lifestyle (functional) causes;
2. Spend three–six months optimizing your lifestyle. For example, increase water intake, activity level, decrease coffee intake or whatever.
3. If, after six months of "cleaning it up," you are still tired all the time, see your doctor for a screening for diabetes (fasting blood sugar), heart disease (EKG), thyroid disease (blood tests), anemia (complete blood count) and so on.

That would be an intelligent approach to building enough stamina to get on with your personal and professional life.

JET-LAG

Making light of jet-lag

Chances are good that your health and professional performance will be compromised by the accumulated stresses of international travel, unless compensated. The scientific evidence continues to accumulate that long distance air travel through multiple time zones can precipitate health problems, ranging from temporary sleep disturbances to debilitating heart disorders.

Call it what you might, "rapid time zone change syndrome," "circadian rhythm shifts secondary to transmeridian travel" or jet-lag, this modern phenomenon introduced with the advent of jet travel is simply another example of how you have voluntarily allowed technology and behavior to override human biology, thereby creating a fundamental mismatch between normal nocturnal sleeping habits and the fast-track business world that expects you to be as alert at 3 a.m. in Tokyo as you were at 9 a.m. in London or New York.

During the past 30 years, great advances have been made in our understanding of the basic underlying neurophysiological processes governing adaptation to light and darkness. An entirely new field of research has been born: chronobiology. Proper functioning of many of the body's vegetative functions, including sleepiness, wakefulness, appetite, intestinal function and body temperature, is directly dependent upon the natural light-dependent cycle known as the circadian (diurnal) rhythm.

Because this circadian or diurnal rhythm generally runs on a 25-hour cycle, it will constantly reset itself on a daily basis instead of lagging behind. This naturally elongated schedule explains one curiosity of jet travel: travelling eastward, say from New York to London, will shorten the calendar day, thereby catapulting the eastbound traveller's biological cycle into the following morning when it says he should be sleeping, resulting in severe fatigue, loss of mental lucidity, and disorientation as the rhythm searches for a new reference point to reset itself by. Using various external prompters such as light, meals, activity and social interaction to bring you back into synch, the brain is generally able to reset only one to two hours of lost cycle per day, so that the trip mentioned above might throw you off for a full week.

Of those external cues used by the body to adapt, **light** is the single most powerful synchronizing agent for resetting the biologic clock in the brain: the suprachiasmic nucleus (SCN), which is connected to light sensing cells in the eye. According to pioneering light research done at Harvard University, resetting the biologic time clock can be practically done by precisely timing exposure to bright light at certain times during the circadian cycle, to reset the clock earlier or later or simply deaden the cycle's peaks and troughs. Related research also shows that the pineal gland, located deep in the brain, Descartes "seat of the soul," actually secretes a powerful light-related hormone – melatonin – which has a fundamental role in the resetting of the body's time clock.

Furthermore, researchers at the Johnson Space Center have shown that the prolonged immobility of overseas flights causes the body to excrete excessive amounts of two substances essential to optimal physical performance: potassium and sodium. This loss accounts for the decreased muscle strength, diminished physical (and mental) reflexes, confusion and, quite possibly, disturbances in heart rhythm. Physical exercise (the day of the flight) helps release potassium into the blood, thus compensating losses resulting from flight immobility.

Given the obvious individual differences between people, a universal remedy to jet-lag is probably unlikely. What follows are practical ways to weave the latest research into your high-tech lives. When I asked several hundred successful travelling managers what strategies they use to battle jet-lag, two strategies came up every time: (1) abstinence from alcohol and (2) exercise. Solutions to battling jet-lag should be divided into three stages: what you can do *before departing*, things you can do *while in flight*, and things you can do *upon arrival*.

Before your departure . . .

First, try to reset your biologic clock. For long trips of a week or more, it really pays to try to gently change your daily rhythm (by one hour a day prior to departure) to simulate your new local time zone. In other words, if you are going from Europe to the west coast of America (where you will be falling to sleep about nine hours earlier), get to sleep one hour earlier every day for three to four days before departing.

For shorter trips of two to three days, attempt to "tough it out" by sticking to the home schedule. That way at least you will not be adapting twice in as many days and you can arrive home hitting the ground running.

While in flight . . .

If you are really serious about beating jet-lag, several "absolutes" must be adhered to religiously. Proper hydration is one such absolute, as the humidity of the plane's cabin air can be uncomfortably low (3%). Rehumidifying the air to more comfortable levels (25 to 35%) requires about 200 liters/hour on a 747 or two tons of water for a ten hour flight: that can get very expensive.

Your strategy should be the same as the flight crew: rehumidify yourself! You can kill two birds with one stone by drinking at least one glass of orange juice (potassium and water) every hour while you are awake. Don't worry, overdosing on orange juice is not possible. Furthermore, resist the seductions of free alcohol and coffee, two substances that will induce lethargy by wringing your system dry and cause potassium loss, and in doing so, set you up for the worst case of jet-lag possible.

Prior to dozing off (something which will be easy for you if you have previously fatigued your body with exercise), do a few arm lifts: using the arm rests, lift your weight (discreetly) off the seat several times. This will help to keep the blood circulating well while you sleep.

After arriving . . .

Make yourself a promise that you will arrange your schedule beforehand (such as by arriving the day before meetings) to accommodate a physical work-out some time before meetings. This will provide the vital organs (including the brain) with well-circulated blood richly saturated in another critical substance: oxygen.

Until the light researchers have found a way to install bright light on aircraft or in hotels in a way that safely dissipates the heat generated and makes it accessible to all desiring it, use exercise and light together to reset the time clock within you. The best time, according to chronobiologists, to do this for eastbound passengers would be to take a jog (or any aerobic work-out) mid-morning of your arrival in bright (artificial or natural sun) light. For the westbound traveller, take a late afternoon or early evening jog or work-out in bright light. This will hold back the clock until you catch up, and do not go to bed until the evening and then stick to local schedules.

"Jet-lag diets" and over-the-counter "anti-jet-lag pills" have little scientific validity according to studies of soldiers involved with large troop maneuvres overseas. Light therapy, combined with an intelligent mixture of hydration and exercise appears to be the highly efficacious drug-free treatment of choice for those whose sleep/activity patterns are disrupted by transmeridian travel.

TRAVEL AND HOTEL WORK-OUT

Weary Traveller: These exercises are designed to provide for you a structure to increase your metabolic rate (i.e. calorie consumption) and to provide the first line of defense against "jet-lag." (If used regularly several days before the trip.)

Regular use of these exercises in your hotel room or gym (three minutes in a.m., three minutes in p.m.), will result in a higher level of fitness and stamina while "on the road."

I. Warm-up stretches

(a) *Arm circles:* Stand up and rotate your arms for ten seconds (as with a backstroke) and reverse direction for ten seconds. This exercise strengthens your shoulder muscles.

(b) *Reach up and stretch:* Still while standing, reach as high as you can for the sky (hold for three seconds). Repeat ten times.

(c) *Towel stretch:* Pick up the towel at both ends and stretch the towel overhead as tight as possible. Repeat ten times. Now stretch the towel behind your buttocks and pull the towel forward. Repeat ten times.

2. 4-minute work-out
(see pages 144–6)

3. Bathroom callisthenics:

(a) *Bathtub push-ups:* Leaning forward with arms extended on the edge of the bathtub (don't slip!) at 45 degrees, hands touching, back straight, perform as many push-ups as possible.

(b) *Bathtub "Crunch":* Get in the tub, arms on the edges, lift your weight straight up (try three times). Add one for every day in that hotel. This exercise strengthens shoulder and abdominal muscles.

IMPROVING MEMORY AND CONCENTRATION

Practice *single-mindedness*
These exercises represent the epitome of the "active searching mind." None of this is to imply that your mind should always be working frantically; it is precisely because the mind will be sharper as a result of these exercises that your mind will not have to work as hard to master the same amount of material. It will pick it *all* up first time round instead of having to go back several times to remember simple material. You only have to *allow* your mind to work for you.

Steps:
1. Do this exercise either when you are "captive" (in your hotel room, on a plane, train, at a bus stop) or when you have ten minutes on your hands.
2. Pick a simple object (i.e. a candle) in front of you and fix your eyes upon it, excluding all other input. Public transportation is especially good for this as we always will have the five or ten minutes necessary to refine concentrative abilities.

At first, this will be exceedingly difficult as people will be walking past and other thoughts in your mind will be vying for your attention. Stick with it. Once this exercise proves no longer challenging to you, try an exercise which is a variation on the same theme: the candle. In a quiet room, sit in a comfortable chair or on a large cushion, with the candle lit in front of you. Focus your mind and your vision on the flame for five minutes, while following your breaths in and out. (This is also a great stress-decompressor.) With practice, you will find that you will be able to focus your concentration on any task like a lazer.

Another powerful exercise for your *concentration* is somewhat more subtle: Suppose that, as you are reading this book, you suddenly realize that you are thinking about watching a wedding ceremony in Bali during a vacation ten years ago. "How did I get here?" you may ask yourself. This daydreaming represents a unique opportunity not only to sharpen your powers of concentration, but also to get to know just how you associate thoughts and feelings.

When you look back you will realize what exactly set off a chain of associated thoughts, sometimes tenuously linked, leading to the episode in Bali. What you will be doing, in effect, will be strengthening the circuits (engrams) that were already established without your knowing it. This is but one of many examples, but as everyone slips pleasantly into daydreaming from time to time, this exercise can be practiced any time and anywhere.

Imagination

Sharpening the imagination may appear more difficult, but, in fact, requires the same basic principle of maintaining a scanning mind, ever strong and nimble.

This exercise is a classic among the artists in the performing arts: role playing. Simply imagine yourself as an actor starring in a movie that you are directing. Even exaggerate in your new powers. It will also enable you to detach yourself from your own little "melodrama" when things get somewhat stressed thereby enabling you to decompress the situation and introduce a bit of levity into an otherwise tense situation.

The Purpose of this section is to improve memory and concentration so as to remain as lucid and active as possible as long as possible.

The true art of memory is in the art of attention.
Samuel Johnson

The exercises are divided into three sections: **Observation**, **Concentration** and **Imagination**. It is a well-established fact that one's memory and concentration are inextricably linked to one's powers of observation, concentration and imagination: being present to the moment. That is, if one does not know how to observe or concentrate on something, that something cannot be registered in the memory. The result is that we waste time trying to relearn something each time.

Observation

In modern life, we are constantly bombarded with information and stimuli, often leaving us confused and tired. Many of the messages that we receive from the outside world are subtle, slipping unnoticed into our subconsciousness and memory. The advertising industry regularly exploits this method of subliminal bombardment to influence our buying decisions, often without us even recognizing it.

In brief: Practice these exercises to

1. improve your memory: both long-term and short-term memories, and
2. regain control over all your buying habits. Here are some proven exercises for learning how to observe through the eye, ear and touch.

Eye

Make a practice of constantly *challenging* yourself to improve your powers of observation and perception, as though it was a game. In fact, make a game of it. For example, in the room in which you are sitting or while waiting for a plane or train, study every detail of your surroundings, as though someone is going to ask you to recite those details several minutes later. Although it is only a simple exercise, solid results *will* quickly follow.

To be a winner at this game (as with any game or activity), you must first believe implicitly in yourself and secondly, while believing in yourself, you must push yourself to the limits. Move outside your "comfort zone" and explore new territory.

Other visual exercises for the memory and your powers of observation include stopping at a store window and scanning the contents quickly. Close your eyes and recite to yourself the contents quickly. Grade yourself each time. What you are doing, in effect, is setting up memory circuits (scientifically known as **engrams**) like highways. Initially, these circuits are somewhat difficult to establish but once set up, other memories fly right along and, therefore, are more easily recalled.

Eventually, a whole network (imagine a three-dimensional spider's nest) will be ready for rapid and sophisticated recall. The important thing throughout these exercises is to always have a scanning mind – nimble and active – never passive and self-indulgent.

Ear

The same principles apply here: be a detective! Sit in a park, close your eyes for five minutes and try to identify all the noises. This is a way of re-acquainting yourself with familiar sounds from a fresh approach. Simultaneously, you are sharpening your "mind's eye."

Touch

With your eyes closed, try to identify objects that are placed in your hand. Appreciate the texture and form. Imagine that you may never see that object again. This makes your mind aware.

THE TEN MOST COMMON DISCOMFORTS AND METHODS OF RELIEF

Discomfort	Relief
1. Constipation	Increase water and juice intake More fruits and roughage (veggies) Increase exercise Practice the "abdominal snap"
2. Insomnia	Warm bath or drink just prior to bed Progressive muscular relaxation + massage Watch a funny movie Talk things over
3. Tired feet or legs	Sit and rest when possible Sensible shoes, not spikes Foot massage
4. Lower back pain	Stretch, arms overhead and breathe deeply Take a yoga course Proper lifting, posture and rest Warm bath
5. Hemorrhoids	Avoid constipation Warm baths with witch hazel Local anesthetic
6. Mild bout of the "blues"	Get some rest Stay active and keep busy Go for a walk Talk it over
7. Leg cramps	Flex and extend calves Leg massage Vegetables and fruits (magnesium)
8. Heartburn (oesophageal reflux)	Loose-fitting clothing Frequent small meals Sleep with head slightly elevated Avoid coffee, chocolates, corn
9. Varicose veins	Elevate legs and feet while seated Move about while standing Support hose Leg draining every night
10. Gas and bloating	Increase water and juice intake More fruits and roughage (veggies) Wash beans before cooking and eating Observe rules of food compatibility

UNDERSTANDING YOUR CHECK-UP

Health Parameter	Normal ranges	Significance
Body mass index (BMI)	19–25	Measurement of Weight = kg/Height^2
Waist-to-hip ratio (WHR)	Men < 0.85, Women < 0.95	Circumference of waist divided by circumference of hips
Body fat percentage	Men < 20%, Women < 23%	Percentage of overall weight taken by fat. Any check-up that does not measure body fat is **incomplete**!
HEART & CIRCULATION		
Blood pressure	< 135/85 mm Hg (or 13.5/8.5 cm Hg) *Note:* Hg is the chemical symbol for Mercury; that is the pressure necessary to push a 135 mm column of mercury.	Pressure generated by the heart and vessels to perfuse the organs: (1) *Systolic:* the higher number, representing the pressure generated by the heart in full contraction; (2) *Diastolic:* the lower number, representing the pressure generated by the heart in full relaxation, filling for the next volley.
Pulse rate	Low 60s	The number of beats that your heart beats in one minute. Most of us have a Cardiac Output in the neighbourhood of five liters per minute at rest. The more efficient the stress, slower the heart, but caffeine, heat and dehydration can all influence this parameter.
Electrocardiogram (ECG or EKG)	* normal rhythms (in 60s); * normal intervals between peaks and troughs; * normal height of peaks and troughs; * no abnormal beats or impulses that might indicate extra or erratic transmissions.	As the heart transmits electrical impulses to its own muscles to contract, we can get a general idea as to the health, not just of the electrical conduction system, but also the heart muscle itself by picking up these signals with an ECG.

Health parameter	Normal ranges	Significance
LUNGS & RESPIRATION		
Forced expiratory volume (FEV)	(> 4 Liters)	FEV measures **the elasticity** of **volume** your **lungs.** An inability to exhale the amounts shown would indicate the presence of small airway obstruction.
Forced vital capacity (FVC)	(> 5 litres)	FVC, as the **amount of air** that you are able to exhale forcefully, measures the total **capacity** of your lungs. An inability to exhale the amounts shown would indicate the presence of small airway obstruction.
FEV(I)/FVC ratio: %	Roughly 90–100%	FEV(I)/FVC ratio is expressed in percentage points. A score below 100% indicates reduced lung function, often due to smoking or lack of exercise.
Aerobic capacity	ml/kg/min	Refers to the ability of the body to extract oxygen from the blood. The higher, the better. Diminishes by ~ 1% per year between 40 and 80 years of age. This is the test you see on TV, with a subject "wired for sound" running on a tread mill, riding a bike to exhaustion.
Chest X-ray	Radiograph of the chest should be free of enlarged organs, fluid infiltrates, radio-opaque masses or other abnormalities	Passage of gamma radiation through the chest onto a film. As the rays do not pass through calcium and metals. Chest radiographs are being phased out and replaced by non-radioactive test of greater precision.
Hematology Hemoglobin – Hgb (grams/100ml)	Women: 14+/– 2.0 Men 16+/–2.0	Low Hemoglobin = anemia due to blood loss or diet poor in iron or vitamin B_{12} or folic acid

Health parameter	Normal ranges	Significance
Hematocrit (%) – Hct	Women: 42% Men: 48%	Low Hematocrit = anemia due to blood loss or diet poor in iron or vitamin B_{12} or folic acid; Hct should be 3× Hgb
MCV (cu μ)	87+/–5	High MCV (> 95) = anemia due to vitamin B_{12} deficiency
White blood cells (WBC) (__ 10^9/Liter)	4–11	WBC or leukocytes increase in number and produce antibodies to combat bacterial or viral infections
Platelets	150–400	Platelets are essential to form clots to stop bleeding
Erythrocyte Sedimentation Rate (ESR) (Wintrobe) (mm/1 hour)	Women: < 15 Men: < 10	ESR or "sed rate" is a sensitive, though non-specific, test of inflammation or infection.
KIDNEY TESTS		
Sodium Na^+ (mmol/l) Potassium K^+ (mmol/l) Urea: BUN (mmol/l) Creatinine (μmol/l) Uric acid (μmol/l) Glucose (mmol/l) Calcium (mmol/l)	135–146 3.5–5.2 1.7–8.8 62–125 100–416 Fasting: 3.9–6.1 2.02–2.6	Overall kidney filtration function Both BUN and Creatinine are increased with poor kidney function and dehydration 80% of high uric acid = poor excretion Screening for diabetes Calcium balance is **critical** and affected by parathyroid dysfunction and other metabolic disorders
LIVER & ENZYME TESTS		
Total Bilirubin Alkaline Phosphatase (U/L) SGOT (U/L) SGPT (U/L) GGT (U/L) Protein (g/l) ALBUMIN TEST(g/l)	< 26 40–135 < 35 < 35 < 58 66–87 38–51	*Elevations:* anemia, liver/GB dis., cancer, drugs *Elevations:* liver and bone disease *Elevations:* liver disease *Elevations:* liver disease and excess alcohol *Elevations:* liver and heart disease *Elevations:* liver disease due to alcohol Normal levels of both Protein and Albumin indicate good overall function of the liver, heart and kidneys.

Health parameter	Normal ranges	Significance
BLOOD FATS		
Triglycerides Cholesterol (mmol/l) LDL Cholesterol (mmol/l) HDL Cholesterol (mmol/l) TC:HDL	< 2.2 < 5.2 1.55–4.6 0.85–2.00 2.5–13	*Elevations:* obesity, diabetes, excess alcohol *Elevations:* excess body fat and dietary fat *Elevations:* associated with heart disease *Depressions:* smoking, inactivity. *Elevations* (> 5) : associated with heart disease
URINALYSIS		
Blood: Glucose: Protein: Microscopy: Culture: Specific gravity (SG)	Negative (none present) Negative (none present) Negative (none present) Trace lining(epithelial) cells Negative 1.005–1.030	Normal kidney filtration should not allow blood cells, glucose or proteins to "get through." Urine should be **sterile** The SG of urine increases as wastes increase in concentration. Water has a SG of 1.000.

THE 5 WS TO HEALTH AND SANITY

	Blood Pressure	Total Cholesterol	HDL Cholesterol	Body Fat%	Cardio Fitness	Resting Heart Rate	Strength Endurance	Energy Stamina
WATER 2–3 L/day (between meals)	↕	↕	↕	↕	↕	↕		←
WALKING 15 minutes (after heaviest meal)	→	→	←	→→	←	→		←
WINE 2–3 units/day (with meals)	↕	↕	←	↕	↕	↕	↕	→
"WIND" 1). Deep breathing	→	↕	↕	↕	↕	→	←	←
2). meditation (5' in a.m. & p.m.)	→	→	↕	↕	↕	→	←	←
WORK-OUT 1). FIT (3×/week @ THR)	→	→	←	→	←	→	←	←
2). 3' work-out every a.m.	→	→	←	→	←	→	←	←

APPENDIX 2: WHAT'S KILLING US?

The statistics gathered herein are incomplete for several reasons. First, some countries were unable to provide reliable figures on the actual health profiles of their people. More importantly, as this book was not meant to be a statistical atlas, an exhaustive effort was not made to compile stacks and stacks of anonymous figures about remote areas. That type of exhaustive work can be readily procured from the World Health Organization (WHO).

The purpose of this section is to provide a brief overview of the health of some major areas of the world, to demonstrate that we can track the wave of certain diseases to the evolution of a country and the influence that aspects like lifestyle and affluence of a region can have on the appearances of diseases.

INTERNATIONAL OVERVIEW

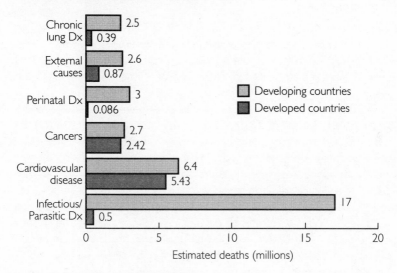

Total = ~ 50 million deaths (1990)
   Developing countries = 38.5 million
   Developed countries = 11.5 million

Annual deaths worldwide

Total = ~ 50 million deaths (early 1990s)

Developing (impoverished) countries = 38.5 million
Infectious diseases: 44%
Cardiovascular and degenerative diseases: 17%
Cancers: 7%
Chronic bronchitis: 6%
The remaining 26% is composed of accidents, maternal and perinatal deaths.

Developed (wealthy) countries = 11.5 million
Cardiovascular and degenerative diseases: 53%
Cancers: 21%
Infectious diseases: 4%
Chronic bronchitis: 3%
The remaining 19% is composed of accidents, maternal and perinatal deaths.

(*Source:* The WHO)

The silent killer

The process responsible for the bulk of coronary heart disease and strokes is known as **arteriosclerosis**, literally "arterial hardening." When choked off, the heart and brain tissue downstream soon die. Together, heart disease and strokes account for 12.5 of the nearly 50 million deaths every year.

But could our Asian colleagues also be at risk from these problems? The statistics are alarming. The World Health Organization (WHO) has reported that coronary heart disease has evolved from a relative rarity in the developing world to the public health epidemic that already exists in affluent developed countries. In short, arteriosclerosis travels without passport across all national boundaries.

Note: throughout my research, I was surprised to see regular use of the term "Third World" to refer to developing countries. Given the richness of the culture, the depth of spiritual traditions, the sheer numbers of peoples in these regions, a more appropriate term might be "First World." To avoid confusion, the author respectfully resists the use of the above terms.

INTERNATIONAL OVERVIEW BY REGION

Asia

What I found in my travels around the world surprised me. Let's start with Asia. When I started researching the whole issue of heart diseases and other preventable diseases I was amazed and shocked that heart disease is not just a major killer in the so-called Western civilized, industrialized world, but is rapidly growing in other parts of the developing world.

What follows is by no means meant to be an exhaustive treatment of the epidemiology of preventable diseases, but rather a snapshot of a killer trend.

Where the term "circulatory diseases" is used, it refers to the following: acute/chronic rheumatic heart disease, high blood pressure and heart attacks.

The double disease burden

While **communicable diseases** (infectious diseases like malaria, tuberculosis, cholera, hepatitis, diarrhoeal diseases, measles, pneumonia and AIDS) are still serious health issues in SE Asia and require constant vigilance, **non-communicable diseases** (cardiovascular diseases, cancers, obesity, lung diseases and diabetes) are on the rise, placing a double disease burden on rapidly developing countries of this region.

In brief, as countries and regions augmented their per capita GNP, the average annual rate of cardiovascular disease rose.

What's the cause for this? There seems to be a sequence of events when it comes to cardiovascular disease emergence in countries making the transition from developing to developed: after a period of time exposed to the multiple risk factors, obesity (*overfatness*) and diabetes mellitus emerge first, followed by high blood pressure, which remains clinically silent and asymptomatic.

This is followed by the first manifestation of the high blood pressure, cerebrovascular diseases and strokes. Then comes angina and heart attacks, rapidly becoming the leading cause of death in most developing countries.

Economic miracle (at what price?)

The increasing prosperity, the national and regional growth rates and the fast pace of life have been without precedent. However, as peoples of the Asian Economic Miracle begin to take stock of their situation, one fact has become painfully clear:

. . . with every wish, there comes a curse.

SE Asia and Oceania

Australia
1992 population = 17,596,000
Life expectancy: 73.2 years
Cause of death # 1: Circulatory diseases (34%)
Cause of death # 2: Cancers (24%)
Cause of death # 3: Strokes (11%)
Note: the coronary artery rates, highest in eastern Australia, peaked in the 1960s and have steadily declined since. This decline is due to smoking cessation and decreased consumption of saturated fats.

China (PRC)
1992 population = 1,187,997,000
Life expectancy: 69.1–72.4 years
Cause of death # 1: Heart disease and stroke (26%)
Cause of death # 2: Cancers (16%)
Cause of death # 3: Chronic lung disease (16%)
Note: given the size, reliable statistics are difficult to come by. Smoking is widespread in PRC, even among doctors and teachers. At the current rate of consumption, it is estimated that by 2025, 2,000,000 will die *every year* from smoking-related diseases. Passive smoking, particularly among children, is also a grave health issue.

Hong Kong
1992 population = 5,800,000
Life expectancy: > 75 years
Cause of death # 1: Cancers (21%)
Cause of death # 2: Cardiovascular disease (15%)
Cause of death # 3: Pneumonia/Lung disease (17%)

India
1992 population = 879, 548,000
Life expectancy:
Cause of death # 1:
Cause of death # 2:
Cause of death # 3:
Note: though data is scarce, several studies indicate that high blood pressure, diabetes and low HDL levels are three major risk factors for coronary disease. Infectious and perinatal diseases are clearly prevalent.

Indonesia
1992 population = 191,170,000
Life expectancy:
Cause of death # 1: Infectious diseases
Cause of death # 2: Cardiovascular diseases
Cause of death # 3: Lung diseases
Cause of death # 4: Accidents
Cause of death # 5: Cancers

Japan
1992 population = 124,491,000
Life expectancy: 75.8 years
Cause of death # 1: Heart disease, high blood pressure and strokes (38%)
Cause of death # 2: Cancers (26.5%)
Cause of death # 3: Pneumonia/Bronchitis (9.1%)

Korean Republic (South Korea)
1987 population = 42,100,000
Life expectancy: > 70 years
Cause of death # 1: Cancer
Cause of death # 2: Heart disease and stroke
Cause of death # 3: Senile diseases

Malaysia
1992 population = 18,792,000
Life expectancy:
Cause of death # 1: Heart/
Cerebrovascular (28.1%)
Cause of death # 2: Cancers (10.8%)
Cause of death # 3: Accidents (8.1%)

New Zealand
1992 population = 3,455,000
Life expectancy: 71.1 years
Cause of death # 1: Heart/
Cerebrovascular (~ 44%)
Cause of death # 2: Cancers (24%)
Cause of death # 3: Accidents (4%)

Philippines
1987 population = 58,400,000
Life expectancy:
Cause of death # 1: Infectious (30%)
Cause of death # 2: Heart disease
(12%)
Cause of death # 3: Cancers (6%)

Singapore
early 1990s population = 2,769,000
Life expectancy: 71.3 years
Cause of death # 1: Heart disease and
stroke (34%)
Cause of death # 2: Cancers (23%)
Cause of death # 3: Pneumonia/
Accidents (10%)

Taiwan
1987 population = 18,300,000
Life expectancy: 71–76 years
Cause of death # 1: Cancer (especially
lung)
Cause of death # 2: Strokes
Cause of death # 3: Accidents
Cause of death # 4: Heart diseases

Thailand
early 1990s population = 56,129,000
Life expectancy:
Cause of death # 1:
Cause of death # 2: Cancers (8%)
Cause of death # 3:

The Americas

My next stop on the research trail brought me to the Americas. As peoples of the developed and developing world rush headlong into the 21st century, one fact must be borne in mind: Around the world about US$1,700 billion is spent every year on health: ~ 8% of the global income. Much of this money is poured into high-tech treatment. Would low-tech education/prevention be a better use of limited funds?

Argentina
1992 population = 33,100,000
Life expectancy: 68.8 years
Cause of death # 1: Circulatory diseases
(34%)
Cause of death # 2: Cancers (17%)
Cause of death # 3: Strokes (10%)
Note: it was estimated that in 1985, approximately 28,100 deaths were caused

by smoking in Argentina: 14,000 deaths due to cardiovascular diseases, 7,000 due to cancers of the lung and trachea.

Brazil:
1992 population = 154,113,000
Life expectancy : 65.3 years
Cause of death # 1: Circulatory diseases
(30%)

Cause of death # 3: Accidents (16%)
Note: the WHO reported that in 1985 Brazil was the first lesser-developed country to have tobacco-related diseases overtake other causes of death in total causes of mortality.

Canada
1992 population = 27,367,000
Life expectancy: 74 years
Cause of death # 1: Circulatory diseases (32%)
Cause of death # 2: Cancers (27%)
Cause of death # 3: Strokes (7%)

Chile
1992 population = 13,600,000
Life expectancy: 69.4 years
Cause of death # 1: Circulatory diseases (19%)
Cause of death # 2: Cancers (18%)
Cause of death # 3: Strokes (9%)
Note: the incidence of deaths due to lung cancer has increased 16 times in men and 10 times in women since 1935.

Colombia
1992 population = 33,424,000
Life expectancy: 73.2 years
Cause of death # 1: Circulatory diseases (34%)
Cause of death # 2: Cancers (24%)
Cause of death # 3: Strokes (11%)
Note: lung cancer deaths have tripled between 1970 and 1980.

Mexico
1992 population = 88,153,000
Life expectancy: 68.6 years
Cause of death # 1: Circulatory diseases (20%)
Cause of death # 2: Infectious diseases (11%)
Cause of death # 3: Accidents (11%)

USA
1992 population = 255,159,000
Life expectancy: 71.6 years
Cause of death # 1: Circulatory diseases (35%)
Cause of death # 2: Cancers (24%)
Cause of death # 3: Strokes (8%)

Europe

Austria
1992 population = 7,776,000
Life expectancy: 72.7 years
Cause of death # 1: Circulatory diseases (40%)
Cause of death # 2: Cancers (23%)
Cause of death # 3: Strokes (13%)

Belgium
1992 population = 9,998,000
Life expectancy: 72.0 years
Cause of death # 1: Circulatory diseases (30%)
Cause of death # 2: Cancers (25%)
Cause of death # 3: Strokes (10%)

Denmark
1992 population = 5,158,000
Life expectancy: 72.6 years
Cause of death # 1: Circulatory diseases (34%)
Cause of death # 2: Cancers (25%)
Cause of death # 3: Strokes (9%)

Finland
1992 population = 5,008,000
Life expectancy: 71.4 years
Cause of death # 1: Circulatory diseases (36%)
Cause of death # 2: Cancers (19%)
Cause of death # 3: Strokes (12%)

France
1992 population = 57,182,000

Life expectancy: 73.4 years
Cause of death # 1: Cancers (26%)
Cause of death # 2: Circulatory diseases (25%)
Cause of death # 3: Strokes (9%)

Germany
1992 population = 80, 253, 000
Life expectancy: 72.7 years
Cause of death # 1: Circulatory diseases (40%)
Cause of death # 2: Cancers (23%)
Cause of death # 3: Strokes (12%)

Italy
1992 population = 57,782,000
Life expectancy: 73.6 years
Cause of death # 1: Circulatory diseases (33%)
Cause of death # 2: Cancers (27%)
Cause of death # 3: Strokes (15%)

Netherlands
1992 population = 15,158,000
Life expectancy: 73.9 years
Cause of death # 1: Circulatory diseases (30%)
Cause of death # 2: Cancers (27%)
Cause of death # 3: Strokes (10%)

Spain
1992 population = 39,092,000
Life expectancy: 73.4 years
Cause of death # 1: Circulatory diseases (28%)
Cause of death # 2: Cancers (20%)
Cause of death # 3: Strokes (14%)

UK
1992 population = 57,696,000
Life expectancy: 73.3 years
Cause of death # 1: Circulatory diseases (34%)
Cause of death # 2: Cancers (25%)
Cause of death #3: Strokes

GLOSSARY OF COMMON TERMS

A

Abdominals: The muscles that form the supporting wall for the organs of the abdomen and pelvic regions. Strong abdominal muscles can prevent back problems.

Adenosine Triphosphate (ATP): A high energy substance found in all cells from which the body gets its energy.

Aerobic Capacity: A functional measure of physical fitness based on the measurement of maximal oxygen uptake. Generally synonymous with the terms maximal oxygen uptake and cardiorespiratory endurance.

Amennorrhea: The absence or abnormal stoppage of the menses (see MENSES).

Amino Acids: The building block components and end-product of the breakdown of the processing of protein.

Anerobic: Means "without oxygen" and refers to the output of energy for muscular contraction when the oxygen supply is insufficient.

Angina Pectoris: Medical term referring to chest pain. A condition in which the heart muscle does not receive enough blood, resulting in pain in the chest.

Angiocardiography: An X-ray examination of the blood vessels or chambers of the heart by tracing the course of a special fluid (called a contrast or dye), visible by X-ray, that's been injected into the bloodstream. The X-ray pictures made are called angiograms.

Angioplasty: A procedure sometimes used to dilate (widen) narrowed arteries. A catheter with a deflated balloon on its tip is passed into the narrowed artery segment, the balloon is inflated and the narrowed segment is widened.

Aorta: The large artery that receives blood from the left ventricle of the heart and distributes it to the body.

Artery: A thick elastic vessel that transports blood away from the heart. Any of a series of blood vessels that carry blood from the heart to the various parts of the body.

Arteriosclerosis or Atherosclerosis: A vascular disease in which the deposits and build-up of fatty substances on the inner walls of the arteries cause the artery walls to thicken and lose elasticity. The arteries become narrow and the flow of blood through them is reduced. This build-up is sometimes called plaque.

Arrhythmia (or Dysrhythmia): An abnormally erratic rhythm of the heart.

Atman: In Sanskrit, " . . . breath, soul, Universal Self, Supreme Spirit . . . ." In Hinduism, "the innermost essence of each individual."

B

Basal Metabolic Rate (BMR): The minimal rate of energy required to maintain the life processes (breathing, heat generation and so on) of the body during a resting state following at least 12 hours of not eating.

Blood Pressure: The force that blood exerts against the walls of the blood vessels and that makes the blood flow through the circulatory system, usually given in units of millimetres of Mercury (mm Hg). For example, a blood pressure of 125/75 (pronounced "125 systolic over 75 diastolic") means that the heart is generating enough pressure to raise a column of mercury 125 millimetres (12.5 cms).

Blood Sugar: The glucose concentration in the blood. This term should not be confused with refined table sugar.

Body Composition: The relative amounts of the structural components of the body, muscle, bone, and fat.

Balloon Angioplasty: See angioplasty.

Blood Clot: A jelly-like mass of blood tissue formed by the clotting factors in the blood. This clot can then stop the flow of blood downstream from the site of an injury. Blood clots can also form inside an artery whose walls are damaged by atherosclerotic build-up and can cause a heart attack or stroke.

Bhagavad Gita: An epic poem, which, along with the Upanishads and the Vedas, form the literary pillars for the magnificent spiritual tradition of India, one of the oldest surviving cultures in the world. The Gita is set on a battlefield between rivalling kinsmen, in a discourse between Arjuna (the troubled hero of the story) and Krishna, who acts as the counselor and charioteer.

Brahma: Chief of the Hindu parathion, the creator and chief of the Hindu triad: Brahma, Shiva and Vishnu.

C

Capilaries: Very small (microscopic) blood vessels between arteries and veins that distribute oxygenated blood to the body's tissues.

Cardiac: Pertaining to the heart.

Cardiac Arrest: A state, incompatible with life, when the heart stops beating.

Cardiology: The study of the heart and its functions in health and disease.

Cardiopulmonary Resuscitation (CPR): A combination of chest compression and mouth-to-mouth breathing, this technique is used during fibrillation or cardiac arrest to keep oxygenated blood flowing to the heart muscle and brain until advanced cardiac life support can be started.

Cardiovascular: Pertaining to the heart and blood vessels. (*Cardio* means heart; *vascular* means blood vessels.) The circulatory system of humans.

Catheterization (cardiac): The process of examining the heart by introducing a thin tube (catheter) into a vein or artery and passing it into the heart.

Cholesterol: A fat-like substance found in animal tissue, it is present only in foods from animal sources such as whole milk dairy products, meat, fish, poultry, animal fats and egg yolks.

Circulatory System: Pertaining to the heart, blood vessels and the circulation of the blood.

Collateral Circulation: A system of smaller arteries not open under normal circumstances that may open up and start to carry blood to a part of the heart when a coronary artery is blocked. They can serve as alternate routes of blood supply.

Coronary Arteries: Two arteries arising from the aorta that arch down over the top of the heart, branch and provide blood to the heart muscle.

Coronary Artery Disease: Conditions that cause narrowing of the coronary arteries so blood flow to the heart muscle is reduced.

Coronary Artery Bypass Graft Surgery (aka CABG): Surgery to improve the blood supply to the heart muscle by bypassing an obstruction with a vessel taken from another part of the body. This surgery is most often performed when narrowed coronary arteries reduce the flow of oxygen-containing blood to the heart itself.

Coronary Care Unit (CCU): A specialized facility in a hospital or an emergency mobile unit equipped with monitoring devices and staffed with trained personnel. It's designed specifically to treat heart attack patients.

Coronary Heart Disease: Damage of the heart muscle due to insufficient blood flow through the coronary arteries.

Coronary Occlusion: An obstruction of one of the coronary arteries that hinder blood flow to some part of the heart muscle.

Coronary Thrombosis: Formation of a clot in one of the arteries that conducts blood to the heart muscle. Also called coronary occlusion.

Callisthenics: Exercise and athletic routines for the purpose of muscular development.

Calorie: A unit of measure for the rate of heat or energy production in the body.

Carbohydrates: A food substance that is the primary energy food for vigorous muscular activity. includes various sugars and starches and is found in the body in the form of glucose and glycogen.

Carbon Dioxide: The waste gas (CO_2) given off during the breakdown of foodstuffs in the cell and transported in the blood to the lungs and exhaled.

Cardio-respiratory Endurance: The capacity of your heart, blood vessels, and lungs to function efficiently during vigorous, sustained activity such as running, swimming, and cycling.

Cardio-respiratory Fitness: The efficient functioning and health of the circulatory and respiratory systems.

Circuit Training: A routine of selected exercises or activities performed in sequence at individual stations, as rapidly as possible.

Conditioning Period: The main exercise portion of a work-out with a training intensity level at a heart rate approximating 75% of the difference between resting and maximal heart rates. See also Training Heart Rate.

Continuous Training: Sustaining a constant tempo of exercise for a period of time. In initial programs, bouts of brisk walking are generally alternated with short bouts of exercise.

Cool-Down: The tapering off period after completion of the main conditioning bout, with activities such as slow jogging, walking, and stretching the major muscle groups.

D

Dehydration: Excessive loss of body fluids.

Diabetes: A chronic disorder of glucose (sugar) metabolism due to a disturbance of the normal insulin mechanism. See INSULIN.

Diastolic Pressure: The lowest force exerted by the arterial blood flow against the walls of the vessels.

Duration: The term used in prescribing exercise that refers to the time length of training sessions. For example, x minutes at an intensity of 75% HR reserve is the recommended duration for developing and maintaining physical fitness.

Defibrillator: An electronic device that helps to re-establish normal contraction rhythms in a heart that is malfunctioning.

Diabetes: A chronic metabolic disorder of carbohydrate (sugar) metabolism due to inadequate insulin production or utilization. Insulin is a vital chemical essential for maintaining proper blood sugar level. The full name for this condition is diabetes mellitus.

Diastolic Blood Pressure: The lowest blood pressure measured in the arteries, it occurs when the heart muscle is relaxed between beats.

Diuretic: A drug that increases the rate of formation of urine by promoting the excretion of water and salts.

Dysrhythmia: See arrhythmia.

E

Echocardiography: A diagnostic method in which pulses of sound are transmitted into the body and the echoes returning from the surfaces of the heart and other structures are electronically plotted and recorded.

Oedema: Swelling due to an abnormally large amount of fluid in body tissues.

Electrocardiogram (ECG or EKG): A graphic record of electrical impulses produced by the heart.

Embolus: A blood clot that forms in the blood vessels in one part of the body and then is carried to another part of the body.

Enzyme: A complex organic substance capable of speeding up specific biochemical processes in the body.

Electrocardiograph (ECG or EKG): The recording of the electrical activity (nervous energy) of the heart.

Endurance: The ability to sustain an activity and resist fatigue. See Muscular Endurance and Cardio-respiratory Endurance.

Ergometer: Generally refers to stationary exercise bicycle that can be adjusted to provide an accurate measurement of the work performed.

Exercise Prescription: Individualizing the exercise work-out based on intensity, duration, frequency, and mode of exercise.

Extensors: Muscles that increase the angle at a joint. For example, the quadriceps extend the knee.

F

Fat: A food substance that is used as a source of energy in the body and is capable of being stored.

Fat Weight: The absolute amount of body fat.

Fatty Acid: The end-product of the breakdown fats.

Fibrillation: Rapid, uncoordinated contractions of individual heart muscle fibres. The heart chamber involved cannot contract at once and pumps blood ineffectively.

Fibrin: A protein in the blood that traps blood cells and other substances during bloodclotting.

Flexibility: The range of movement of a specific joint and its corresponding muscle groups.

Flexors: Muscles that decrease the angle at a joint, for example, the hamstrings flex the knee (bend it).

Frequency: The number of work-outs needed to reach a training effect in conjunction with the intensity and duration factors recommended.

G

Glucose: The end-product of carbohydrate that is transported in the blood (blood sugar) and metabolized in the cell.

Glycogen: The form in which carbohydrates are stored in the muscles and liver.

Gram: A unit of mass and weight in the metric system. An ounce equals 28.3 grams, whereas 1,000 grams equals one kilogram or 2.2 pounds.

H

Heart Attack: Death of, or damage to, part of the heart muscle due to an insufficient blood supply.

Heredity: The genetic transmission of a particular quality or trait from parent to offspring.

High Blood Pressure: A chronic increase in blood pressure above its normal range.

High Density Lipoprotein (HDL): A carrier of cholesterol believed to transport cholesterol away from the tissues and to the liver where it can be excreted. High levels of HDL-cholesterol are associated with increased protection for heart disease. Exercise tends to elevate this lipoprotein and may be a protective mechanism against heart disease.

Hypertension: A blood pressure higher than normal blood pressure, usually defined as any systolic pressure above 135 mm Hg and a diastolic pressure in excess of 85 mm Hg.

Heat Stroke: A potentially fatal condition due to excessive exposure to heat characterised by the body temperature being dangerously elevated, a cessation of sweating, and total confusion or unconsciousness.

Haemoglobin: The iron-containing protein in the red blood cell that combines readily with carbon dioxide and oxygen and acts as a carrier of these gases throughout the circulatory system.

Humidity: The degree of moisture in the air.

I

Insulin: A storage hormone that controls the rate of glucose entry into the cell.

Intensity: The physiological stress on the body during exercise. Your level of intensity can be readily determined by measuring your pulse rate (heart rate) immediately following an exercise bout.

Interval Training: Successive bouts of exercise at near-maximal intensity, alternated with lighter periods of rest or exercise such as brisk walking.

Isokinetic: A muscle contraction at a constant speed with the muscle generating force against a variable resistance.

Isometric: A muscle contraction with the muscle generating force that does not allow significant shortening of the muscle (e.g. pushing against a wall).

Isotonic: A muscle contraction with the muscle generating force against a constant resistance with a shortening of the muscle (e.g. curling a dumb-bell).

Incidence: The number of new cases of a disease that develop in a population during a specified period of time, such as a year.

Ischaemic Heart Disease: Also called coronary artery disease and coronary heart disease, this term is usually applied to heart ailments caused by narrowing of the coronary arteries.

K

Kilogram: Metric measure of weight; 2.2. pounds equals one kilogram or 1,000 grams.

Koran or "Qur'an": the sacred scriptures of Islam, containing the revelations of the prophet Mohammed. It is divided into 114 suras or chapters, which give the basis for all spiritual, social, commercial, legal, and military activities in the Muslim world.

Krishna: one of the most important deities of Hinduism, the eighth avatar (reincarnation) of the god Vishnu.

L

Lactic Acid: The end-product of anaerobic (oxygen-absent) metabolism.

Lean Body Weight: The body weight minus the percent of body weight that is stored fat.

Ligament: The connective tissue that binds bones together.

Lipid: A fat, or fat-like substance, such as fatty acids, triglycerides, and cholesterol.

Lipoprotein: A type of protein that carries cholesterol and triglycerides in the bloodstream.

Low Density Lipoprotein (LDL): The main carrier of harmful cholesterol in the blood.

Liter: Basic metric unit of capacity, 1,000 milliliters.

Load: The poundage used for a particular weight training exercise.

Lower Back Pain: The term used to describe the pain resulting from a general overall weakness of the structures in the lower spinal region.

Lungs: Located within the rib cage, these two organs regulate the exchange of air between the blood and external environment.

M

Marathon: A foot race covering the distance of 26.2 miles (42.185 km).

Mantra: a Sanskrit term used in Hinduism to denote a sound or syllable which when sung or chanted repeatedly throughout life is reputed to purify and liberate the soul from bondage.

Maximal Heart Rate: The highest attainable heart rate for an individual, defined as 220 − age.

Maximal Oxygen Uptake: The largest amount of oxygen that can be consumed per minute. It is the best physiological index of cardiorespiratory endurance. Often referred to as maximal aerobic capacity, maximal oxygen intake, or maximal oxygen consumption.

Mean: Commonly understood as the arithmetic average (computed by dividing the sum of all scores by the number of scores).

Menses: The monthly flow of blood from the female genital tract often called the menstrual period.

Menstruation: The periodic cycle in the uterus of the female associated with preparation of the uterus to receive a fertilized egg.

Met: The rate of energy expended at rest; used to rate activities in multiples above rest.

Metabolism: All chemical processes of the body that make it possible for the cells to function.

Metabolic Rate: The rate, in calories/time, at which the body consumes its calories.

Minerals: A group of 22 metallic elements vital to proper cell functioning; for example, minerals are part of enzymes, hormones, and vitamins.

Mitochondria: The compartments within the cell where energy is produced to carry out body functions such as muscular movement.

Muscular Endurance: The capacity of a muscle to exert a force repeatedly or to hold a fixed or static contraction over a period of time.

Mono-unsaturated Fat: A type of fat found in many foods but predominantly in canola, olive and peanut oil, and avocados.

Myocardial Infarction: The damaging or death of an area of the heart muscle (myocardium) resulting from a reduced blood supply to that area.

Myocardial Ischemia: Deficient blood flow to a part of the heart muscle.

Myocardium: The muscular wall of the heart. It contracts in order to pump blood out of the heart and then relaxes as the heart refills with returning blood.

N

Nitroglycerine: A drug that causes dilation of blood vessels and is often used in treating angina pectoris.

Norm: A standard of achievement represented by the average achievement of a large group.

O

Overload Principle: The physiological fact that a muscle subjected to a greater-than-normal load will increase in size and strength.

Oxidative: The breakdown of foodstuffs with oxygen to produce energy for reforming ATP. The krebs cycle is another name for this process.

Oxygenated: Mixed or combined with oxygen, such as the combining of oxygen with the red blood cells in the lungs.

Oxygen Uptake: Indicates the amount of energy the body uses; can be easily converted to calories.

Obesity: An increase in body weight beyond physical and skeletal requirements due to an accumulation of excess fat. It's usually applied to a condition of 20% or more over ideal body weight. Obesity puts a strain on the heart and can increase the chance of developing high blood pressure and diabetes.

Obstructed artery: An artery In which the flow of blood has been impaired by a blockage.

Open Heart Surgery: Surgery performed on the opened heart while the bloodstream is diverted through a heart-lung machine.

P

Percutaneous Transluminal Coronary Angioplasty (PCA): See angioplasty.

Plaque: Also called atheroma, this is a deposit of fatty (and other) substances in the inner lining of the artery wall, characteristic of atherosclerosis.

Plasma Lipid: The lipid (fat) carried in blood.

Platelets: One of the three kinds of formed elements found in the blood, and one which aids in the clotting of the blood.

Polyunsaturated Fats: These fats are liquid oils of vegetable origin such as corn, safflower sunflower or soybean oil.

Potassium (aka "katrium": K$^+$): Another mineral essential to human life.

Prevalence: The total number of cases of a given disease existing in a population at a specific time.

Prophylaxis: Preventive treatment.

Power: The rate at which force can be produced or the product of force and velocity; sometimes referred to as the explosive ability to apply force.

Protein: A food substance that provides the basic structural properties of the cells; also the source for enzymes and hormones in the body.

R

Ramayana: Estimated to have been written some time around the 2nd century BC, an ancient Sanskrit epic poem which tells the tale of Rama, Vishnu's incarnation.

Relative Body Fat: The proportion of fat tissue in your body, often expressed as a percentage of body weight (body fat percentage).

Repetitions (or reps): The number of consecutive contractions performed during each weight training exercise. See Sets.

Respiration: The process of gas exchange in the lungs and cells of the body.

Rheumatic Heart Disease: Damage done to the heart, particularly the heart valves, by one or more attacks of rheumatic fever.

S

Sanskrit: The ancient sacred Aryan (Indo-Persian) language of the Hindus of India.

Saturated Fats: Types of fat found in foods of animal origin and a few of vegetable origin.

Shiva: Along with Brahma and Vishnu, an integral part of Hinduism triad of gods.

Silent Ischaemia: Episodes of ischaemia that aren't accompanied by pain.

Sodium: A mineral essential to life, found in nearly all plant and animal tissue. Table salt (sodium chloride) is nearly half sodium.

Sphygmomanometer: An instrument for measuring blood pressure.

Stenosis: The narrowing or constriction of an opening, such as a blood vessel or heart valve.

Stethoscope: An instrument for listening to sounds within the body.

Stroke (also called Apoplexy, Cerebrovascular Accident or Cerebral Vascular Accident): A sudden and often severe attack caused by an insufficient supply of blood to part of the brain.

Systolic Blood Pressure: The highest blood pressure measured in the arteries. It occurs when the heart contracts and ejects blood with each heartbeat.

Saturated Fats: A food source found in meat, milk, cheese, and butter. This type of fat does not melt at room temperature.

Set: The number of bouts performed for each weight training exercise (e.g, three sets of six reps) (see Repetitions).

Shiva: along with Vishnu and Brahma, one of the three deities of the classic triad of Hindu gods. The so-called "Dance of Shiva" figure in Hindu religion, with a four-armed god dancing in a circle of fire, represents the playing out of the cycle of creation and destruction of the Universe.

Skin Fold Callipers: An instrument used to measure selected thickness of fat folds that have been pinched up on the body.

Standard Deviation: A measure of variability that indicates the scatter and spread of approximately two-thirds of a distribution of scores around a mean (see Mean and Norm).

Step Test: A testing procedure for assessing the heart-rate recovery after stepping on and off a bench for a three-minute time period at a pre-determined cadence.

Strength: The capacity of a muscle to exert a force against a resistance.

Stretching: Increasing the length of a particular muscle or muscle group.

Stoke Volume: The volume of blood ejected from the left ventricle during one heart beat.

Sugar: A term often misused; in this book it refers to refined sugar or table sugar. The scientific name for sugar is sucrose (see Blood Sugar).

Systolic Pressure: The greatest force exerted by the arterial blood flow against the walls of the vessels.

T

Tendon: An extension of muscle tissue that attaches to the bone.

T-Score: A score that enables you to interpret and compare raw scores from various fitness tests. It provides a simple way to describe the deviation of a test result from the average score for the particular test (see Mean, Standard Deviation, and Normal).

Training Heart Rate: A heart-beat rate (or pulse rate) per minute during exercise that will produce significant cardiorespiratory benefits.

Treadmill: A testing device consisting of a motor-driven conveyor belt constructed so that the speed and angle of incline can be regulated to produce varying workloads.

Triglycerides: Fat particles that are stored in the body. They provide the main means for fat to be transported in the blood. Recent evidence has revealed an association with atherosclerosis (see Cholesterol).

Type A Behavior: The term used to describe people who exhibit an excessive competitive drive and time urgency. This behavior tends to predispose people to heart disease.

Thrombolysis: The breaking up of a blood clot.

Thrombosis: The formation or presence of a blood clot (thrombus) inside a blood vessel or cavity of the heart.

Thrombus: A blood clot which forms inside a blood vessel or cavity of the heart.

Triglyceride: The chemical form in which most fat exists. Fat comes from the food we eat or is made in the body from other energy sources like carbohydrates.

U

Ultrasound: High-frequency sound vibrations, not audible to the human ear, used in medical diagnosis.

Upanishads: Spiritual treatises, 112 in number, dating back as far as the 8th century BC.

Unsaturated Fats: A liquid type of fat found in peanut oil and olive oil.

V

Ventilation: The movement of volumes of air into and out of the lungs.

Ventricle: The chamber of the heart that pumps blood to the lungs (right ventricle) or to all the systems of the body (left ventricle).

Vitamins: Word stemming from "vital amines," which are organic substances that perform vital functions within the cells.

Vein: Any one of a series of blood vessels of the vascular system that carry blood from various parts of the body back to the heart.

Ventricle: One of the lower chambers of the heart.

Ventricular Fibrillation: A condition in which the ventricles contract in a rapid, unsynchronized, uncoordinated fashion so that no blood is pumped from the heart.

Ventricular Tachycardia: A condition in which an area of the ventricle muscle develops pacemaker activity, resulting in a very fast, abnormal heartbeat.

Vishnu: One of the triad of Hinduism deities: Vishnu, Shiva and Brahma.

W

Warm-Up: The exercise portion of your work-out that is geared to preparing your body for a more vigorous exercise bout. Generally, walking, stretching major muscle groups, and exercises that stimulate the heart, lungs, and muscles moderately and progressively are engaged in during warm-up periods.

White Blood Cells (aka Leukocytes): The blood cells that provide a rapid and potent defence against infectious agents present in the body.

Y

Yoga: Literally, "to be one, united with God." Yoga consists of various mental and physical disciplines wherein the breath and posture are controlled so as to achieve a profound state of meditation. A series of body positions that are held without motion or with slow continuous motion while the mind is held in attention of some object.

SELECTED READINGS

Note to Reader: The choice included here for your reading pleasure is by no means exhaustive. To initiate and maintain personal transformation, food for the Mind and Soul will have to accompany, and probably predate, food for the Body. Accordingly, I have divided the selected readings into those for the body (technical guides or 'how to' books), as well as more transcendent manna for the mind and the soul.

Food for the Body . . .

Benyo, Richard, *Making the Marathon Your Event*, Random House Publishers, New York, 1992.

Chapman, Mr Simon & Wong Wai Leng, *Tobacco Control in the Third World*: *A Resource Atlas*, International Organization of Consumer Unions, Penang, Malaysia, 1990.

Clarke, Ron, *Total Living*: *The Complete Guide to Fitness & Well Being*, Pavilion Books London, 1995.

Cooper, Dr Kenneth H, *Controlling Cholesterol*, Bantam Books, 1988.

Dawood, Dr Richard, *How to Stay Healthy Abroad*, Penguin Publishers, 1987.

Davenport, Dr Horace W; *A Digest of Digestion*, YearBook Medical Publishers, 1975.

Dunne, Lavon J *Nutrition Almanac*, (Third Edition) McGraw-Hill Publishers, 1990.

Eaton, MD, Dr S Boyd, *The Paleolithic Prescription*, Harper & Row Publishers, New York, 1988.

Fries, James and Crapo, Lawrence M, *Vitality and Aging*, Freeman Publishers, 1981.

Getchell, Bud, *Physical Fitness – A Way of Life* (3rd Edition), Wiley Publishers, 1983

Hales, Dianne, *A Complete Book of Sleep*, Addison Wesley Publishers, 1981.

Harper, H A et al, *Review of Physiological Chemistry*, Lange Medical Publications, 1979.

Johnson, Barry L and Nelson, Jack K, *Practical Measurements for Evaluation in Physical Education*, (4th Edition), Macmillan Publishers, 1986.

Longstaff, Roberta and Mann, Jim, *The Healthy Heart Diet Book*, Macdonald & Sons, 1986.

Mackay, Dr Judith, *The State of Health Atlas*, Simon & Schuster, 1993.

Nieman, Dr David C *Fitness and Sports Medicine*, Bull Publishing, 1990.

Ornish, Dean, *Stress, Diet & Your Heart*, Signet Books, 1982.

Reid, Tom, *The Tao of Health, Sex and Longevity*.

Sharkey, Dr Brian, *Physiology of Fitness*, Human Kinetics Books, 1990.

Guidelines for Exercise Testing and Prescription (4th Edition), The American College of Sports Medicine, Lea & Febiger, 1991.

Wallach, Dr Jacques, *Interpretation of Diagnostic Tests: A Handbook Synopsis of Laboratory Medicine*, 3rd Edition, Little Brown, Boston, 1978.

American Heart Association, *Textbook of Advanced Cardiac Life Support*, 1981.

Resource Manual for Guidelines for Exercise Testing and Prescription, American College of Sports Medicine, Lea & Febiger, Philadelphia, 1988.

International Travel and Health: Vaccine Requirements and Health Advise, World Health Organization, Geneva, 1990.

Report of the United States Preventative Services Task Force, *Guide to Clinical Preventative Services*, 1989.

United States Department of Agriculture, *Handbook of the Nutritional Value of Foods in Common Units*, Dover Publishers, 1986

World Health Organization, *World Health Statistics*, Geneva, 1994.

Food for the Mind . . .

Adams, Douglas *A Hitchhiker's Guide to the Galaxy*, Omnibus Edition, Harmony Books, 1983.

Albrecht, Karl, *Stress and the Manager, Making it Work for You*, Simon and Schuster, New York, 1979.

Covey, Mr Stephen, *The Seven Habits of Highly Effective People*, Simon & Schuster, 1989.

Dickens, Charles, *A Christmas Carol*, Penguin Publishers, 1843.

Donne, John, *The Complete English Poems*, edited by A.J. Smith, Penguin Books, 1971.

Edelman, Gerald M, *Bright Air, Brilliant Fire: On the Matter of the Mind*, Basic Books, 1992.

Gray, Spalding, *Swimming to Cambodia*, Picador Publishers, 1986.

Hanson, Dr Peter G, *The Joy of Stress*, Andrews, McMeel & Parker, 1986.

Jones, Judy and Wilson, William, *An Incomplete Education*, Ballantine Books, 1987.

Kirsta, Alix, *The Book of Stress Survival*, Gaia Books, London 1986.

Kofodimos, Joan, *Balancing Act*, Jossey-Bass Publishers, San Francisco, 1993.

Kushner, Harold S *When Bad Things Happen to Good People*, Avon Publishers, New York, 1981.

Lansing, Alfred, *Endurance, Shackleton's Incredible Voyage*, Carroll & Graf Publishers, 1959.

O'Toole, John Kennedy, *A Confederacy of Dunces*, Grove Press, New York, 1980

Payer, Lynn, *Medicine and Culture*, Penguin, 1988.

Watson, Lyall, *Supernature*, Sceptre Press, 1986.

Wee Chow Hou, *Sun Tzu: War & Management*, Addison Wesley Publishers, 1991.

Suzuki, Shunryu, *Zen Mind, Beginner's Mind*, Weatherhill, New York, 1970

Stress and Coping: An Anthology, edited by Monat & Lazarus, Columbia University Press, New York, 1977.

Food for the Soul . . .

Fox, Matthew, *The Coming of the Cosmic Christ*, Harper & Row Publishers, New York, 1988.

Eadie, Betty J, *Embraced by the Light*, Bantam Books, 1992.

Easwaran, Eknath, *The Upanishads*, Penguin Classics, 1987.

Fields, Rick, *Chop Wood, Carry Water*, Tarcher Publishers, 1984.

Gandhi, M K, *Gandhi Interprets the Baghavad Gita*, Orient Paperbacks, New Delhi, 1994.

Gabran, Kahlil, *The Prophet*, Alfred A. Knopf Publishers, 1923, New York.

Krishnamurti, J, *Meditations*, Harper & Row Publishers, New York, 1979.

Kübler-Ross, MD, Elisabeth, *On Death and Dying*, MacMillan Publishers, 1969.

Lao Tzu, *Tao Tê Ching (The Way of Life)*

Levine, Steven *Who Dies?, An Investigation into Conscious Living and Conscious Dying*, Anchor Books, 1982.

Mascaro, Juan, *The Baghavad Gita*, Penguin Classics, 1962.

Millman, Dan, *Way of the Peaceful Warrior*, Kramer Publishers, 1984.

Peck, MD, Dr M Scott, *The Road Less Travelled, A New Psychology of Love, Traditional Values and Spiritual Growth*, Touchstone Book (Simon and Schuster), New York, 1978.

Siegel, MD, Dr Bernie S *Love Medicine & Miracles*, Harper & Row, 1986.

Thich Nhat Hanh, *The Sun in My Heart*, Parallax Press, 1988.

Trungpa, Chögyam, *Cutting Through Spiritual Materialism*, Shambala Press, 1973.

The Holy Bible, King James Version.

The Qur'an, The Great Word of God.

The Asian Journal of Thomas Merton, New Directions Book, 1973.

World Masterpieces (3rd Edition), Norton Publishers, New York, 1974.

INDEX

Note to Reader: all entries that are included in the glossary appear in *italics*.